THE VIETNAM WAR
IN
LITERATURE

THE
MAGILL
BIBLIOGRAPHIES

Other Magill Bibliographies:

American Theatre History—Thomas J. Taylor
Biography—Carl Rollyson
Black American Women Novelists—Craig Werner
Classical Greek and Roman Drama—Robert J. Forman
Contemporary Latin American Fiction—Keith H. Brower
English Romantic Poetry—Bryan Aubrey
The Modern American Novel—Steven G. Kellman
Resources for Writers—R. Baird Shuman
Shakespeare—Joseph Rosenblum
The Victorian Novel—Laurence W. Mazzeno

THE VIETNAM WAR
IN
LITERATURE

An Annotated Bibliography of Criticism

Philip K. Jason

Professor of English
United States Naval Academy

SALEM PRESS

Pasadena, California   Englewood Cliffs, New Jersey

Library of Congress Cataloging-in-Publication Data

Jason, Philip K., 1941–
    The Vietnam War in literature / Philip K. Jason
        p. cm.—(Magill bibliographies)
    Includes bibliographical references and index
    ISBN 0-89356-679-9
    1. American literature—20th century—History and
criticism—Bibliography.   2.   Vietnamese   conflict,
1961–1975—Literature and the conflict—Bibliography.
3. American literature—20th century—Bibliography. 4.
Vietnamese conflict, 1961–1975—Bibliography. 5. War
stories.   American—Bibliography.   6.   War   poetry,
American—Bibliography I. Title.   II. Series.
Z1227.J37   1992
[PS228.V5]   92-12898
016.8108'0358—dc20   CIP

For Hope and Daniel

Editorial Staff

Publisher
FRANK N. MAGILL

Advisory Board
KENNETH T. BURLES
DAWN P. DAWSON

Series Editor
JOHN WILSON

Production Editor
CYNTHIA BRESLIN BERES

Copy Editor
Philip Wong

CONTENTS

CONTENTS

THE VIETNAM WAR
IN
LITERATURE

INTRODUCTION

Because the Vietnam War is a living memory for thousands of men and women who participated in it, who witnessed it from near or far, or who otherwise felt its impact on their lives and on their cultural environment, the imaginative responses to the war are still being written. Even as the critical enterprise has begun to give the large body of creative work already in print an initial winnowing and judgment, new novels, stories, poems, plays, and memoirs alter the literary landscape. Thus, while the creative "field" is not fully sown, the critical harvest is itself already abundant and rich, a fact to which the following pages will testify.

The imaginative literature of the Vietnam War participates—whether overtly or covertly, consciously or unconsciously—in a struggle for the national memory. Through interaction with these imaginative works, readers individually and the society as a whole will most likely come to an "understanding"—a gradually built and deeply ingrained consensus—of the place and meaning of the Vietnam War in the American experience. Critics, as they raise the banner of one or another work and offer responses to artistic endeavor, participate in this struggle as well.

Even aesthetic discussion can have a political bias. Genre, structure, and style make a difference not simply in our pleasure or appreciation but in the ways in which we absorb the issues that literature addresses. Literature makes things happen inside of readers. What lasts—what becomes part of future generations' required reading lists—is accommodated to an ongoing definition of American values and American myth. At the same time, what is newly absorbed becomes a new factor in the mythic equation. The critics whose comments are annotated here are arguing the terms of the adjusted equation and the adjusted myth of who we are as a people and where we have been.

Critics have raised a wide range of questions about particular works and about the growing body of Vietnam War literature. Some have searched for the distinctive features, both in vision and in technique, that separate this literature from either other contemporary writing or the literature of other wars. This inquiry has been conducted on the most general level and also within the various genres. Students of fiction, nonfiction, poetry, and drama have examined how the major themes, experiences, and understandings regarding United States involvement in Vietnam extend or reshape the boundaries of genre. They have also argued the relative success of each genre in expressing the essential truths of what is too tritely labeled the "Vietnam experience."

Among the genre issues is a special concern that many critics have voiced with erasing the conventional distinction between fiction and nonfiction, especially autobiography. Indeed, the concern goes back to authors such as Michael Herr, John Sack, W. D. Ehrhart—and to their publishers. Each of these writers (but not only these) has created autobiographical works that have come very close to being offered as novels. Of course, even earlier, Norman Mailer was instrumental in creating the hybrid "nonfiction novel" and earning status for the oxymoronic term that straddles the inherited categories.

While this issue of an encompassing genre of narrative has a life outside the interest in Vietnam War fiction, the literature of the war and the commentaries on it have focused and amplified the problem. The suggestion is often implicit, and sometimes explicit, that when it comes to war stories—at least those written by participants or witnesses—the distinction is not serviceable and perhaps not even real. In his landmark study *The Great War and Modern Memory* (New York: Oxford University Press, 1975), Paul Fussell argued that "the memoir is a kind of fiction, differing from the 'first novel' . . . only by the continuous implicit attestations of veracity or appeals to documented historical fact." Critics such as Thomas Myers and Lloyd Lewis have chosen to examine Vietnam "narratives"; for their purposes, the old distinction is not particularly relevant. Although Myers usually pairs titles that have generic identity, he examines Herr's *Dispatches* and O'Brien's *Going After Cacciato* together as examples of "a revised American romanticism." In her provocative essay "Disarming the War Story," Lorrie Smith is more concerned with the power of "mimetic stories" than with whether they present themselves as fiction or fact.

As suggested above, another set of questions is concerned with the ways in which the literature of the war challenges and adjusts American myths. The work of Philip D. Beidler and John Hellmann has been influential here. Much has been made in the criticism (and in the literature itself) of Vietnam as an extension of the powerful frontier myth. Others, such as Philip H. Melling, write of how the literature reveals the continued unfolding of America's Puritan past. Myths of innocence and invincibility, myths of home and homecoming, and myths of race and gender all have powerful representation and, more often, counterrepresentation in the literature.

It is a high but productive irony that the Vietnam War and the women's rights movement gained momentum at the same time. One consequence of this dichotomous parallel is that the literature of the Vietnam War and feminist criticism have matured together and some sort of symbiotic relationship has developed. Perhaps no other contemporary body of literature has found itself as susceptible to the perceptions and methods of feminist criticism (and, more broadly, gender criticism). Much attention in the criticism has been drawn to representations of and by women in what, at first sight, would seem an unlikely arena. More importantly, the range of Vietnam War representation has been a fertile ground (no sexist metaphor here) on which to dramatize the central issues in the feminist cultural critique of patriarchal society. No critic has been more constructive in this endeavor than Susan Jeffords. One major adjustment in vision between Philip Beidler's trailblazing study of 1982 and his broader and richer study of 1991 derives, arguably, from the influence of feminist thinking on Beidler's own understanding.

The field of Vietnam War literature can be narrowly or broadly defined. John Newman, for the purposes of his excellent *Vietnam War Literature: An Annotated*

Bibliography of Imaginative Works About Americans Fighting in Vietnam, does not choose to include personal narratives or nonfiction novels. Moreover, to be included by Newman, a work must have a substantial segment set in Vietnam during the war years. Aiming for comprehensiveness, Newman sets limits that make comprehensiveness possible. The current venture defines Vietnam War literature more broadly, including within its scope commentary on literary nonfiction; works that treat the veteran's return, the stateside impact, and the aftermath of the war; works that treat the war allegorically or otherwise obliquely; and works that deal with the protest against the war. The agenda of selectivity regarding titles that fit the broad parameters of possible inclusion has been set, in part, by the shape that critics have been giving to the emerging canon. If a creative literary work receives no mention here, that is probably because no significant critical treatment has yet found its way into print.

Other criteria are also at work. Though a published script of Ronald Ribman's *The Final War of Olly Winter* exists, no commentary on that significant drama appears because of a decision to exclude commentary on creative works written for television. This limitation places a number of other intriguing representations of the war out of bounds. Also, the enormous body of scholarship on Vietnam War films is not included here (it needs its own bibliography), except for a handful of the major studies that are listed to help the interested student get started. Studies of films that are based on included literary works are listed when they help our understanding of those texts.

Even though this is a selected bibliography, for most of the included authors the range of critical commentary here is reasonably thorough for book-length studies and subsections, and for essays in collections, and scholarly periodicals—with certain exceptions. Because the field is so new and the publication of book-length critical material so recent, no attempt is made to provide information on various editions and printings of a book title. Generally, the citation is to the latest clothbound American edition (which in most cases is the first and only edition). Students should know, however, that there are paperback reprints of many of the titles listed here—especially of those listed in the section "General Studies—Background."

For established figures such as Graham Greene and Norman Mailer, writers deserving of their own annotated bibliographies of criticism, the listings are much more highly selective than they are for emerging figures such as Caputo, O'Brien, and most of the others. For all writers, interviews (both printed and recorded) are treated less comprehensively, and no attempt has been made to cover book reviews, newspaper articles, or material in popular magazines in a systematic way. A number of omnibus reviews in which Vietnam titles are grouped together have been included. Of single-work reviews, only those that seemed especially significant and/or especially accessible because reprinted in collections are included. Students can consult *The Reader's Guide to Periodical Literature*, *Book Review Digest*, *Book Review Index*, and major newspaper indexes such as *The New York Times Index* for additional interviews, reviews, and news articles. Reviews of play productions are not treated at all, nor are commentaries in foreign languages, theses, or dissertations. A number of standard reference works contain biographical materials and critical comment on Vietnam War writers. Many are included in one or another volume of the *Dictionary of Literary Biography*, its yearbooks, or its Documentary Series. See the cumulative index of the most recent volume (Detroit: Gale Research). Such readily available items are not treated in this bibliography.

No body of literature exists in a vacuum. The student of Vietnam War literature must become a student of the historical and cultural background out of which the literature grows. For that reason, this bibliography begins with a section called "General Studies—Background" in which one can find representative studies from various disciplines concerning the war as well as useful reference tools such as specialized dictionaries and bibliographies. Also, one will find skeletal representation of certain kinds of works that are neither scholarly nor literary but crucial to our understanding of the war: oral histories and personal histories. The titles presented in this section are only a small sampling of the thousands of titles that have been published on all aspects of the war. The next section, "Criticism—General," lists those works that attend to the literature broadly or thematically while cutting across genre lines. Book-length studies of Vietnam War literature are treated here, along with critical anthologies. Next comes a listing of critical works that focus on writings in a particular genre; this section is subdivided into "Nonfiction," "Fiction," "Poetry," "Drama," and "Film." Finally, the section on "Authors and Works" presents commentary on individual writers and titles. Since many of the studies found under the sections "Criticism—General" and "Criticism—Genre" treat individual authors and titles briefly, the student should consult the index to find material not listed under the author entries. Only those commentaries that give singular or extended attention to a specific work are listed under that work's title.

Special Collections

The student of Vietnam War literature should know that several specialized collections of Vietnam War material exist. The holdings in these collections lend themselves to a wide variety of studies. Of these collections, the first two listed below are of greatest value to literary scholars.

1. "Imaginative Representations of the Vietnam War." Special Collections Department, Connelly Library, La Salle University, 20th Street and Olney Avenue, Philadelphia, PA 19141. This collection is limited to imaginative literature and the visual arts. It stresses novels, short stories, poetry, drama, film scripts, graphic art, painting, video recordings of films, TV productions, and sound recordings. Other holdings include curriculum guides for teaching the war through literature, runs of

comic books, cartoon art, Vietnam War strategy games, and software. Standard editions of literary works are supplemented by variant editions, limited editions, manuscripts, galley and page proofs, and holograph copies. Approximately five thousand items.

2. "Vietnam War Literature Collection." Special Collections Department, Colorado State University Library, Fort Collins, CO 80523. The "original" collection and the basis for John Newman's bibliography *Vietnam War Literature* (2d ed., 1988), this project intends to be the major resource for imaginative accounts of the war that stay within the boundaries of Newman's subtitle, that is, works "About Americans Fighting in Vietnam." The collection also contains theses and dissertations that examine such accounts. Scholars should arrange in advance to use the collection. Some materials can be borrowed through interlibrary loan.

3. Bailey/Howe Library, University of Vermont, Burlington, VT 05405-0036. Holds approximately 220 titles in first edition of Vietnam War fiction along with a small manuscript collection that contains the papers of David Huddle, among others. Most of the fiction volumes are found in the rare book collection. Contact Connell B. Gallagher, Assistant Director for Research Collections, at 802-656-2595.

4. The Indochina Archive, University of California, 6701 San Pablo Avenue, 4th Floor, Oakland, CA 94608. Has an estimated three million pages of documents as well as approximately forty thousand maps, photographs, and other graphics and ten thousand books and monographs. The archive was initiated by Douglas Pike, who heads the Indochina Studies Program, part of the University of California Institute of East Asian Studies, 2223 Fulton Street, 6th Floor, University of California, Berkeley, CA 94720. The documents include government publications (from various governments), foreign language documents, publications of nongovernmental organizations, interviews, propaganda leaflets, posters, interviews, and public opinion polls. Those holdings most pertinent to Vietnam War research are being made commercially available to other libraries (see entry under "Pike" in the section "General Studies—Background").

5. The John M. Echols Collection on Southeast Asia, Cornell University, 107E Olin Library, Ithaca, NY 14853. Regarded as the premier North American repository of material on Southeast Asia. This collection, begun in the 1950s by Echols, a former foreign service officer, when he chaired Cornell's Department of Far Eastern Studies, developed under Echols' direction until his death. Echols' co-developer, curator Giok Po Oey, continued to build the collection after Echols' death in 1982. With a focus on the humanities and social sciences, the collection contains some 225,000 monographs and serial titles plus another 200,000 titles in microformats. Of these, approximately 5,000 items are related to the Vietnam War.

The *Vietnam War Bibliography* by Sugnet and Hickey lists the majority of these items and is the basis for the microformat *The Echols Collection: Selections from the Vietnam War* (both listed under the section "General Studies—Background"). The collection publishes a monthly *Southeast Asian Accessions List*.

6. The Vietnam Archive, Special Collections, University Library, Texas Tech University, Lubbock, TX 79409-0002. Stated purpose: "to collect, house, and preserve information related to the American experience in Vietnam, with special emphasis on the experiences of people of Texas and the Southwest." All kinds of print and nonprint materials are being collected, including literature, music, diaries, letters, photographs, maps, sound recordings, scrapbooks, oral histories, and albums. Because this collection is a new one, cataloging is incomplete. The Vietnam Archive has microfilm copies of relevant material from other major collections.

7. The William Joiner Center for the Study of War and Social Consequences, University of Massachusetts, Boston, MA 02125-3393. The Joiner Center has a wide range of collections on the Vietnam War, its causes, and its consequences. These include a film and video collection (especially strong on documentary materials), oral history tapes and files, photographs taken by veterans, declassified documents, captured documents, records and other materials of service organizations, command reports, and many other gatherings of interest to students and researchers. The university library holds eight hundred Vietnam War titles purchased from the collection built by the specialist bookseller Ken Lopez. Contact Kevin Bowen at 617-287-5850.

8. Lyndon Baines Johnson Library and Museum, 2313 Red River, Austin, TX 78705-5702. This collection houses White House papers pertaining to U.S. involvement in Vietnam from 1963-1969 as part of its archival function for the Johnson presidency. Includes also papers of Secretary of Defense Clark Clifford, General William Westmoreland, and other important government officials. This facility is a branch of the National Archives and Records Administration. Phone: 512-482-5137.

There are many Vietnam War collections under the jurisdiction of branches of the Armed Forces.

Students of Vietnam War literature will have to depend not only on specialized libraries and interlibrary loan services but also in some cases on the services of specialist booksellers. The catalogs of three such booksellers are found at the end of the section "General Studies—Background." In addition, two other booksellers are important for the Vietnam War researcher. These are The Cellar Book Shop, 18090 Wyoming, Detroit, MI 48221, and Tom Hebert, "Vietnam Bookman," 5 Marlene Drive, Burlington, CT 06013. The Cellar Book Shop publishes *Cellar*

Arrivals, a newsletter of recent listings, by subscription. Mainland Southeast Asia is one of the four areas of specialization covered. Hebert, who operated the Vietnam Bookstore for a decade, has reshaped his business to serve Vietnam book collectors. That is, he will conduct specialized searches.

The literature of the Vietnam War and the growing body of comment on that literature offer diverse lenses through which to perceive a major epoch in recent American history. Each student, through careful reading and diligent reflection, can make a contribution to these perceptions and understandings. What follows is a handbook or guide to what has already been done.

GENERAL STUDIES—BACKGROUND

Allen, Douglas, and Ngo Vinh Long, eds. *Coming to Terms: Indochina, the United States, and the War*. Boulder, Colo.: Westview Press, 1991.
One of the few and perhaps the strongest attempt to see the war and its aftermath from non-Western and antiwar perspectives. Essays on the Laotian and Cambodian experiences make this collection particular useful, as do the contributions by Noam Chomsky, George R. Vickers, and Kevin Bowen. There is a section on "Films and Scholarly Literature on Vietnam" that includes Marvin E. Gettleman's "Three Generations of Vietnam Scholarship." Illustrated.

Alvarez, Everett, Jr., and Anthony S. Pitch. *Chained Eagle*. New York: Donald I. Fine, 1989.
Though there is a large, imposing body of POW (prisoner of war) literature, this memoir is more intent than most on telling a representative, as well as personal, story. Not begun until many years after the events, *Chained Eagle* gains its useful distance also by the fact that co-author Pitch has handled much of the research, including interviews, necessary to tell Alvarez's story. Illustrated.

Anzenberger, Joseph F., Jr., ed. *Combat Art of the Vietnam War*. Jefferson, N.C.: McFarland, 1986.
A representation of the work of combat artists drawn from various military historical and art museums, this book gives more of a "feel" for the war than the many well-known photographic representations. Chapters include "Action," "Support," "Air War," "Portraits," "POWs," and "Humor." Anzenberger's introductions and his excerpts from interviews with many of the combat artists are particularly useful. These renderings were done under the auspices of the various military services.

Baritz, Loren. *Backfire: American Culture and the Vietnam War*. New York: William Morrow, 1985.
Baritz argues "that there is an American way of war that is congruent with the American way of life" and that we must understand the culture in order to understand the war. His major sections discuss cultural myths, political assumptions, and bureaucratic behavior. Though Baritz is not concerned with the imaginative literature of the Vietnam War, this study is enormously useful for anyone wishing to explore the connections between that literature and American culture.

Bowman, John S., ed. *The Vietnam War: An Almanac*. Introduction by Fox Butterfield. New York: World Almanac, 1985.
A handy, detailed chronology, with almost daily entries for the period of

American involvement, this reference is perhaps the most convenient way to discover what happened and when. The chronology is followed by essays on "The Price of the War," "Land Forces in Vietnam and Their Weapons," "Air Forces in Vietnam," "The Naval War in Vietnam," and "Irregular Forces of the Vietnam War." Includes a section of thumbnail biographies, a bibliography, and an index.

Braestrup, Peter. "Vietnam as History." *Wilson Quarterly* 2, no. 2 (Spring, 1978): 178-187.
This review essay treats a wide range of studies on various aspects of the war, setting newer works against selected earlier works on each subject. The scope includes foreign policy, military and diplomatic history, key biographies and autobiographies, and Vietnamese perspectives. Braestrup provides an authoritative overview of the dimensions of Vietnam War studies at an early stage of their development. Includes "A Vietnam Booklist."

Budge, Alice, and Pam Did r. "Women and War: A Selected Bibliography." *Mosaic* 23, no. 3 (Summer, 1990): 151-173.
This annotated bibliography lists scholarly books, articles, journalistic accounts, and memoirs published between 1974 and 1989 that treat the relationship between women and war. Since a number of the entries refer to the Vietnam War, this survey provides a useful intersection between Vietnam War studies and Women's Studies.

Burns, Richard Dean, and Milton Leitenberg. *The Wars in Vietnam, Cambodia, and Laos, 1945-1982: A Bibliographic Guide*. Santa Barbara, Calif.: ABC-Clio, 1984.
Updates and expands the work listed below under Leitenberg. With more than six thousand entries, this bibliography groups materials under such headings as "General Reference Aids," "Combat Operations," "United States and the Politics of Intervention," "Congress, International Law, and Negotiations," "Strategy, Tactics and Support Efforts," and "The War at Home." Includes maps, tables, and a useful introductory essay.

Cable, Larry E. *Conflict of Myths: The Development of American Counterinsurgency Doctrine and the Vietnam War*. New York: New York University Press, 1986.
At the center of this valuable study is an attempt to understand "the American theory of victory" in order to evaluate America's sense of its abilities "to define and achieve policy goals in Southeast Asia." In particular, Cable examines the means to victory in guerilla warfare, citing such precursor conflicts as the Greek Civil War, the Korean Conflict, and political/military situations in the Philippines, Malaysia, and Central America.

Camp, Norman M., Robert H. Stretch, and William C. Marshall. *Stress, Strain, and Vietnam: An Annotated Bibliography of Two Decades of Psychiatric and Social Sciences Literature Reflecting the Effect of the War on the American Soldier.* New York: Greenwood Press, 1988.
The three main divisions are "Vietnam Service," "Veteran Adaptation," and "Social and Institutional Context." The 851 citations span the years 1965-1987 and include the findings of mental health professionals and social scientists supplemented by relevant reports of war correspondents and personal narratives of veterans. Subtopics include abusive violence, substance abuse, psychiatric treatment, military organization, and public attitudes. Excellent annotations.

Chen, John H. M. *Vietnam: A Comprehensive Bibliography.* Metuchen, N.J.: Scarecrow Press, 1973.
This listing (alphabetical by author) covers all publications in book form in all written languages. Its early completion date (before the end of American involvement) limits utility, but the comprehensive subject and title indexes make it easy to use. Not annotated.

Cima, Ronald J., ed. *Vietnam: A Country Study.* Washington, D.C.: Library of Congress Federal Research Division, 1989.
The essays collected here are "Historical Setting," "The Society and Its Environment," "The Economy," "Government and Politics," and "National Security." This interdisciplinary study focuses on the years between 1975 and the mid-1980s "when a nascent and newly reunified nation struggled to develop a postwar identity." Appendices on demographic and industrial data.

Cincinnatus [pseudonym]. *Self-Destruction: The Disintegration and Decay of the United States Army During the Vietnam Era.* New York: W. W. Norton, 1981.
The argument is that although the war was fought for political purposes and under certain limitations imposed by political situations, it was still a war that could have been won. The army had sufficient latitude and opportunity for victory but failed to adopt appropriate strategy and tactics. Careerism and self-perpetuation handicapped effective decision making. The detailed underpinnings of this indictment give credibility to many of the situations and experiences developed in the imaginative literature.

Clark, Gregory R. *Words of the Vietnam War.* Jefferson, N.C.: McFarland, 1990.
Contains ten thousand entries (including cross-references) and more than forty-three hundred definitions relating to the Vietnam War: "persons, places, events, terrain features; military installations, operations, units, equipment, specifications and weapons; euphemisms, slang, graffiti, acronyms, and abbreviations; and foreign words and phrases." Also included is the language of the antiwar movement of the late 1960s. A crucial resource for explicating the specialized

references and jargon of the literary responses to the war. More comprehensive than James S. Olson's *Dictionary of the Vietnam War* and with more extended definitions than Reinberg's *In the Field*.

DeBenedetti, Charles, with Charles Chatfield. *An American Ordeal: The Antiwar Movement of the Vietnam Era*. Syracuse, N.Y.: Syracuse University Press, 1990.
This detailed "interpretive history" examines how the momentum to foster a foreign policy conducive to peace became transformed into organized opposition to the Vietnam War. Main divisions are "The Reconstruction of the Peace Movement, 1955-1963," "The Construction of an Antiwar Movement, 1963-1965," "The Contest for the Center, 1966-1970," "The War and The American Way, 1970-1975," and concluding "Reflections."

Dicks, Shirley. *From Vietnam to Hell: Interviews with Victims of Post-Traumatic Stress Disorder*. Jefferson, N.C.: McFarland, 1990.
These two dozen narratives, a mixture of the interviewer's summaries of taped telephone interviews and the words of those interviewed, are an important supplement to the clinical and otherwise professional discussions of this problem available elsewhere. Some of those interviewed are wives of PTSD sufferers.

Doyle, Jeff, and Jeffrey Grey, eds. *Australian R & R: Representations and Reinterpretations of Australia's War in Vietnam*. Chevy Chase, Md.: Burning Cities Press, 1991. Also available as *Vietnam Generation* 3, no. 2 (1991).
This collection offers to American readers "versions of the history of the Vietnam War as experienced by one of its principal allies." Essays include "The Australian Government and Involvement in the Vietnam War," "Policy Contradictions of the Australian Task Force," "Dismembering the Anzac Legend: Australian Popular Culture and the Vietnam War," and "Australia and the Vietnam War—A Select Bibliography."

Duiker, William J. *Historical Dictionary of Vietnam*. Metuchen, N.J., Scarecrow Press, 1989.
More selective but wider in range than the dictionaries of war terms is this dictionary of Vietnam's complex history. It includes names of important personages, dynasties, political groups, and events such as "Annamese Communist Party" and "Convention of 1925." Duiker includes an extensive bibliography with works grouped under such headings as history, society, economy, culture, and official documents. Includes maps, chronologies, and tables.

The Echols Collection: Selections on the Vietnam War. Microform. Ann Arbor, ich.: UMI Research Press, 1990-

More than five thousand volumes of material on American involvement in
Vietnam have been selected from the John M. Echols Collection on Southeast
Asia located at Cornell University. The first four units include, respectively: (1)
four hundred titles, mostly monographs, including propaganda, factual accounts,
and after-the-fact analyses; (2) four hundred pamphlets from organizations and
documents from North and South Vietnamese government agencies; (3) three
hundred titles on the economics of Vietnam and Southeast Asia; (4) three
hundred titles on Vietnamese culture, economics, and politics (pre- and postwar). These are all English language materials; French and Vietnamese materials
are forthcoming.

Eckert, Edward. "The Vietnam War: A Selective Bibliography." *Choice* 24, no.
1 (September, 1986): 51-71.
Eckert comments on nonfiction works in the following categories: "Vietnamese
Background," "American Politics and the Vietnam War," "The Battles and
Soldiers," "Veterans and Resisters," and "General Histories and Anthologies."
This discussion touches upon many of the important memoirs and oral histories.
An excellent overview of the broad field of Vietnam War studies.

Edelman, Bernard, ed. *Dear America: Letters Home from Vietnam*. New York: W.
W. Norton, 1985.
This collection was prepared for the New York Vietnam Veterans Memorial
Commission in order to heighten public awareness and to raise funds for
veterans' programs. The representative letters are grouped into thematic
chapters: "'Cherries': First Impressions," "'Humping the Boonies,'" "Beyond
the Body Count," "Base Camp: War at the Rear," "'World of Hurt,'" "What
Am I Doing Here?" "'We Gotta Get Out of the Place,'" and "Last Letters."
Edelman includes 208 letters by 125 people. Brief biographical notes.

Ellsberg, Daniel. *Papers on the War*. New York: Simon & Schuster, 1972.
A collection of essays notable for their analyses of U.S. government decision-
making policies. Most important is "The Quagmire Myth and the Stalemate
Machine." Other topics include the invasion of Laos, the failure of rural
pacification, and "The Responsibility of Officials in a Criminal War." Ellsberg's
opinions are based, in part, on his readings of the Pentagon Papers, which he
brought to the public's attention by making them available to the press.

Elwood-Akers, Virginia. *Woman War Correspondents in the Vietnam War, 1961-
1975*. Metuchen, N.J.: Scarecrow Press, 1988.
In chronologically delimited chapters, the author profiles the activities of woman
journalists who covered the war. Her emphasis is on their professionalism, the
range of attitudes toward their presence in the combat arena, and the wide
spectrum of their political and journalistic styles. Each chapter presents a

sampling of one or more journalists' work. Marguerite Higgins, Martha Gellhorn, and Frances FitzGerald are among those discussed and represented.

Engelmann, Larry. *Tears Before the Rain: An Oral History of the Fall of South Vietnam.* New York: Oxford University Press, 1990.
Because of the large amount of imaginative literature that treats the fall of Saigon, Engelmann's compilation is valuable to the literary student. Based on interviews with more than three hundred individuals, this study includes such topics as "Last Flight from Da Nang," "The Congressional Delegation," "American Embassy," "Media," and "Military Sealift Command." Engelmann interviewed both Americans and Vietnamese.

Fall, Bernard F. *Viet-Nam Witness, 1953-66,* New York: Praeger, 1966.
The writings of this French journalist are considered to be among the prophetic books. Rooting his observations in the disastrous experience of French colonialism, Fall argues that the American phase of Vietnam's tragedy was entirely avoidable. A series of individual, shortsighted decisions led America step-by-step into further involvement—and, as Fall sees it, would lead to even further escalations. This volume is a collection of newspaper and magazine articles. Fall's other books include *The Two Viet-Nams* and *Street Without Joy.*

Figley, Charles R., and Seymour Leventman, eds. *Strangers at Home: Vietnam Veterans Since the War.* New York: Praeger, 1980.
This collection of essays gives comprehensive coverage to all aspects of the Vietnam veteran situation: estrangement and victimization, oral history as therapy, attitudes toward race, psychosocial adjustment, drug use, economic (job) situations, government programs, and legal issues. Many of the individual essays are classics in their field. Among the contributors include Charles Moskos, Norma Wikler, John P. Wilson, and Dean K. Phillips.

FitzGerald, Frances. *Fire in the Lake: The Vietnamese and the Americans in Vietnam.* Boston: Atlantic Monthly Press/Little, Brown, 1972.
This award-winning history explores the attempts by the Vietnamese to find their own solution to their complex problems. FitzGerald places the American intercession into a rich context of bewildering social, religious, economic, and political forces indigenous to Vietnam and largely misinterpreted by American officials. By examining the causes and mutual misunderstanding and suspicion, FitzGerald lays bare the futile, hopelessly destructive nature of U.S. involvement there. Essentially, FitzGerald felt that the emergence of a united Vietnam cleansed of Western contamination was desirable and inevitable, and that the communist-dominated National Liberation Front, a committed organization of Vietnamese, held the winning hand.

Frey-Wouters, Ellen, and Robert S. Laufer. *Legacy of a War: The American Soldier in Vietnam.* Armonk, N.Y.: M. E. Sharpe, 1986.
The authors conducted more than twelve hundred interviews with men of the Vietnam generation in order to examine the social, psychological, and political effects of the war. Major sections are "War Stress and Its Aftermath," "Views of the War," "Perceptions of the Conduct of the War," and "Vietnam and Beyond." Unusually fascinating appendices include detailed tables and an overview of the sampling and analytic methodologies. The authors' data "suggest that the question of participation in future wars like Vietnam will be carefully scrutinized."

Gettleman, Marvin E., Jane Franklin, Marilyn Young, and H. Bruce Franklin, eds. *Vietnam and America: A Documented History.* New York: Grove Press, 1985.
Each of the eight sections begins with an editor's introduction, often followed by an interpretative essay. Then come the selected documents: official pronouncements or government records. The sections are: "Background to Revolution," " "War and Independence," "Geneva—The Peace Subverted," "The Revolution Against Diem," "The Americanization of the War," "The Movement Against the War," "The Decisive Year, 1968," and "Vietnamization, 1969-1975."

Gibson, James William. *The Perfect War: Technowar in Vietnam.* Boston: Atlantic Monthly Press, 1986.
Gibson defines "technowar" as the "military mode of strategy and organization in which war is conceptualized and organized as a high-technology, capital-intensive production process." The managers of this system operated in "closed, self-referential universe" in which technological, economic, and production superiority was deemed sufficient to assure victory. They were wrong. Gibson's analysis is persuasive, and his presentation is marked by many allusions to literary works.

Gilbert, Marc Jason, ed. *The Vietnam War: Teaching Approaches and Resources.* New York: Greenwood Press, 1991.
Designed to help instructors pressed into service for the burgeoning field of Vietnam War studies, this collection assesses primary and secondary sources from a wide variety of perspectives. Historical, literary, and documentary materials are reviewed in the various essays. Includes an appendix of course syllabi and "A Guide to Curriculum Development Resources" prepared by the editor.

Gray, J. Glenn. *The Warriors: Reflections on Men in Battle.* New York: Harcourt, Brace, 1959. Reprint, with an introduction by Hannah Arendt. New York: Harper & Row, 1967. Reprint, with a new foreword by the author. 1970.

Drawing largely upon his personal experiences in World War II, Gray tries to determine "what the practice of total war did to man as warrior." His insights into such topics as "The Enduring Appeal of Battle," "The Soldier's Relations to Death," "Images of the Enemy," and "The Ache of Guilt" have been found useful by scholars studying the Vietnam War and its aftermath.

Gruening, Ernest, and Herbert W. Beaser. *Vietnam Folly*. Washington, D.C.: The National Press, 1968.
The senator from Alaska examines decisions and assumptions that led to "the tragic involvement of the United States military in Vietnam" and the gradual expansion of the military role. Gruening sees many of these decisions as based on honest miscalculation as well as congressional cowardice. A vivid insider's view of how executive and congressional conduct and misconduct shaped American participation in Vietnam's civil war.

Halberstam, David. *The Best and the Brightest*. New York: Random House, 1972.
Based on hundreds of interviews conducted on the heels of the 1968 election campaign, Halberstam's study attempts to trace the history of the decision-making process that led to our active involvement in Vietnam and the escalation of that involvement. Halberstam examines the major personalities in American government during the Vietnam era in order to discover what combination of strengths and weaknesses led them and the United States into what he considers a disastrous policy. This book may be considered a successor to Halberstam's *The Making of a Quagmire* (New York: Random House, 1965).

Hallin, Daniel C. *The "Uncensored War": The Media and Vietnam*. New York: Oxford University Press, 1986. Reprint, with a new preface. Berkeley: University of California Press, 1989.
Hallin explores the generally accepted notion of conflict between the media and the government during the Vietnam War. He examines the freedom of the media in reporting the war and the consequences of this freedom. The period was one in which the media gained autonomy in its relationship to government and the professional journalist became "more autonomous within the news organization." This study's two major sections are "Escalation and News Management, 1961-1975" and "The War on Television, 1965-1973." Tables provide statistical analyses of coverage.

Heath, G. Louis. *Mutiny Does Not Happen Lightly: The Literature of the American Resistance to the Vietnam War*. Metuchen, N.J.: Scarecrow Press, 1976.
Introductory matter includes a brief overview of the war resistance movement. The body of the work is a collection of 118 representative "flyers, leaflets, letters, reports, manuals, and documents produced by or relating to the antiwar

movement in the United States from 1964 to 1974." Includes also a list of protest organizations and a "Select Bibliography on Vietnam."

Ho Chi Minh. *On Revolution: Selected Writings, 1920-66*. Edited, and with an introduction, by Bernard B. Fall. New York: Praeger, 1967.
Here are gathered the most eloquent and authoritative assertions of the "enemy" point of view. Ho Chi Minh's hatred of colonialism and his vision of its worldwide exploitation of underdeveloped countries are captured in this assemblage that covers half a century of Vietnamese history. These writings clarify his reasons for joining the Communist Party. The focus, of course, is on the imperialist French rather than the Americans. Most of the selections were designed as speeches rather than formal writings.

Indochina Chronology. Published quarterly by the Institute of East Asian Studies at the University of California, Berkeley.
Reports on current events in or related to Indochina. The "Chronology" sections on Vietnam, Cambodia, and Laos are supplemented by a "Bibliography" of Indochina-related monographs as well as articles in periodicals. *Indochina Chronology* also provides news on recent conferences and lists new documents received by the Indochina Archive.

Johnson, Donald Clay. *A Guide to Reference Materials on Southeast Asia Based on the Collections in the Yale and Cornell University Libraries*. New Haven, Conn.: Yale University Press, 1970.
Examples of the groupings in this listing are biographies, dictionaries, guidebooks, economics, anthropology, archaeology, religion, and agriculture. It includes many references that are primarily statistical but omits government publications and yearbooks. Not annotated.

Karnow, Stanley. *Vietnam: A History*. New York: Viking Press, 1983. Rev. ed. New York: Penguin Books, 1991.
Probably the most judicious and most attractively written discourse on Vietnam at war written from a Western perspective, this study reaches back to the longer history of conflict in Vietnam. From this vantage point, America's late engagement and partial reshaping of the Vietnamese people's ongoing struggle for national identity is treated in laborious yet lucid detail. Illustrated, with "Chronology" and "Cast of Principal Characters," this text is the companion to the Public Television series of the same name.

Kimball, Jeffrey P., ed. *To Reason Why: The Debate About the Causes of U.S. Involvement in the Vietnam War*. New York: McGraw-Hill, 1990.
Kimball "brings together readings that best exemplify the widely varying answers that historians, political scientists, social scientists, policymakers,

journalists, and novelists have given to the essential question of American involvement." Major divisions represent the official view, idealistic and strategic concepts, analyses of process, presidential influence, managers and bureaucrats, economic concerns, and cultural misunderstandings. A rich, far-ranging survey.

Kolko, Gabriel. *Anatomy of a War: Vietnam, the United States, and the Modern Historical Experience*. New York: Pantheon Books, 1985.
Kolko's analysis gives far more detailed attention to South Vietnamese politics and economics than other histories. He also examines the leadership, strategies, and assumptions of the Communist Party. U.S. failure stemmed from fatal dependence on a client military government that was "an intrinsically dysfunctional hybrid order that the United States had constructed both by default and by accretion."

Lacouture, Jean. *Vietnam: Between Two Truces*. Translated by Konrad Kellen and Joel Carmichael. New York: Random House, 1966.
Based on his experiences as a French journalist covering Southeast Asia for many years, Lacouture's analysis rests on a detailed knowledge of local political phenomena that have escaped the attention of most other writers. The general argument of this book, the original edition of which was written even as American forces were building, is that an essentially local struggle demands a settlement of local issues. The overlay of foreign and global concerns can only make things worse.

Lansdale, Edward G. *In the Midst of Wars: An American's Mission to Southeast Asia*. New York: Harper & Row, 1972.
Lansdale's mission to Vietnam during the 1950s made him a central figure in American involvement at that time. The events that he recounts and the attitude that he defends are familiar to readers of Graham Greene's *The Quiet American* and Lederer and Burdick's *The Ugly American*. Indeed, Lansdale is the "original" of the main American character in each. Illustrated.

Leitenberg, Milton, and Richard Dean Burns. *The Vietnam Conflict: Its Geographical Dimensions, Political Traumas, and Military Developments*. Santa Barbara, Calif.: ABC-Clio, 1973.
This bibliography is divided into the following topic areas: "General References," "Area Dimensions," "Vietnam: History and Politics," "U.S. Involvement," "Military Operations," and "Domestic Impact of the War." Each major division has several subdivisions—such as "Private Journals," "War Crimes," and "Draft Protest"—under which works are listed alphabetically by author. More than twenty-three hundred entries. Not annotated. Updated in Burns, above.

Lewy, Guenter. *America in Vietnam*. New York: Oxford University Press, 1978.
One of the first histories to make extensive use of classified records of the
armed forces. Lewy hopes that his empirical evidence will "clear away the
cobwebs of mythology" regarding the kind of actions that were officially
condoned. Lewy focuses attention on miscalculations and ineffectively
implemented strategies and tactics. Public opinion was swayed more by the
ineffectual conduct of the war than by issues of principle.

Lifton, Robert Jay. *Home from the War: Vietnam Veterans, Neither Victims nor
Executioners*. New York: Simon & Schuster, 1973.
A classic study of the psychological dilemmas of Vietnam War veterans. Lifton
explores the pain and alienation of these veterans, the ways in which their
experience and homecoming was different from that of veterans of other wars,
and especially the lingering guilt over their involvement in a tainted enterprise.
Based in part on extensive interviews, Lifton's study provides a context for
understanding and assessing the literary responses to the plight of the Vietnam
War veteran. Far-ranging discussions of the psychology of the warrior in
Western culture and of the "gook syndrome" in American culture.

Lippard, Lucy R. *A Different War: Vietnam in Art*. Seattle: Real Comet Press,
1990.
Based on an exhibit held at the Whatcom Museum of History and Art, this book
contains a detailed narrative on artistic responses to the Vietnam War as well as
reproductions of the works in the exhibit. The majority of works take an antiwar
stance. Unlike the by-and-large representational sketches, drawings, and
paintings in the Anzenberger collection, these are often nonrepresentational and
employ a wide range of techniques and media. Includes list for further reading,
exhibition checklist, and artist index.

McDonald, Ben. *The Vietnam Book List*. 3d ed. Conifer, Colo.: Bibliographies
Unlimited, 1991.
More than thirty-four hundred entries are listed in a single alphabet. The index
groups books by their entry numbers into more than seventy categories including
"Air War, " "Fiction," "Helicopters," "North Vietnam," "PTSD," "Refugees,"
"War Crimes," and "Women and War." McDonald often fails to indicate
whether a listed title is an edited work or a translation. No annotations.

Maclear, Michael. *The Ten Thousand Day War: Vietnam, 1945-1975*. New York:
St. Martin's Press, 1981.
Maclear's is one of the earliest "complete histories" of American involvement
in Vietnam, and still one of the best in balance and readability. The basis for a
major television series, the book relies heavily on Peter Arnett's reports and on
his interviews with the principal figures in the Vietnam War. Each chapter is a

short, manageable framing of some significant episode or aspect. Aimed at the general reader rather than the specialist.

MacPherson, Myra. *Long Time Passing: Vietnam and the Haunted Generation.* New York: Doubleday, 1984.
This dazzling exploration of Vietnam generation culture orchestrates more than five hundred interviews with veterans (wounded, traumatized, and well), protesters, draft dodgers, parents, and representatives of various minority groups, regions, and socioeconomic classes. MacPherson allows the various components in the chorus of attitudes each to have its own voice. An essential text.

Marshall, Kathryn, ed. *In the Combat Zone: An Oral History of American Women in Vietnam, 1966-1975.* Boston: Little, Brown, 1987.
The women whose voices are heard here were involved in many of the activities reviewed in Marshall's introduction. Women worked as nurses, American Red Cross field service staff and members of the Red Cross Supplemental Recreational Activities Overseas ("donut dollies"), Army Special Services and USO volunteers, employees of airlines under military contracts, government staff, and workers for religious organizations.

Marshall, S. L. A. *Fields of Bamboo: Three Battles Just Beyond the China Sea.* New York: Dial Press, 1971. Reprinted as *Vietnam: Three Battles.* New York: Da Capo Press, 1982.
Marshall's detailed narratives of small-scale operations provide a unique feel for the day-to-day flavor of the war. Reconstructing operations carried out in 1966, veteran observer-participant Marshall portrays the ironic contrast between American air mobile forces and the Vietcong tactics. The text is supplemented by photographs, drawings, and a brief glossary. One of several studies of the Vietnam War written or co-written by Marshall.

Martin, Charles E. "'A Good One Is a Dead One': The Combat Soldiers' View of Vietnam and the Indian Wars." *Kentucky Folklore Record* 26, no. 3/4 (July-December, 1980): 114-132.
Martin points out striking parallels between the perceptions of combat circumstances and of the enemy in the Vietnam War and in the Indian Wars of one hundred years earlier. Low morale, substance abuse, desertion, racism, and a frequently invisible enemy who had mastered its home territory are among the many connecting links.

Matthews, Lloyd J., and Dale E. Brown, eds. *Assessing the Vietnam War: A Collection from the Journal of the U.S. Army War College.* Washington, D.C.: Pergamon-Brassey's International Defense Publishers, 1987.

Reprints reviews and articles in five categories: "The Literature of the War," "The Strategy and Nature of the War," "The Conduct of the War," "The Lessons of the War," and "The Aftermath of the War." Contributors include Harry G. Summers, Jr., Joe P. Dunn, Guenter Lewy, and W. W. Rostow. Introduction by Gen. Bruce Palmer, Jr. Notable for its breadth and authority, this collection has a wider range of opinion than its source journal might suggest.

Miller, Robert Hopkins. *The United States and Vietnam, 1787-1941.* Washington, D.C.: National Defense University Press, 1990.
Miller documents the tides of American diplomatic, economic, and strategic interests in Vietnam beginning with Thomas Jefferson's interest in trading for rice in Cochinchina. The six chapters cover "Merchant Ships and Their Captains," "Diplomats and Naval Vessels," "Commerce, Strategic Thinking, and Colonial Expansion," "The United States' Good Offices," "The United States and Japan: Prelude to Confrontation," and "Japan's Southward Advance." His study traces the gradual evolution of U.S. "perceptions of Vietnam as a country and people" and the slow process by which Vietnam's importance to American interests became perceived.

Morris, Richard, and Peter Ehrenhaus, eds. *Cultural Legacies of Vietnam: Uses of the Past in the Present.* Norwood, N.J.: Ablex, 1990.
This stimulating collection grew out of a conference held at Rutgers University. The essays are gathered in three sections: "Vietnam as Political Metaphor," "Vietnam and the Shaping of Popular Imagination," and "Vietnam and the Shaping of American Cultures." Includes Adi Wimmer on protest poetry and an adaptation of part of Susan Jeffords' *The Remasculinization of America* titled "Reproducing Fathers: Gender and the Vietnam War in American Culture" (focus here on film representation).

Moss, George Donelson, ed. *A Vietnam Reader: Sources and Essays.* Englewood Cliffs, N.J.: Prentice-Hall, 1991.
Designed as a college text, this exciting reader is divided into two parts. The first organizes sixty primary source documents into five chronological groupings. These documents include presidential speeches, reports of cabinet secretaries, letters, declarations, and testimony. The second part gathers five interpretive essays on the Cold War "domino theory" myth, Nixon's responses to shifts in public opinion, the Vietnam War in American movies, television coverage, and "The Vietnamization of Nicaragua." Moss's thirty-page introduction is a solid overview of "U.S. Involvement in Indochina, 1942-1975." Includes a chronology, a glossary, and a disappointing list of further readings.

Nixon, Richard M. *No More Vietnams*. New York: Arbor House, 1985.
The heart of Nixon's argument is to counter the following "myths": that the war was immoral, that it was unwinnable, that diplomacy without force is the best answer to Communist aggression and Communist-inspired or -supported revolution, and that the United States was on the wrong side in Vietnam. Nixon believes that America tried and failed in a just cause; he argues the justice and explores the failure in political, military, and personal terms.

Norman, Elizabeth. *Woman at War: The Story of Fifty Military Nurses Who Served in Vietnam*. Philadelphia: University of Pennsylvania Press, 1990.
Based on extensive interviews, Norman's study illuminates the wide range of professional and personal experiences of women who served in the Army, Navy, and Air Force Nurse Corps. Loosely structured around a tour of duty, the chapters include "Professional Strains and Moral Dilemmas," "Status of Female Military Nurses," and "Homecoming." Norman provides an authoritative context for assessing the literary treatments of nurses and the armed forces medical establishment in Vietnam during the war.

Olson, James S. *Dictionary of the Vietnam War*. New York: Greenwood Press, 1988.
The major focus is on the period 1945-1975 in this cross-referenced, alphabetical compendium of "brief descriptive essays on most of the people, legislation, military operations, and controversies important to military participation in the Vietnam War." Entries include references for further reading. The appendices encompass demography, acronyms and slang, a selected bibliography, a chronology of the war, and maps. The entries here are fewer in number but generally longer than the ones in Clark's *Words of the Vietnam War*.

Peake, Louis A. *The United States in the Vietnam War, 1954-1975: A Selected, Annotated Bibliography*. New York: Garland, 1986.
Peake lists and describes all kinds of sources, including primary documents, under the following ten headings: "General Reference," "Southeast Asia," "Vietnam," "Vietnam and the United States Government," "The Vietnam War," "The American Military Experience in Vietnam," "The Media War," "The Vietnam War in Literature, Film, Music, and Art," "The Domestic Impact of the War," and "The Consequences of the Vietnam War." Unfortunately, some of Peake's annotations replicate those of an earlier scholarly work.

The Pentagon Papers (The Senator Gravel Edition). 5 vols. Introduction by Senator Mike Gravel. Boston: Beacon Press, 1971-1972.
The history of U.S. decision making regarding Vietnam made available in these volumes includes twenty-nine hundred pages of narrative, one thousand pages of appended documents, and a two-hundred-page collection of official justifica-

tions. Volume 5 is a collection of interpretive essays drawing upon the Pentagon Papers. Contributors include James Aronson, Gabriel Kolko, and Noam Chomsky ("The Pentagon Papers as Propaganda and as History"). Also included is "The Tonkin Gulf Narrative and Resolutions."

Pike, Douglas, comp. *The History of the Vietnam War*. Microform. Ann Arbor, Mich.: UMI Research Press, 1988-   .
An ongoing project that draws upon the Indochina Archives at the University of California, Berkeley, the "history" includes 365,000 pages of materials of every conceivable kind relevant to a rounded picture of the war. The project has ten units, each with a printed guide prepared by Pike: "Grand Strategy and General Assessment of the War," "General History of the War," "Topical History of the War" (in fifteen sections), "Political Settlement Efforts," "The National Liberation Front," "The Democratic Republic of Vietnam," "Indochina," "The Asian Region During the Vietnam War," and "Chronology of the Vietnam War."

Pratt, John Clark. *Vietnam Voices: Perspectives on the War Years, 1941-1982*. New York: Viking Press, 1984.
Pratt represents the full range of participants, from policymakers to grunts, in this ambitious survey of opinion. The materials are organized into a five-act dramatic structure, surrounded by prologue and epilogue. Such a mixture of cablegram, oral history, North Vietnamese propaganda, letters home, journalistic accounts, and government documents is simultaneously bewildering and illuminating. Pratt's weaving gives us both "the facts" and the feel.

Raskin, Marcus G., and Bernard B. Fall, eds. *The Viet-Nam Reader*. New York: Random House, 1965.
An early gathering of "articles and documents on American foreign policy and the Viet-Nam crisis" that shows a noninterventionist bent. Section titles are "The Crisis of American Foreign Policy," "The Rise of the Viet-Nam Problem," "The Second Indochina War," and "The Negotiating Positions." Opinions include those of American, European, and Southeast Asian statesmen, journalists, and scholars.

Reinberg, Linda. *In the Field: The Language of the Vietnam War*. New York: Facts on File, 1991.
This dictionary has even more entries than Clark's, but its entries tend to be shorter (handled in a total of 288 pages against Clark's 616). Reinberg includes code names, place names, the names of events and campaigns, the names of weapons, slang expressions, acronyms, and nicknames as well as Vietnamese words and phrases adopted by American military personnel.

Sayres, Sohnya, Anders Stephanson, Stanley Aronowitz, and Fredric Jameson, eds. *The 60s Without Apology*. Minneapolis: University of Minnesota Press, 1984. In shaping left-leaning response to the right wing's trashing of the 1960s, the editors have chosen materials to affirm the spirit and value of a historical moment when there was a liberating "disruption of the late-capitalist ideological and political hegemony." The emerging portrait of 1960s political struggles is important to an understanding of what is often called "the war at home." Most useful for students of the war and its literature are Herman Rapaport's "Vietnam: The Thousand Plateaus" and Jay Boyer's "Why You Will Never Read the Novel You Might Like To." Includes a lexicon of 1960s argot.

Schell, Jonathan. *The Real War*. New York: Pantheon Books, 1987. This book brings together Schell's two classic journalistic accounts: "The Village of Ben Suc" (1967) and "The Military Half" (1968). The former describes the destruction of a village as part of a major American military operation. The latter recounts American bombing and ground operations that destroyed two provinces in South Vietnam. A new essay, "The Real War," is a succinct, retrospective account of the causes of American failure in Vietnam.

Shafer, D. Michael, ed. *The Vietnam War in the American Imagination*. Boston: Beacon Press, 1990. The major assumption of this gathering is that the Vietnam War was not an aberration in American history. The book "probes how and how much Vietnam shapes America and Americans today." Major divisions are "The Importance of Remembering," "Going to War: The Human Legacy," "The Recreation of Vietnam and America," and "Facing the Future." One essay each on the media, film, and literature (the latter by Richard A. Sullivan).

Sheehan, Neil. *A Bright Shining Lie: John Paul Vann and America in Vietnam*. New York: Random House, 1988. A unique and engagingly written blend of biography and history that uses the character and career of Col. John Paul Vann as a window on American failure, frustration, and corruption and on the growing magnitude of destruction consequent upon American involvement in Vietnam. Vann's ambivalent relationship to "the system" echoes America's ambivalent relationship to its goals and methods in Vietnam. Sheehan seems torn between his desire to uphold an understanding of the war that echoes his own and his realization that Vann was a habitual liar. A stylistic masterwork, with extensive documentation and bibliography.

Sheehan, Neil, Hedrick Smith, E. W. Kenworthy, and Fox Butterfield. *The Pentagon Papers as Published by The New York Times*. New York: Quadrangle Books, 1971.

Based on the incomplete texts of the Pentagon Papers that were published in *The New York Times* in the summer of 1971, these ten essays, chronologically arranged, review and interpret the material. Chapter titles include "The Consensus to Bomb North Vietnam," "Secretary McNamara's Disenchantment," and "The Tet Offensive and the Turnaround." This volume also includes key documents, court records, and biographies.

Sheehan, Susan. *Ten Vietnamese*. New York: Alfred A. Knopf, 1969.
Recognizing that the news media had made the Vietnam War "more of an American than a Vietnamese story" and that reporters' contacts were "usually limited to the country's leaders and would-be leaders," Sheehan set out to capture the lives of the ordinary people. Her representative sketches include a peasant, a landlord, a refugee, a politician, a Montagnard, an orphan, a Buddhist monk, a South Vietnamese soldier, a Viet Cong, and a North Vietnamese prisoner.

Spector, Ronald H. *Researching the Vietnam War*. Washington, D.C.: Analysis Branch, U.S. Army Center of Military History, 1984.
In narrative form, Spector gives an account of what kinds of documents are found and where. He divides his account by chronological periods and topics, locating the various governmental and private collections, archives, and libraries that hold relevant materials. Official documents, oral histories, and firsthand accounts are the kinds of materials surveyed here. Select bibliography.

Sugnet, Christopher, and John T. Hickey. *Vietnam War Bibliography*. Lexington, Mass.: Lexington Books, 1983.
Though this bibliographical register and its companion index were prepared to aid researchers using the John M. Echols Collection in Cornell University's Olin Library, it can be of benefit to any scholar. Four thousand items were selected from the seven thousand or so in the collection, and these are listed alphabetically by title with brief annotations for those whose titles are not self-explanatory. Includes French and Vietnamese titles as well as English ones. The index contains subjects, personal and organizational names, and alternate titles. The focus is on the political, military, and economic aspects of the collection.

Summers, Harry G., Jr. *On Strategy: A Critical Analysis of the Vietnam War*. Rev. ed. Novato, Calif.: Presidio, 1982.
Summers' treatment is considered by many to be a classic treatment of U.S. strategy in Vietnam. His discussion supports the assertion that "we failed to properly employ our armed forces so as to secure U.S. national objectives in Vietnam." Summers further observes that America's unwillingness to declare war hindered the clear articulation of objectives; thus it was difficult to keep such objectives in view. Moreover, the United States' reluctance to engage the

North Vietnamese ("the root of the trouble") in its initial military efforts made victory unlikely.

_____. *Vietnam War Almanac*. New York: Facts on File, 1985.
Part 1 concerns the setting of the war, with brief sections on misperceptions, physical and historical realities, French occupations, the First Indochina War, and the Republic of Vietnam. Part 2 is a handy chronology of the war, 1959-1975. Part 3, "The Vietnam War: A to Z," is a dictionary of terms. Some of the entries are quite detailed. Representative entries: "Chinook Helicopter," "Morality," "Sapper," and "Tactics." This work has more in common with the dictionaries by Clark, Olson, and Reinberg than it does with the similarly named "almanac" by Bowman.

Tal, Kali, gen. ed. *Vietnam Generation*. Chevy Chase, Md.: Vietnam Generation and Burning Cities Press, 1989-
Each issue of *Vietnam Generation* highlights some aspect of the Vietnam War era or the Vietnam War generation. Each of the publications is simultaneously an issue of the journal and a book, and most have guest editors. Representative titles are *GI Resistance: Soldiers and Veterans Against the War*, *Kent and Jackson State: 1970-1990*, *Southeast Asian American Communities*, and *A White Man's War: Race Issues and Vietnam*. Many of the *Vietnam Generation* issues and essays related to literary study are entered elsewhere in this bibliography. A must for any serious student of the war, its context, its cultural representations, and its consequences. This publisher's *Vietnam Generation Newsletter*, edited by Dan Duffy, 2921 Terrace Drive, Chevy Chase, MD 20815, is an important source of reviews and comment on Vietnam-related concerns.

Taylor, Clyde, ed. *Vietnam and Black America: An Anthology of Protest and Resistance*. Garden City, N.Y.: Anchor, 1973.
The editor argues that the writings collected here—creative works, essays, speeches, and autobiography—"contain the truest and most meaningful understanding of the American involvement in Vietnam." Though the claim is inflated, the perspectives here gathered are indispensable for building a rounded understanding of that involvement. Included are works by James Baldwin, Julian Bond, Stokely Carmichael, Etheridge Knight, Malcolm X, and Ronald Dellums.

Trujillo, Charley, ed. *Soldados: Chicanos in Viet Nam*. San Jose, Calif.: Chusma House, 1990.
Noting the lack of attention to the Chicano experience in Vietnam, Trujillo gathered the testimony of nineteen Chicano veterans from his hometown of Corcoran, California. Trujillo founded Chusma House after failing to interest a major publisher in the book. Nonetheless, it is a major contribution to the oral

literature of the war and a necessary reminder of the disproportionate numbers of minority group members who served.

Truong Nhu Tang. *A Vietcong Memoir.* San Diego: Harcourt Brace Jovanovich, 1985.
The author was a Vietcong urban organizer and later a cabinet member. His two decades of involvement in the political side of the war demonstrated to him that "the Vietcong was no monolith." His narrative stresses "the human motives, the internal struggle, the bitter resolution." Truong feels that "the national democratic revolution" succumbed to "the arrogance of power" and to an undesirable dependence on the Soviets.

Vietnam Remembered. CD-ROM database. St. Paul, Minn.: Quanta Press, 1989.
Contains both information and images compiled from private and public sources covering the U.S. involvement in Southeast Asia from 1946 through 1976. Major sections include biographies, equipment, glossaries, statistics, battle information, chronologies, and bibliographies. Includes items retrievable by various subject categories to provide flexible searching.

Vietnam Veterans Against the War. *The Winter Soldier Investigation: An Inquiry into American War Crimes.* Boston: Beacon Press, 1972.
Convened in Detroit from January 31 through February 2, 1971, The Winter Soldier Investigation presented participants' testimony regarding alleged war crimes and the de facto policies that led to such actions. One thousand pages of transcripts lie behind this abridged published version. These veterans maintain that the My Lai massacre was hardly an isolated incident, and that the punishment of those involved is hypocritical when one considers the lack of condemnation for those whose policies created the environment that made My Lai—and other atrocities—possible and likely.

Vogelgesang, Sandy. *The Long Dark Night of the Soul: The American Intellectual Left and the Vietnam War.* New York: Harper & Row, 1974.
Beginning with a sketch of who the major left-wing intellectuals were and where they published, Vogelgesang goes on to mark out three stages of the liberal critique. In the first stage, the war is seen as a lapse in judgment, in the second as an exercise in immorality, in the third as a reflection of political illegitimacy. Vogelgesang believes that the intellectual left's outcries did not have a significant effect on mainstream public opinion or on policymakers.

Wagner, Christine. "Women and the U. S. Military: Invisible Soldier and Veteran, An Annotated Bibliography." *Feminist Teacher* 5, no. 3 (Winter, 1991): 34-39.
This guide is divided into two sections: "Women and the Military" and "Women and Vietnam." Neither section is particularly strong, and Wagner fails to include

such essential material as Butler's *American Women Writers on Vietnam*.Though far less useful than the Budge and Didur "Women and War: A Selected Bibliography" listed above, Wagner's compilation includes sources that other bibliographies miss.

Weisner, Louis A. *Victims and Survivors: Displaced Persons and Other War Victims in Viet-Nam, 1954-1975*. New York: Greenwood Press, 1988.
Forced relocations and massive civilian casualties weakened South Vietnamese society and contributed to the country's defeat. Weisner gives a detailed account of population displacements at different stages of the war, examining their causes and consequences. The creation of a refugee population brings further tragedy to those who have already suffered the trauma of war and dislocation. An excellent, well-documented study.

Westmoreland, William C. *A Soldier Reports*. Garden City, N.Y.: Doubleday, 1976.
This autobiography focuses on Westmoreland's role as Vietnam field commander from 1964 to 1968 and as Army Chief of Staff from 1968 to 1972. Westmoreland's position may be summed up in his own words: "Despite the final failure of the South Vietnamese, the record of the American military services of never having lost a war is still intact." Westmoreland believes that the military did what it was asked, and that its leaders "adhered to a basic tenet of our Constitution prescribing civilian control of the military."

Whitfield, Danny J. *Historical and Cultural Dictionary of Vietnam*. Metuchen, N.J.: Scarecrow Press, 1976.
This reference volume emphasizes transliterated Vietnamese terms in order to make information on Vietnamese cultural documents, movements, places, and personalities available to scholars who do not read Vietnamese. The entries are brief but not sketchy. This dictionary is not centered on the American war experience there, but on the wider sweep of Vietnam's history. Appendices include a historical outline, dynastic chronology, and maps.

Wilcox, Fred A. *Waiting for an Army to Die: The Tragedy of Agent Orange*. New York: Vintage Books, 1983. Reprint. Cabin John, Md.: Seven Locks Press, 1990.
Wilcox records the testimony of veterans who suffer from dioxin poisoning consequent to their exposure to its use in the defoliant Agent Orange. The catastrophic aftereffects of our herbicidal activities (severe skin rashes, cancer, birth defects), the government denials and stonewalling, and the ongoing legal battles for veterans' rights are examined. The Seven Locks Press edition carries a new, updated introduction.

Willenson, Kim. *The Bad War: An Oral History of the Vietnam War*. New York: New American Library, 1987.
Most of the interviews collected here were conducted as part of the preparation for a special issue of *Newsweek* commemorating the tenth anniversary of the fall of Saigon. The voices heard were involved in making and implementing policy. They include Clark Clifford, William Sullivan, Walt Rostow, Herman Kahn, Henry Kissinger, James B. Stockdale, Alexander Haig, Casper Weinberger, James Schlesinger, and a number of Vietnamese officials.

Williams, Reese, ed. *Unwinding the Vietnam War: From War into Peace*. Seattle: Real Comet Press, 1987.
This collection of essays, memoirs, poems, and stories "is grounded in the political, cultural, and aesthetic issues of the mid-1980s." It is a collection of voices joined by "the need to speak out against war." A fascinating mixture of primary and secondary materials, *Unwinding the Vietnam War* was published as a companion to the Washington Project for the Arts programs on "War and Memory: In the Aftermath of Vietnam." Illustrated.

Woolf, Cecil, and John Bagguley, eds. *Authors Take Sides on Vietnam*. New York: Simon & Schuster, 1967.
Close to two hundred American and European authors respond to two questions: "Are you for, or against, the intervention of the United States in Vietnam?" and "How, in your opinion, should the conflict in Vietnam be resolved?" The answers are predominantly and predictably antiwar, but the collection is large enough to have significant range and provides useful insights about mid-1960s attitudes.

Young, Marilyn B. *The Vietnam Wars, 1945-1990*. New York: HarperCollins, 1990.
In fifteen neatly shaped chapters, Young reviews and assesses the competing understandings of American military involvement in Vietnam. Her title refers both to these competing versions of the story and to the fact that the American military activity in Vietnam is one thing from the perspective of American history and quite another from the perspective of Vietnam history. This lucidly written account is a work of synthesis in the best sense. It is among the very best of the shorter treatments, and the most attractively written. Illustrated.

Zaroulis, Nancy, and Gerald Sullivan. *Who Spoke Up? American Protest Against the War in Vietnam, 1963-1975*. Garden City, N.Y.: Doubleday, 1984.
The authors argue that the antiwar movement was homegrown, included a large swath of the political spectrum, and was dominated by ordinary adult citizens rather than counterculture youths. Furthermore, the movement, while not monolithic, was never anti-American. This chronological treatment discusses

such luminaries as Benjamin Spock, Tom Hayden, Rennie Davis, and the Berrigan brothers, along the way explaining and correcting false myths.

Booksellers' Catalogs

Books on Southeast Asia and the Indochina Wars. Christianburg, Va.: Dalley Book Service, July, 1992.
The first two categories in this catalogue are "Vietnam: Non-Fiction" and "Vietnam: Fiction" (333 items in the fiction category). Others are "Cambodia, Laos, Thailand," "Southeast Asia: History and Political," "OSS, CIA, and Intelligence," and "Guerilla Warfare." Includes physical descriptions and occasional, extremely brief annotations. Contains 1825 items. Updated regularly. Address: 90 Kimball Lane, Christianburg, VA 24073.

Howard, Esme Joy. *Vietnam War Literature: The Garry Lepper Collection*. Serendipity Books Catalogue 46. Berkeley, Calif.: Serendipity Books, 1989.
An unclassified, alphabetized list of 417 items with physical descriptions and brief annotations. Mostly narratives, fiction and nonfiction. First editions. Where appropriate, items are cross-referenced to John Newman's *Vietnam War Literature* (1st ed., 1982). Address: 1201 University Avenue, Berkeley, CA 94702.

Lopez, Ken. *Vietnam War Literature: A Catalogue*. Introduction by Robert Olen Butler. Hadley, Ma.: Ken Lopez, Bookseller, 1990.
Part 1 includes nonfiction subdivided as "personal accounts" and "general nonfiction." Part 2 includes drama (plays and screenplays), poetry, and fiction. Part 3 includes visual material, manuscripts, brochures, and literature from foreign presses. Contains 2,342 items with physical descriptions and occasional brief annotations. In 1991, Lopez produced a supplement to this catalog listing an additional 366 items and including his brief assessment of "The 25 Best Books on Vietnam." Address: 51 Huntington Road, Hadley, MA 01035.

CRITICISM—GENERAL

Bates, Milton J. "Men, Women, and Vietnam." In *America Rediscovered: Critical Essays on Literature and Film of the Vietnam War*, edited by Owen W. Gilman, Jr., and Lorrie Smith. New York: Garland, 1990.
After providing a concise history of gender relationships before, during, and after the war, Bates examines films, novels, and memoirs that reflect three different stances toward these relationships. One group does not challenge conventional notions. A second "presupposes the same mythology of gender" but asks that something be done about it. The third, including Donald Pfarrer's novel *Neverlight* (which receives detailed attention), explores "those areas where social constructions of gender overlap or fail to account for feelings and behavior."

Baughman, Ronald, ed. *American Writers of the Vietnam War*. Vol. 9 in the *Dictionary of Literary Biography Documentary Series*. Detroit: Gale Research, 1991.
This reference volume treats John Del Vecchio, W. D. Ehrhart, Larry Heinemann, Walter McDonald, and Tim O'Brien. Each entry includes representative previously published reviews and critical articles, as well as previously unpublished material from the authors' private papers: photographs, letters, journal entries, hand-corrected manuscript or typescript pages, military or literary awards, and recently conducted interviews.

Beidler, Philip D. *American Literature and the Experience of Vietnam*. Athens: University of Georgia Press, 1982.
One of the trailblazing attempts to discover the truly literary, as distinguished from political or moral, ways in which people have discussed the Vietnam War, this overview sees the literary consciousness "in relation to the larger process of cultural myth-making." After first providing an overview of the Vietnam experience on American culture, Beidler then establishes a notion of American literature characterized by "prophecy and context." The next three chapters examine three chronological periods of writings about the Vietnam War. Beidler is concerned with how the literature is "sense-making"; he awaits the emergence of a "new architecture of consciousness" that will release the definitive literature of the Vietnam War.

_____. *Re-writing America: Vietnam Authors in Their Generation*. Athens: University of Georgia Press, 1991.
A significant self-critique of American culture and myth began with a group of writers who first came to prominence through literary responses to the Vietnam War. Beidler traces the careers of those writers, examining the further

developments of their vision and art in works that sometimes maintain Vietnam as a central setting, theme, or metaphor and as frequently depart from Vietnam but nonetheless continue the "re-writing" of America's mythic history.

Bell, Pearl K. "Writing About Vietnam." *Commentary* 66 (October, 1978): 74-77.
This brief overview of Vietnam War narratives touches upon Herr's *Dispatches*, Caputo's *A Rumor of War*, Groom's *Better Times Than These*, Stone's *Dog Soldiers*, and O'Brien's *Going After Cacciato*. The latter is considered the most successful, while *Dispatches* is found wanting.

Bellamy, Michael. "Carnival and Carnage: Falling Like Rock Stars and Second Lieutenants." In *America Rediscovered: Critical Essays on Literature and Film of the Vietnam War*, edited by Owen W. Gilman, Jr., and Lorrie Smith. New York: Garland, 1990.
There is a "conflation of carnival and war" in many of the key novels, personal narratives, and films about Vietnam. Their significance, especially what they tell us about America in the 1960s, is illuminated by examining them against the background of America's Puritan heritage. Hawthorne's short story "The Maypole of Marymount" reveals "the official American attitude toward carnival" that opposes merrymaking and adult responsibility. Without the Puritan dialectic, carnival and war become identified.

Bellhouse, Mary L., and Lawrence Litchfield. "Vietnam and Loss of Innocence: An Analysis of the Political Implications of the Popular Literature of the Vietnam War." *Journal of Popular Culture* 16, no. 3 (Winter, 1982): 157-174.
One common thread in the popular literature shows the idealistic youth, who identifies national values with military heroism, turned into a ruthless killer. Many writers testify to seeing the Vietnamese as a problem to be exterminated and not as a people. The war and the literature responsive to it cracked America's national myth of omnipotence and virtue. Treats works by Webb, Kovic, Hasford, Heinemann, and others on issues of brutality, moral choice, war-loving, and class.

Brown, Constance A. "Severed Ears: An Image of the Vietnam War." *War, Literature, and the Arts* 4, no. 1 (Spring, 1992): 25-42.
Brown treats the uses and significance of this provocative image in Caputo's *A Rumor of War*, O'Brien's *If I Die in a Combat Zone*, Herr's *Dispatches*, Heinemann's *Paco's Story*, and Stephanie Vaughn's short story "Kid Mac-Arthur." She is concerned with the aesthetic and moral dimensions of an image that has had its shock value undermined by familiarity.

Bryan, C. D. B. "Barely Suppressed Screams: Getting a Bead on Vietnam War Literature." *Harper's*, June, 1984, 67-72.

This detailed omnibus treatment is less a review and more Bryan's attempt at establishing a core list of important titles. He argues for, among others, Wright's *Meditations in Green*, Fuller's *Fragments*, Caputo's *A Rumor of War*, Glasser's *365 Days*, Kovic's *Born on the Fourth of July*, Baker's *Nam*, Emerson's *Winners and Losers*, and Herr's *Dispatches*. Bryan feels that "Vietnam War literature is concerned with something more than form. The writers want to give historical coordinates to the landscape the war occupies in their minds."

Butler, Deborah A. *American Women Writers on Vietnam: Unheard Voices—A Selected Annotated Bibliography*. New York: Garland, 1989.
Annotations of various length follow the nearly eight hundred entries in this listing of imaginative, biographical, and scholarly writings by women on all facets of the Vietnam experience. Within each major division, entries are grouped by decade. What emerges is a sense of a different range of experience and concern, a different kind of selection and emphasis, in the writings of women. Author, title, and subject indexes.

Calloway, Catherine. "American Literature and Film of the Vietnam War: Classroom Strategies and Critical Choices." In *The Vietnam War: Teaching Approaches and Resources*, edited by Marc Jason Gilbert. New York: Greenwood Press, 1991.
While considering the various texts and approaches through which teachers can build a course on representations of the Vietnam War, Calloway briefly reviews the major primary and secondary sources. Calloway's comments on the major critical works and on such issues as gender awareness and stereotyping are especially useful, as is her sense of the emerging canon.

_____. "Vietnam War Literature and Film: A Bibliography of Secondary Sources." *Bulletin of Bibliography* 43, no. 3 (September, 1986): 149-158.
In her essential precursor to the present volume, Calloway lists the commentaries by genre of subject: drama, film, poetry, and prose (choosing not to distinguish fiction from nonfiction). Includes dissertations and foreign language publications, but not brief reviews. Calloway is intentionally selective on Greene and Mailer.

Carton, Evan. "Vietnam and the Limits of Masculinity." *American Literary History* 3, no. 2 (Summer, 1991): 294-318.
Carton develops the striking thesis that "writings about the war betray a Vietnam experience that is an enacted dream of *undifferentiation*—of a human solidarity beyond (or before) ideological, linguistic, and sexual division." Parrying expertly with John Carlos Rowe and particularly Susan Jeffords, Carton explores Webb's *Fields of Fire*, William Broyles's *Brothers in Arms*, and most extensively Mason's *In Country* to develop his point. Mason demystifies the Vietnam experience by "deterritorializing it, denaturalizing it—resisting its recuperability

for patriarchy and imperialism." A very important essay. See separate annotation under Mason, *In Country*, in the section "Authors and Works."

Casciato, Arthur D. "Teaching the Literature of the Vietnam War." *Review* 9 (1987): 125-147.
This intelligent review essay examines Walsh's *American War Literature*, Wilson's *Vietnam in Prose and Film*, Beidler's *American Literature and the Experience of Vietnam*, Lomperis' *"Reading the Wind": The Literature of the Vietnam War*, Lewis' *The Tainted War*, and Hellmann's *American Myth and the Legacy of Vietnam*. An astute appraiser of the directions that book-length criticism has taken, Casciato gives high marks to Pratt's "Bibliographical Commentary" (in Lomperis) and to Hellmann's study as he isolates critical issues and approaches.

Christie, N. Bradley. "Teaching Our Longest War: Constructive Lessons from Vietnam." *English Journal* 78, no. 4 (April, 1989): 35-38.
Teachers will enjoy the ideas for course design and the brief comments on individual narratives and films that Christie offers. He addresses the formal, moral, and cultural issues that the literature raises.

Clifton, Merritt, ed. *Those Who Were There: Eyewitness Accounts of the War in Southeast Asia, 1956-1975, and Aftermath*. Paradise, Calif.: Dustbooks, 1984.
This annotated bibliography includes entries on authors "whose writings describe or reflect their first-hand experience." Clifton begins with book-length works: memoirs and other nonfiction, fiction, and poetry. Then he lists contributions to periodicals classified by subject: prisoners of war, coming home, war crimes, and so forth. There is also a list of special interest periodicals. Unfortunately, this richly informative reference work is not indexed.

Colonnese, Tom, and Jerry Hogan. "Vietnam War Literature, 1958-1979: A First Checklist." *Bulletin of Bibliography* 38, no. 1 (January-March, 1981): 26-31, 51.
This checklist includes two alphabets of primary sources: one for book-length titles, the other for short fiction in collections and periodicals. The book section is not classified by genre but includes novels, poetry collections, plays, and "new journalism." Derived in part from the special collection at Colorado State University.

Cronin, Cornelius A. "Line of Departure: The Atrocity in Vietnam War Litera-ture." In *Fourteen Landing Zones: Approaches to Vietnam War Literature*, edited by Philip K. Jason. Iowa City: University of Iowa Press, 1991.
Cronin maintains that differences between the self-consciousness of Vietnam War participants and participants in World War II are acutely registered in narratives

of atrocity. By contrasting parallel scenes in Charles B. MacDonald's World
War II memoir *Company Commander* with Caputo's *A Rumor of War* and
Heinemann's *Close Quarters*, Cronin points out how the literatures reflect
differing military cultures. For various reasons, the Vietnam soldier was forced
to take individual responsibility for his actions.

Dunn, Joe P. "The Vietnam War POW/MIAs: An Annotated Bibliography."
Bulletin of Bibliography 45, no. 2 (June, 1988): 152-157.
Dunn classifies his materials under such headings as "POW Memoirs,"
"Collective POW Accounts," "Collective Vietnam Memoirs That Contain
Segments on Individual POWs," memoirs of civilian captives, materials on the
MIA issue, rescue narratives, and novels. There are twelve entries under the last
heading. The listings are preceded by a brief description of the circumstances
that produced the literature and the general nature of the literature.

_____. "Women and the Vietnam War: A Bibliographical Review."
Journal of American Culture 12, no. 1 (Spring, 1989): 79-86.
A good starting place for exploring the women's perspectives on the Vietnam
War. Dunn surveys the major primary and secondary texts—fiction, memoir,
oral history, and analysis—by and about women who worked in Vietnam as
nurses, reporters, and in various other roles. He also includes works by
nonparticipant woman writers that deal with the war. Includes comments on Van
Devanter's *Home Before Morning*, Walsh's *Forever Sad the Hearts*, Hawkins'
Vietnam Nurse, and Mason's *In Country*.

Eckert, Edward K., and William J. Searle. "Creative Literature of the Vietnam
War: A Selective Bibliography." *Choice* 24, no. 5 (January, 1987): 725-735.
Limiting their discussion to those literary and dramatic works that "make
important statements about the nature or meaning of the war," Eckert and Searle
provide what is probably the most effective short introduction to the field. Their
essay is organized by genre and includes both well-known works and those such
as Jocelyn Hollis' *Collected Vietnam Poems and Other Poems* and Rob Riggan's
novel *Free Fire Zone*, that linger in undeserved obscurity. Giving more attention
to short fiction than most other treatments, this essay may be the best single
place to begin for newcomers to the study of Vietnam War literature.

Gaspar, Charles J. "Searching for Closure: Vietnam War Literature and the
Veterans Memorial." *War, Literature, and the Arts* 1, no. 1 (Spring, 1989): 19-
34.
On both the personal and national levels, there is a need "to reconnect, to
reunify." The Vietnam Veterans Memorial in Washington, with its open and
inclusive shape, provides an opportunity for psychological enclosure. Many of
the Vietnam War narratives, whether fiction or memoir, demonstrate the need

for, and frequently attempt a similar enactment of, closure through reader involvement and participation.

Gerster, Robin. *Big-Noting: The Heroic Theme in Australian War Writing.* Carlton, Victoria, Australia: Melbourne University Press, 1987.
Gerster surveys and assesses the literature of the Australian military experience from 1890 to the present. His chapter "Vietnam Survived" examines the key narratives of Australian forces in Vietnam. Included are treatments of David Alexander's *When the Buffalo Fight*, William Nagle's *The Odd Angry Shot*, and John Rowe's *Count Your Dead*.

Gilman, Owen W., Jr., and Lorrie Smith, eds. *America Rediscovered: Critical Essays on Literature and Film of the Vietnam War.* New York: Garland, 1990.
These twenty-four essays provide a generous range of perspectives on the literature, drama, and film of the war. Those in the first section attempt to place the Vietnam experience in American culture. The second section focuses on individual writers and works, while the third, called "Genre Overviews," is composed of bibliographical commentary. Gilman's introduction asserts that the collection's shaping principle has to do with "the condition of being an American—past, present, and future."

Grant, Zalin. "Vietnam as Fable." *The New Republic*, March 25, 1978, 21-24.
After a long preamble on the history of Vietnam War book publishing, Grant comments briefly on Bryan's *Friendly Fire*, Caputo's *A Rumor of War*, Herr's *Dispatches*, Kovic's *Born on the Fourth of July* and other titles. He praises Huggett's *Body Count* and Rabe's *Streamers*, but generally feels that Vietnam War veterans deserve better than what had been written about their experiences to date. Films also discussed.

Hall, H. Palmer. "The Helicopter and the Punji Stick: Central Symbols of the Vietnam War." In *America Rediscovered: Critical Essays on Literature and Film of the Vietnam War*, edited by Owen W. Gilman, Jr., and Lorrie Smith. New York: Garland, 1990.
In both films and narratives, the helicopter serves as the "symbol of the American Army and the American war effort." The enemy is first represented by the punji stick, later transformed (by the time of the Tet Offensive) into the land mine. The high-tech helicopter "flies frantically" after an illusive enemy, frequently becoming a victim, while the more primitive punji stick and the land mine patiently wait for victims.

Hansen, J. T. "Vocabularies of Experience." In *America Rediscovered: Critical Essays on Literature and Film of the Vietnam War*, edited by Owen W. Gilman, Jr., and Lorrie Smith. New York: Garland, 1990.

There is no useful distinction between fiction and autobiography in Vietnam War narratives. They all share a layering of three broad categories of vocabulary: "Standard American English, military, and conversational." The particular orchestration of these vocabularies gives distinction to individual works, while the mixed vocabularies become "an objective correlative for the entire Vietnam experience." By mastering the languages, the reader is able to share that experience.

Hellmann, John. *American Myth and the Legacy of Vietnam.* New York: Columbia University Press, 1986.
Hellmann examines dominant American myths and then explores the way America's Vietnam experience undermined those myths. The frontier hero, the good son, and the Kennedy promise are among the myths questioned by the significant literary and cinematic responses to the war. Hellmann argues that American myths must now be reshaped to accommodate the Vietnam experience in a way that allows the United States to find new and wiser strength and purpose. Many of the major literary texts are treated.

Herzog, Tobey C. "John Wayne in a Modern Heart of Darkness: The American Soldier in Vietnam." In *Search and Clear: Critical Responses to Selected Literature and Films of the Vietnam War,* edited by William J. Searle. Bowling Green, Ohio: Bowling Green State University Popular Press, 1988.
By the 1960s, the John Wayne persona had been well established "as a cultural icon representing traditional American values of patriotism, courage, confidence, leadership, and manliness." Various memoirs and novels of the war attest to the influence of this icon, grafted onto Vietnam by the film version of *The Green Berets*. Ironic references to the John Wayne myth reveal the extent to which this image was undermined by the experiences of those who served in the Vietnam War.

_____. "Writing About Vietnam: A Heavy Heart-of-Darkness Trip." *College English* 41, no. 6 (February, 1980): 680-695.
This early overview of both fiction and nonfiction is concerned with the "dichotomy of fact and truth" that links Conrad's *Heart of Darkness* to the growing corpus of Vietnam War narratives. Herzog stresses the differences between World War II narratives and Downs's *The Killing Zone*, Bryan's *Friendly Fire*, Herr's *Dispatches*, Caputo's *A Rumor of War*, Groom's *Better Times Than These*, Webb's *Fields of Fire*, and O'Brien's *Going After Cacciato*. Herzog outlines the different approaches to the unique elements in the Vietnam experience in terms of "styles, techniques, and conventions."

Howard, Victor, ed. "Focus on the Vietnam War." Special section of *Journal of American Culture* 4, no. 2 (Summer, 1981): 54-200.

This interdisciplinary collection of essays includes treatments of the literature and drama, film, protest music, television coverage, G.I. slang, and such issues as amnesty and Nixon's first year in office.

Jason, Philip K., ed. *Fourteen Landing Zones: Approaches to Vietnam War Literature*. Iowa City: University of Iowa Press, 1991.
These essays exemplify a wide range of approaches to the imaginative literature—the fiction, poetry, and drama—of the war. Historical, American studies, feminist, mythic, comparative, genre, and psychological perspectives illuminate a significant sampling of the literature. The introduction gives an overview of the burgeoning body of Vietnam War writings and traces its peculiar life in the literary and academic marketplace.

Jeffords, Susan. "Debriding Vietnam: The Resurrection of the White American Male." *Feminist Studies* 14, no. 3 (Fall, 1988): 525-543.
Recent images of the Vietnam veteran tend toward "the display and regeneration of a victimized American masculinity" as a response "to recent feminist challenges to patriarchal structures." Though Jeffords draws her evidence primarily from popular films, her argument can be applied to literary treatments as well (and is discussed in her book *The Remasculinization of America*, below). A related essay is her "Reproducing Fathers: Gender and the Vietnam War in U.S. Culture" found in *From Hanoi to Hollywood*, edited by Linda Dittmar and Gene Michaud (New Brunswick, N.J.: Rutgers University Press, 1990).

_____. *The Remasculinization of America: Gender and the Vietnam War*. Bloomington: Indiana University Press, 1989.
Jeffords employs cinematic, literary, and other representations of the Vietnam War to argue that there had been, in the 1980s, a revival of "the interests, values, and projects of patriarchy" in the United States following challenges to patriarchal power in the preceding decades. The principal purpose of this study is "to elucidate the gendered structure of representations of the Vietnam War in America through readings of films, personal narratives, criticism, novels, essays, and short stories, the bulk of them written by men who are themselves veterans of the war," and "to broaden avenues of feminist criticism." One of the key studies of the relationships between war and gender.

_____. "Whose Point Is It Anyway?" *American Literary History* 3, no. 1 (Spring, 1991): 162-171.
Thomas Myers' *Walking Point*, Jeffords contends, is representative of academic projects that maintain "a tacit policy of exclusion" of women and minorities. Myers' search for canonical Vietnam texts leads him to examine those authors who share attributes with those (male) writers already enshrined in the American

literature canon. Jeffords worries that such approaches to Vietnam War literature valorize the very traditions of canonicity that need to be challenged.

_____. "Women, Gender, and the War." *Critical Studies in Mass Communication* 6, no. 1 (March, 1989): 83-89.
Representations of the Vietnam War tend to "change the gender of women involved in the Vietnam War and its cultural effects by subsuming their experiences under those of men." Jeffords surveys both literary and cinematic images of women that support her assertion. She also reviews the growing body of critical works that "focus on women and war." Excellent reference list.

Klein, Michael, ed. *The Vietnam Era: Media and Popular Culture in the U.S. and Vietnam.* London: Pluto Press, 1990.
The first part of this essay collection concerns itself with the impact of the war on American culture as reflected in the popular media and in serious art forms. The second section examines the impact of the war on the Vietnamese. Topics include the alternative press, popular song, film, and the changing position of women in Vietnamese society. Includes contributions by Vietnamese writers. Walter Holbling's essay on fiction and John Balaban's piece on poetry are listed in the appropriate subsections in the section "Criticism—Genre."

Kroll, Barry M. *Teaching Hearts and Minds: College Students Reflect on the Vietnam War in Literature.* Carbondale: Southern Illinois University Press, 1992.
Although this book explores "college students' processes of reflective inquiry" and is not by any measure a foray into literary criticism, it must be included here for Kroll's presentation of a fascinating array of youthful responses to major texts. These include Caputo's *A Rumor of War*, Herr's *Dispatches*, Komunyakaa's *Dien Cai Dau*, O'Brien's *Going After Cacciato*, Van Devanter's *Home Before Morning*, and Webb's *Fields of Fire*.

Lawson, Jacqueline, ed. *Gender and the War: Men, Women, and Vietnam.* Special issue of *Vietnam Generation* 1, no. 3/4 (Summer/Fall, 1989).
This collection is solid evidence of the fruitful interaction between scholars working in feminism, masculinism, and gender studies on the one hand and Vietnam studies on the other. Topics include oral histories and personal narratives by women veterans, paramilitary fantasy culture, women in the protest/peace movement, and several treatments of the literature of the Vietnam War. There is a "Bibliography of Unusual Sources on Women and the Vietnam War."

Leland, John C., and Tobey C. Herzog. "Comment and Response: Writing About Vietnam." *College English* 43, no. 7 (November, 1981): 739-744.

Leland argues that Herzog's *College English* article "Writing About Vietnam" (listed above) is misguided in minimizing the universal features of the Vietnam conflict and the traditional elements in the literature. Herzog responds by giving some ground but maintaining that important distinctions exist. An interesting encapsulated version of an ongoing debate.

Lewis, Lloyd B. *The Tainted War: Culture and Identity in Vietnam War Narratives.* Westport, Conn.: Greenwood Press, 1985.
Like the more recent study by Thomas Myers, this book flattens the distinction between fiction and nonfiction. After an introductory chapter on the sociology of knowledge, Lewis examines the shared "symbolic universe" of Americans who were sent off to fight in Vietnam, the "dysfunctional socialization" consequent upon their experience, and the difficult adjustments to civilian life. Though no single work is examined in detail, nineteen important narratives provide the evidence for Lewis' discussion.

Lomperis, Timothy J. *"Reading the Wind": The Literature of the Vietnam War.* Durham, N.C.: Duke University Press, 1987.
Essentially a narrative and commentary on the May, 1985, conference on "The Vietnam Experience in American Literature" sponsored by The Asia Society, these unofficial proceedings cover a wide range of political, moral, and aesthetic issues. The participants include James Webb, John Del Vecchio, Jack Fuller, William Pelfrey, Tim O'Brien, Wallace Terry, Bruce Weigl, Stephen Wright, Joseph Ferrandino, W. D. Ehrhart, Ron Kovic, John Balaban, Myra McPherson, Asa Baber, Philip Beidler, and others. Includes John Clark Pratt's important "Bibliographic Commentary" (listed separately in the "Fiction" subsection in the section "Criticism—Genre").

Lopez, Ken. "The Literature of the Vietnam War Experience." *A B Bookman's Weekly*, June 26, 1989, 2809-2810.
Written more for book dealers and collectors than scholars, Lopez's essay considers the reasons for the great number of titles in this area as well as the difficulties in finding many of them. His discussion divides the material into various categories including "paperback originals," "plays and scripts," and the inevitably subdivided "novels." Lopez attaches then-current market prices to the titles that he mentions.

Louvre, Alf, and Jeffrey Walsh, eds. *Tell Me Lies About Vietnam: Cultural Battles for the Meaning of the War.* Philadelphia: Open University Press, 1988.
This collection of essays on the cultural products about the Vietnam War is self-admittedly an "attempt to offer alternatives to the contemporary rightward revision of the war in America." Like Walsh and Aulich's *Vietnam Images* (several of whose individual authors it includes), this volume includes essays on

film, drama, popular music, poetry, and narrative literature. The introduction traces the shifting focal points in both the cultural production and critical evaluation of that production.

Luckett, Perry D. "The Black Soldier in Vietnam War Literature and Film." *War, Literature, and the Arts* 1, no. 2 (1989/1990): 1-27.
Luckett demonstrates that, notwithstanding claims to the contrary, there are many positive depictions of black soldiers in Vietnam narratives. He includes among these Oscar Johnson in *Going After Cacciato*, Day Tripper in *Dispatches*, Cannonball and Sergeant Sadler in *Fields of Fire*, Lieutenant Brooks in *The 13th Valley*, Roscoe Jackson in Thomas Taylor's *A Piece of This Country*, and Santee in Loyd Little's *Parthian Shot*.

Ludington, Townsend. "Comprehending the American Experience in Vietnam—A Review Essay." *Southern Humanities Review* 18, no. 4 (Fall, 1984): 339-349.
This engaging discussion, occasioned by the appearance of Beidler's *American Literature and the Experience of Vietnam*, asks whether Beidler's stance is "revisionism of a conservative stripe" and then assures readers that it is not. While praising Beidler's work, Ludington reviews a number of other studies in terms of their political vision of the Vietnam experience. In assessing the shift from a literature of description to one of explanation, Ludington comments on titles by Webb, Hasford, Herr, and O'Brien.

McCarthy, Gerald. "Static Essentials: Voices of Vietnam War Literature." *Mid-American Review* 4 (Fall, 1984): 96-100.
The voices in such representative works as Kovic's *Born on the Fourth of July*, O'Brien's *Going After Cacciato*, and Wright's *Meditations in Green* are haunted by questions of reconciliation and healing, charged with rage at their role in America's catastrophe, and bewildered by the easy acceptance of conventional answers to a unique set of problems. These voices demand an impossible "day of reckoning" toward which they offer accountings of their own transformation and self-discovery.

McInerney, Peter. "'Straight' and 'Secret' History in Vietnam War Literature." *Contemporary Literature* 22, no. 2 (Spring, 1981): 187-204.
McInerney applies Hayden White's notion of "metahistory" to discuss the interplay of narrative modes (history and fiction) in Vietnam War literature. 'Straight' history is represented by Guenter Lewy's *America in Vietnam*, which is judged a fiction by other writers. 'Secret' history includes the fictional and biographical writings that blur conventional lines. These works, characterized by self-conscious narrators, include Greene's *The Quiet American*, Mailer's *The Armies of the Night*, Kovic's *Born on the Fourth of July*, and Caputo's *A Rumor of War*. Many reporters, such as David Halberstam, turned fictioneers to tell the

story right. Herr's *Dispatches* is the paradigm of the secret history mode, and almost its parody.

Marin, Peter. "Coming to Terms with Vietnam: Settling Our Moral Debts." *Harper's*, December, 1980, 41-56.
While discussing many of the literary responses to the war, Marin argues that "none of these books, for all their obvious passion and truth, suggest a way out of our present moral predicament or confronts the reader with his own responsibilities." Gloria Emerson comes closest. Films come off even worse than literature. The essay looks at the creative works to argue that America is not yet ready to make a full moral assessment of the Vietnam experience.

Melling, Philip H. "Old History, New History, No History at All? The Vietnam War as Affirmation of American Values." *American Studies International* 28, no. 2 (October, 1990): 93-105.
Melling refers to many well-known Vietnam War texts in this discussion of how American cultural ideology assumes "the Americanness of the world." While much of the earlier Vietnam War literature dissents from this perspective, more recent works "recuperate the American cause in Vietnam." Melling reviews the perspectives of many important critics of the literature and introduces students to an exceptional British novel, Mark Frankland's *The Mother-of-Pearl Men*, which continues the Graham Greene vision of the American in Vietnam as intruder.

_____. *Vietnam in American Literature*. Boston: Twayne, 1990.
Melling draws parallels between the spiritual autobiographies of colonial New England and the major literary responses to the Vietnam War. Both bodies of work share "the problem of the disturbing journey," though in the Vietnam works the process is doubled: one journey to war, another back to an uncaring America. The two major parts of Melling's study are called "The Narrative Voice" and "Errand in a Wilderness." In many places, Melling's analogies and parallels seem either forced or irrelevant, but he provides many provocative insights while arguing that in American literary responses to Vietnam, Puritanism reigns.

Myers, Thomas. "Recent Books on War Literature: An Essay-Review." *Modern Fiction Studies* 30, no. 1 (Spring, 1984): 165-171.
Treats John Cruickshanks' *Variations on Catastrophe: Some French Responses to the Great War*, J. M. Ritchie's *German Literature Under National Socialism*, Frederick J. Harris' *Encounters with Darkness: French and German Writers on World War II*, Jeffrey Walsh's *American War Literature, 1914 to Vietnam*, and Philip D. Beidler's *American Literature and the Experience of Vietnam*.

_____. *Walking Point: American Narratives of Vietnam*. New York: Oxford University Press, 1988.

Myers pairs texts that he judges to be the most successful examples of five literary types: realistic narrative, classical memoir, black humor, revised American romanticism, and explorations of American memory. These works tap aesthetic and cultural traditions even while demonstrating that traditions themselves have been irrevocably altered by the nature of the Vietnam War. Their shared goal is "to re-create fully and imaginatively how the American soldier became both agent and victim of the narrow interpretive spectrum by which the conflict was illuminated."

Newman, John. *Vietnam War Literature: An Annotated Bibliography of Imaginative Works About Americans Fighting in Vietnam*. 2d ed. Metuchen, N.J.: Scarecrow Press, 1988.

This most authoritative bibliography of primary materials is divided into sections by genre (novels, short stories, poetry, drama, miscellaneous), then into years of publication in which works are listed alphabetically by author. The annotations are especially useful, being both descriptive and evaluative. Excludes nonfiction and, generally, works set outside Vietnam, Laos, and Cambodia and those that, though they reflect the impact of the war, are predominantly postwar in orientation. Nonetheless, Newman amasses 752 entries. Author and title indexes.

Newman, John, and Julie Wessling. "Vietnam War Literature: A Guide to Resources at Colorado State University." *War, Literature, and the Arts* 1, no. 2 (1989/1990): 73-76.

The authors trace the history, purpose, and scope of this trailblazing collection. The Vietnam War Literature Collection of approximately twelve hundred items "contains fiction, plays, poetry, sketches, cartoons, and miscellaneous works of imagination" as well as academic studies of these materials. See additional comments in the "Introduction" and in its "Special Collections" subsection.

Oldham, Perry. "On Teaching Vietnam War Literature." *English Journal* 75, no. 2 (February, 1986): 55-56.

Oldham's narrative records his high school seniors' reactions to Caputo's *A Rumor of War*, Webb's *Fields of Fire*, O'Brien's *Going After Cacciato*, Herr's *Dispatches*, Santoli's *Everything We Had*, and *Tim Page's Vietnam* (photos). Oldham, a veteran and poet of the war, briefly explores his motives and methods.

Pierce, Peter. "A Checklist of Australian Literature of the Vietnam War." *Australian Literary Studies* 12, no. 2 (October, 1985): 287-288.

Lists poetry, fiction, memoirs, and articles by Australian writers. Part of a special issue on Australian Literature and War.

_____. "'The Funny Place': Australian Literature and the War in Vietnam." In *Australian R & R: Representations and Reinterpretations of Australia's War in Vietnam*, edited by Jeff Doyle and Jeffrey Grey. Chevy Chase, Md.: Burning Cities Press, 1991. Also available as *Vietnam Generation* 3, no. 2 (1991).
This brief overview considers the dominant themes of Australian fiction and poetry of the Vietnam War. The literature reveals a "lost cause" experience while also reflecting Australia's complex xenophobia toward Asians. Pierce describes indirect depictions of Vietnam through other Asian settings. He claims that no more than a dozen novels that deal directly with the war have so far been published. On the whole, Australia's ten-year involvement in Vietnam has produced a scanty record in its imaginative literature.

_____. "Perceptions of the Enemy in Australian War Literature." *Australian Literary Studies* 12, no. 2 (October, 1985): 287-288.
Includes comments on a number of Vietnam War titles and makes comparisons to American literature of the Vietnam War. Traces perceptions from 1885 through Vietnam, noting that the latter pays scant attention to the enemy but rather "concentrates upon the destructiveness of the language" of those in officialdom who fostered the war.

Reynolds, Clay. "Vietnam's Artistic Legacy: The Need to Understand." *Journal of American Culture* 14, no. 1 (Spring, 1991): 9-11.
In this personal essay, Reynolds, a writer and teacher, addresses how and why nonveterans depend on literature and popular media to understand the nature of the Vietnam War and to perceive the cultural roots of its causes.

Rollins, Peter C. "The Vietnam War: Perceptions Through Literature, Film, and Television." *American Quarterly* 36, no. 3 (1984): 419-432.
Rollins reviews the public perceptions of the war as shaped by print and visual media. His section on "The War in Literature" stresses "the motif of corruption of innocence" in personal narratives and autobiographical fictions. He comments on Kovic's *Born on the Fourth of July*, Caputo's *A Rumor of War*, Robert Mason's *Chickenhawk*, Ehrhart's *Vietnam-Perkasie*, O'Brien's *If I Die in a Combat Zone*, and Del Vecchio's *The 13th Valley*, which he calls "a novel of ideas." Rollins notes that some of these works examine commitment and heroism.

Rowe, John Carlos. "Eye Witness: Documentary Styles in the American Representations of Vietnam." *Cultural Critique*, no. 3 (Spring, 1986): 126-150. Reprinted

in *The Vietnam War and American Culture*, edited by Rowe and Rick Berg. New York: Columbia University Press, 1991.
Rowe discusses our "tendency to transform particular incidents into exemplary events, to transform individual experience into cultural fact" in both film and prose narrative. He illustrates his points with reference to works in a wide range of genre, including the oral histories by Mark Baker (*Nam*) and Al Santoli (*Everything We Had*).

Rowe, John Carlos, and Rick Berg, eds. *American Representations of Vietnam*. Special issue of *Cultural Critique,* no. 3 (Spring, 1986).
One of the best collections of commentaries on a wide range of artistic and cultural responses to the Vietnam War, this gathering pays attention to major literary texts as well as film, oral history, drama, and memoir. Some of the items are revised and reprinted in the editors' *The Vietnam War and American Culture*, below.

_____. *The Vietnam War and American Culture*. New York: Columbia University Press, 1991.
An updating of the *Cultural Critique* special issue listed above, this collection is notable for its concern with the stateside effects of the war. Carol Lynn Mithers' "Missing in Action: Women Warriors in Vietnam" makes passing reference to Vietnam writings by women. David James explores the impact of Vietnam on American music. Susan Jeffords treats Larry Heinemann's *Paco's Story*. The essays that first appeared in *Cultural Critique* have been revised.

Scheurer, Timothy E. "Myth to Madness: America, Vietnam, and Popular Culture." *Journal of American Culture* 4, no. 2 (Summer, 1981): 149-165.
Scheurer perceives a "new myth of Vietnam . . . marked by three distinct phases": innocence and disillusionment, madness, and survival. His elaboration of these categories draws upon film, fiction, and personal narratives including O'Brien's *Going After Cacciato*, Groom's *Better Times Than These*, Caputo's *A Rumor of War*, and Webb's *Fields of Fire*. The new myth may be "a paradigm for our gradual slide into a rapt concern and absorption of the 'self' in the 1970s."

Searle, William J., ed. *Search and Clear: Critical Responses to Selected Literature and Films of the Vietnam War*. Bowling Green, Ohio: Bowling Green State University Popular Press, 1988.
Sixteen essays explore the range of literary and cinematic responses to the war under these headings: "The Quest," "Differences and Debts," "Craft and Techniques," "Return and Partial Recovery," and "Wider Perspectives." Good coverage of the major themes, issues, and genres. Searle's introduction gives

both a general overview of the field and specific comments on the selections that he has included.

Slocock, Caroline. "Winning Hearts and Minds: The 1st Casualty Press." *Journal of American Studies* 16, no. 1 (1982): 107-118.
Because commercial publishers were unwilling during the early 1970s to risk bringing the writings of Vietnam War veterans to the public, a group of veterans edited and published two anthologies under the logo of 1st Casualty Press. These anthologies, *Winning Hearts and Minds* (1972) and *Free Fire Zone* (1973), brought together poetry and short fiction, respectively. The key figures in this enterprise were Larry Rottmann, Jan Barry, Basil T. Paquet, and Wayne Karlin. Slocock outlines the political and economic factors at work during the short life of this important moment in American literary protest.

Smith, Lorrie. "Back Against the Wall: Anti-Feminist Backlash in Vietnam War Literature." *Vietnam Generation* 1, no. 3/4 (Summer/Fall, 1989): 115-126.
Recent treatments of the war "reveal more about the cultural and political climate of the 1980s than about the war itself." While many works create illusions of political neutrality, these illusions "mask agendas driven by the conservative politics of the eighties." Steve Mason's poetry is blatantly misogynistic; Heinemann's *Paco's Story* and O'Brien's "How to Tell a True War Story" compensate their characters' losses with "anger directed at women, who are not only excluded from the male domain of war, but punished for their absence."

_____. "Disarming the War Story." In *America Rediscovered: Critical Essays on Literature and Film of the Vietnam War*, edited by Owen W. Gilman, Jr., and Lorrie Smith. New York: Garland, 1990.
Realistic narratives provide either overt (as in Webb's *Fields of Fire* and Del Vecchio's *The 13th Valley*) or "more complicated subtextual conflicts" (as in Caputo's *A Rumor of War*) between language and reality. Writings by Heinemann, Wright, Herr, and O'Brien involve "linguistic dislocations and formal indeterminacy [to] destabilize the very modes of thinking which permitted American involvement in Vietnam in the first place."

Spark, Alasdair. "Flight Controls: The Social History of the Helicopter as a Symbol of Vietnam." In *Vietnam Images: War and Representation*, edited by Jeffrey Walsh and James Aulich. New York: St. Martin's Press, 1989.
References to literary and cinematic works abound in this fascinating survey of the Vietnam War's dominant icon. Spark stresses the unifying omnipresence of the Huey "in a war characterized by great variety in terrain, climate, types of privation and types of combat." Spark also considers the ramifications of the

war's key symbol being technological rather than human. References to Herr, Caputo, Del Vecchio, and William Holland's *Let a Soldier Die*, among others.

Stephens, Michael G. *Back in the World: Writing After Viet Nam.* 2 vols. Sound recording. New York: American Arts Project, 1984.
Stephens is the moderator for a panel of Vietnam veteran writers who read from their works and discuss issues relating to the literature of the war. The panelists are John Del Vecchio, W. D. Ehrhart, Larry Heinemann, John Clark Pratt, Robert Olen Butler, Smith Hempstone, Chuck Wachtel, Joseph Ferrandino, William C. Woods, and Stephen Wright. Recorded in March, 1984, at the West Side YMCA in New York City.

_____. "Vietnam: The American Ronin." In his *The Dramaturgy of Style: Voice in Short Fiction.* Carbondale: Southern Illinois University Press, 1986.
After setting the historical stage to discuss Vietnam War literature, Stephens begins by examining the use of voice in John Clark Pratt's *Vietnam Voices* and *The Laotian Fragments*. Stephens further exemplifies his concern with voice by reference to many of the leading Vietnam War authors, who are mostly poets and novelists rather than short-story writers. Extended discussions on W. D. Ehrhart, John Balaban, Bruce Weigl, and John Del Vecchio.

Sullivan, Richard A. "The Recreation of Vietnam: The War in American Fiction, Poetry, and Drama." In *The Vietnam War in the American Imagination*, edited by D. Michael Shafer. Boston: Beacon Press, 1990.
Sullivan emphasizes the works of those writers who were participants. For him, most of the literature presents Vietnam "as a personal or individual experience" and locates the reader in the mind of the participant or observer. Sullivan first cuts across literary kinds to address topics and issues, then gives a historical account of the war in literature. He concludes with a brief discussion of Heinemann's *Paco's Story*. A useful, concise overview.

Tal, Kali. "Feminist Criticism and the Literature of the Vietnam Combat Veteran." *Vietnam Generation* 1, no. 3/4 (Summer/Fall, 1989): 190-201.
The writings of Vietnam War veterans show that they encountered "some of the same problems of poor self-image and perceived powerlessness as women traditionally face," and that "the process which these men were going through on the way toward healing and reintegration is a similar process to feminist consciousness-raising." Both processes involve relocations and redefinitions of power.

_____. "Speaking the Language of Pain: Vietnam War Literature in the Context of a Literature of Trauma." In *Fourteen Landing Zones: Approaches to*

Vietnam War Literature, edited by Philip K. Jason. Iowa City: University of Iowa Press, 1991.
Tal's is a detailed and passionate exploration of the links between Vietnam War literature, rape literature, holocaust literature, and other literary responses to trauma for which she posits an embracing critical theory. Tal insists that we must distinguish between participant and nonparticipant literatures, and that each demands a distinct set of critical tools.

Taylor, Gordon O. "Cacciato's Grassy Hill." *Genre* 21, no. 4 (Winter, 1988): 393-407.
This survey of the emerging Vietnam War literary canon finds a connecting thread: "that the war *cannot* be written, or at least not yet or in traditional ways." Taylor touches upon the writings of Herr, Halberstam, O'Brien, Heinemann, Hasford, Kopit, and Alain Arias-Misson ("Vietnam-Superfiction"), providing terse, penetrating insights into how each deals with the business of saying the unsayable.

_____, ed. *The Vietnam War and Postmodern Memory*. Special issue of *Genre* 21, no. 4 (Winter, 1988).
An attractive mix of critical and creative writing, this special issue features excerpts from a novel by Robert Olen Butler; poems by R. S. Carlson; literary studies by Thomas Myers, Philip D. Beidler, Kate Beaird Meyers, and Taylor; film criticism by Claudia Springer and Susan Jeffords; and television criticism by John Carlos Rowe.

Taylor, Sandra C. "The Vietnam War as Meta-History." *Peace and Change* 11, no. 2 (1986): 67-79.
Taylor considers literary texts in terms of "their relationship to the history of the war and their values as reflections of or elaborations on history." She assesses the various writings as pieces of a puzzle that includes the war itself, the home front, and the war's aftermath. She considers three categories of fiction: those that use time-honored traditions of the war novel with a more or less traditional vision, those that stress the unique features of this war, and those that blend realism and fantasy. Taylor hopes for a multidimensional picture to which historians and literary artists contribute.

Walsh, Jeffrey. "Towards Vietnam: Portraying Modern War." In his *American War Literature, 1914 to Vietnam*. New York: St. Martin's Press, 1982.
Walsh notes that the development of Vietnam War literature parallels the rise of postmodernism in the United States. Thus, many of the books written in response to the war are marked by technical innovation and the blurring of genre lines. Joseph Heller's novel of World War II, *Catch-22* (1961), is viewed as a precursor of much Vietnam War Literature, as is Kurt Vonnegut's *Slaughter-*

house-Five (1969). Walsh includes brief comments on the formal strategies of Caputo's *A Rumor of War* and Herr's *Dispatches*, both of which he categorizes as "epic biography." Both writers portray "collective endurance and suffering as an extension of their own experience."

Walsh, Jeffrey, and James Aulich, eds. *Vietnam Images: War and Representation.* New York: St. Martin's Press, 1989.
This wide-ranging anthology considers the images through which the Vietnam War is remembered in the popular media and in the fine arts: "filmic, literary, televisual, photographic, musical and auditory" as well as posters, comic books, and sculpture. There are three essays on the Vietnam Veterans Memorial, one on black music. Visual images get the most attention, but there is much here for the literary scholar, especially Walsh's essay on John Balaban's poetry. Illustrated.

Willson, David A., moderator. *Vietnam War Writers Symposium.* Video. Auburn, Wash.: Green River Community College, 1987-
The videocassette recordings of this annual symposium are available from the moderator (see *Willson's Bibliography*, below); they are also held by the special collection on "Imaginative Representations of the Vietnam War" at La Salle University in Philadelphia (see the "Special Collections" subsection in the "Introduction"). Participants include W. D. Ehrhart, Jerome Gold, Michael Lee Lanning, Richard E. Baker, Eva Bowman, and William E. Merritt. Readings and discussion.

_____. *Willson's Bibliography: War in Southeast Asia.* 3d ed. Auburn, Wash.: Private printing, 1991.
Though privately printed and circulated, this bibliography is the most comprehensive and authoritative listing of literary texts connected with the Vietnam War. Willson not only lists titles but also indicates various printings and editions. The nearly three thousand entries are grouped as follows: "Novels," "Proofs," "Pornography," "Children's Books," "Graphic Novels," "Cartoons," "Short Stories," "Poetry," "Drama," "Screenplays," "Reviews," and "Miscellaneous." Available from Willson at Green River Community College, Auburn, WA 98002.

Wilson, James C. *Vietnam in Prose and Film.* Jefferson, N.C.: McFarland, 1982.
Wilson's study is concerned with literary and cinematic responses to the war as they "attempt to correct distortions and to clarify important historical, moral, and political questions." Thus, he gives little attention to formal analyses and much to what the works reveal about American culture. Though many of his discussions are valuable, there is a problem in evaluating works by testing them against one's own sense of the truth: what should be said and either was or was

not. Wilson is worried about apocalyptic endings without revelation, with visions that "imply the destruction of human values and human morality."

Wittman, Sandra M. *Writing About Vietnam: A Bibliography of the Literature of the Vietnam Conflict*. Boston: G. K. Hall, 1989.
This study annotates a wide range of responses to the Vietnam experience. Aside from publications in the major literary genres, Wittman includes anthologies, criticism, bibliographies, dissertations, and teaching materials. The seventeen hundred entries are followed by author and title indexes. The reader cannot conveniently discover which texts are treated by the critical writings, however, because the *subjects* of the criticism are not indexed. There is a high degree of inaccuracy in what otherwise would be an essential reference tool.

Wright, Robert A. "History's Heavy Attrition: Literature, Historical Consciousness, and the Impact of Vietnam." *Canadian Review of American Studies* 17, no. 3 (Fall, 1986): 301-316.
Wright examines "literary artists' attitudes toward the historical study of the war." He finds that "the belief that the truth of the Vietnam War is accessible to the powers of historical rational analysis" is "not only erroneous but contemptible" to most of the war's literary artists. Wright touches upon many important historical and literary works in this thoughtful, provocative analysis.

The Writer in Our World. Sound recording. Columbia, Mo.: American Audio Prose Library, 1985.
These excerpts from *TriQuarterly*'s 1984 symposium include comments by Gloria Emerson, Ward Just, and Robert Stone. The full printed version is in *TriQuarterly* 65 (Winter, 1986).

Young, Perry Deane. "Nightmares in Print." *Saturday Review*, October 7, 1972, 54-58.
This early look at the state of Vietnam War literature publication develops through an interview with Basil T. Paquet and Larry Rottmann, who are, along with Jan Barry, the founders of 1st Casualty Press. Young draws useful biographical information from these men and facts about the making of the companion anthologies *Winning Hearts and Minds* and *Free Fire Zone*. There is also intriguing material on a stage version of poems from *Winning Hearts and Minds* called *Warplay*. Following the article is a one-page "Art from the War" bibliography that lists literary books, film, and photo collections.

CRITICISM—GENRE

Nonfiction

Brown, F. C. *POW/MIA: Indochina, 1946-86. An Annotated Bibliography of Non-Fiction Works Dealing with Prisoners of War/Missing in Action*. Mesa, Ariz.: Rice-Paddy Press, 1988.
According to the listing in The Cellar Book Shop (Detroit) brochure, this reference provides "excellent coverage of its subject, with annotations that are based on reading and evaluation rather than is so usual, on cribbing from file cards or tables of contents." Unavailable for examination.

Hellmann, John. *American Myth and the Legacy of Vietnam*, pp. 103-188. New York: Columbia University Press, 1986.
Within a chapter called "Good Sons," Hellmann treats together Caputo's *A Rumor of War*, Kovic's *Born on the Fourth of July*, and O'Brien's *If I Die in a Combat Zone*. In these memoirs, "the special conditions of the war do not allow the protagonists to identify themselves with the ideals of American myth." The patterns of the memoirs are paralleled in two novels: Webb's *Fields of Fire* and Huggett's *Body Count*.

Herring, George C. "Vietnam Remembered." *Journal of American History* 73, no. 1 (June, 1986): 152-164.
This review essay treats John Ketwig's *. . . And a Hard Rain Fell*, Bernard Edelman's *Dear America: Letters Home from Vietnam*, David Donovan's *Once a Warrior King*, James R. McDonough's *Platoon Leader*, Al Santoli's *To Bear Any Burden*, T. Mangold and J. Penycate's *The Tunnels of Cu Chi*, and Truong Nhu Tang's *A Vietcong Memoir*. Herring values these books for the glimpses of Vietcong perceptions and for insights into American interactions with South Vietnamese. He finds various degrees of revisionism in each while worrying over the lack of historical perspective.

Lawson, Jacqueline E. "'Old Kids': The Adolescent Experience in the Nonfiction Narratives of the Vietnam War." In *Search and Clear: Critical Responses to Selected Literature and Films of the Vietnam War*, edited by William J. Searle. Bowling Green, Ohio: Bowling Green State University Popular Press, 1988.
The Vietnam soldier underwent an especially accelerated version of the premature aging process characteristic of all combat experience. Lawson discerns and illustrates five stages of this process—preinduction mystique, boot camp initiation, dislocation in Vietnam, confrontation with mortality, and coming home—as she draws upon memoirs by Caputo, Ehrhart, Ketwig, and Kovic as well as oral history collections by Mark Baker (*Nam*) and Al Santoli (*Everything We Had*).

_____. "'She's a Pretty Woman . . . for a Gook': The Misogyny of the Vietnam War." In *Fourteen Landing Zones: Approaches to Vietnam War Literature*, edited by Philip K. Jason. Iowa City: University of Iowa Press, 1991.
Lawson extracts from memoirs and oral histories the rampant misogyny that fuels the male military enterprise. In Vietnam, the age-old tendency for crimes against women during wartime to not even be considered as crimes occurred again. This time, the number of atrocities was enormous, as is the available documentation. Lawson pays particular attention to the misogynistic rites of basic training. This essay first appeared in the *Journal of American Culture* 12, no. 3 (Fall, 1989): 55-65.

_____. "Telling It Like It Was: The Nonfiction Literature of the Vietnam War." In *America Rediscovered: Critical Essays on Literature and Film of the Vietnam War*, edited by Owen W. Gilman, Jr., and Lorrie Smith. New York: Garland, 1990.
Lawson describes the proliferation of Vietnam narratives, then divides them into three categories, analyzing examples of each: "works of confession and meditation (memoirs), of wartime witness (diaries, journals, chronicles), and of postwar remembrance, both individual and collective (oral histories and letters)." After giving the value and characteristics of each type, Lawson observes common threads, which include tracing "a process of deterioration, an erosion of belief and a disintegration of illusion."

Meyers, Kate Beaird. "Fragmentary Mosaics: Vietnam War 'Histories' and Postmodern Epistemology." *Genre* 21, no. 4 (Winter, 1988): 535-552.
The accounts by Stanley Karnow and Frances FitzGerald exemplify the shortcomings of traditional history writing—its distance from what actually happened, from experience. Journalistic memoirs by Gloria Emerson and Michael Herr move closer to rendering experience, while participant accounts by Tim O'Brien and Lynda Van Devanter move closer yet. The fragmented character of war experience is captured by the structure and style of some of these narratives and also by the mosaics of many voices—the documentary and oral histories such as John Clark Pratt's *Vietnam Voices*, Gareth Porter's *Vietnam: A History in Documents*, Mark Baker's *Nam*, and Al Santoli's *Everything We Had*. Contains references to many other works in these categories.

Morgan, Thomas B. "Reporters of the Lost War." *Esquire*, July, 1984, 49-60.
This interview-based essay summarizes the experiences, and comments on the significance, of ten key Vietnam War correspondents, many of whom became major writers of fiction and literary nonfiction. The writers are Ward Just,

David Halberstam, Michael Herr, Peter Arnett, Tim Page, Charles Mohr, John Laurence, Neil Sheehan, Gloria Emerson, and H. D. S. Greenway.

Taylor, Gordon O. *Chapters of Experience: Studies in Twentieth Century American Autobiography.* New York: St. Martin's Press, 1983.
In this impressive examination of the importance of autobiography to American literary culture, Taylor explores the work of three authors important to the student of Vietnam War literature: Norman Mailer, Mary McCarthy, and Michael Herr. Published in London by Macmillan as *Studies in Modern American Autobiography.*

Fiction

Aichinger, Peter. *The American Soldier in Fiction, 1880-1963: A History of Attitudes Toward Warfare and the Military.* Ames: Iowa State University Press, 1975.
Aichinger is concerned less with the aesthetic dimension than with the cultural one in his examination of major American war fiction. Though his study (of necessity) stopped short of treating the Vietnam War, his survey provides a context for examining the literature of our most recent war. Aichinger discusses the attraction that war has for the writer and strives to describe the war novel as an identifiable genre. Chapters include "The War as Metaphor," "The Professional Officer," and "The Nonhero."

Anisfield, Nancy. "Sexist Subscript in Vietnam Narratives." *Vietnam Generation* 1, no. 3/4 (Summer/Fall, 1989): 107-114.
The focus is on "gender-biased language" in Vietnam War fiction. "Dominance and abuse rest more easily on the speaker's conscience if they follow objectification and distancing." Such devices are employed in Hasford's *The Short-Timers*, Del Vecchio's *The 13th Valley*, Pelfrey's *The Big V*, and even Elizabeth Ann Scarborough's *The Healer's War*. Ironic uses of sexist language give only the illusion, and not the reality, of control.

_____. "Words and Fragments: Narrative Style in Vietnam War Novels." In *Search and Clear: Critical Responses to Selected Literature and Films of the Vietnam War*, edited by William J. Searle. Bowling Green, Ohio: Bowling Green State University Popular Press, 1988.
Anisfield gives a brief overview of traditional, chronological narratives and "fragmented" ones that mix events, tones, and jargons. She writes, "The combination of the fragmented style and in-country tone create a fictional environment which not only shows the physical and psychic atmosphere of the

war, but gives the writer more dimensions through which to comment on the war."

Baldwin, Neil. "Going After the War: Books About Vietnam." *Publishers Weekly*, February 11, 1983, 34-38.
Baldwin reviews the literary and economic status of Vietnam narratives ten years after the Paris Peace agreement. He presents information on the decision-making process in publishing houses regarding books on Vietnam, along the way telling stories about how such books as Del Vecchio's *The 13th Valley* and Butler's *The Alleys of Eden* came to the marketplace. Having interviewed twenty-five writers and publishers, Baldwin summarizes their expectations and provides a list of "Best of the Lost Books" (fiction) based on their opinions.

Beidler, Philip D. *American Literature and the Experience of Vietnam*, pp. 161-172. Athens: University of Georgia Press, 1982.
Charles Durden's *No Bugles, No Drums* is treated together with Hasford's *The Short-Timers*, Webb's *Fields of Fire*, Heinemann's *Close Quarters*, and Groom's *Better Times Than These*. They share a "dynamic of sense-making" that involves a "movement through consciousness toward confrontation with a vision of horror so arresting in its sense of awful completeness and finality as to possess at once both a terrible individual significance and a kind of iconographic representativeness within the context of American sensibility at large." The books by Groom and Webb point backward to the traditional war novel. Those by Durden, Hasford, and Heinemann "incline toward a vision more explicitly experimental."

_____. "Bad Business: Vietnam and Recent Mass-Market Fiction." *College English* 54, no. 1 (January, 1992): 64-75.
Beidler examines Franklin Allen Leib's *The Fire Dream*, Danielle Steel's *Message from Nam*, and Kurt Vonnegut, Jr.'s *Hocus Pocus*. He argues that the first two "mine from the war a new pornography of popular desire" that reinforces those cultural frailties that engendered the American venture in Vietnam. Vonnegut's satirical genius, on the other hand, deepens our understanding of who we are and how we let the Vietnam War happen. Beidler attends to how these books were marketed and how each exploits or succumbs to the clichés.

_____. "Truth-Telling and Literary Values in the Vietnam Novel." *South Atlantic Quarterly* 78, no. 2 (Spring, 1979): 141-156.
Beidler examines the "balance between experiential truth-telling and inherited literary values" in Halberstam's *One Very Hot Day*, Bunting's *The Lionheads*, Eastlake's *The Bamboo Bed*, and Durden's *No Bugles, No Drums*. Halberstam and Bunting are more traditional, Eastlake and Durden more modishly and self-

consciously literary, thus more overtly concerned with the business of writing the war. Fine explorations of the essential manner of each book.

_____. "The Vietnam Novel: An Overview with a Brief Checklist of Vietnam War Narrative." *Southern Humanities Review* 12, no. 1 (Winter, 1978): 45-55.
Many significant Vietnam War novels are the testaments "of tired men" whose loss of innocence brings "sad acceptance of moral and spiritual exhaustion." Beidler comments on Eastlake's *The Bamboo Bed*, Kolpacoff's *The Prisoners of Quai Dong*, and other novels to support his point. His "Checklist" is itself a short essay comparing and contrasting familiar and unfamiliar narratives. This brief article is a good starting place for the beginning student as well as a good place to begin following Beidler's career as a major critical voice in this field.

Bergonzi, Robert. "Vietnam Novels: First Draft." *Commonweal*, October 27, 1972, 84-88.
In one of the earliest review articles on Vietnam War fiction, Bergonzi comments on James Reston, Jr.'s *To Defend, to Destroy*, Joan Silver and Linda Gottlieb's *Limbo*, Tom Mayer's *The Weary Falcon*, Josiah Bunting's *The Lionheads*, Joe W. Haldeman's *War Year*, and James Park Sloan's *War Games*. The last two are praised most highly. Bergonzi notes: "Great novels don't usually emerge from wars while they are still being fought." (The first two titles touch Vietnam very lightly.)

Berkley, Gerald W. "Novels About the 'Other Side.'" In *The Vietnam War: Teaching Approaches and Resources*, edited by Marc Jason Gilbert. New York: Greenwood Press, 1991.
In the context of teaching the war through fiction, Berkley briefly discusses three novels that develop Vietnamese characters who are more than Western stereotypes. These are Michael Peterson's *The Immortal Dragon*, Anthony Grey's *Saigon*, and Tran Van Dinh's *Blue Dragon, White Tiger: A Tet Story*. Berkley considers the strengths and weaknesses of each novel as a version of history and as a text for classroom use.

Brown, F. C., and B. Laurie. *Annotated Bibliography of Viet Nam Fiction: Five Hundred Titles Dealing with the Conflict in Viet Nam, Cambodia, and Laos*. Mesa, Ariz.: Rice-Paddy Press/Cyclo-Dap Archives, 1987.
Brief annotations accompany the entries in this cheaply produced, unbound list. Many entries are more likely to be classified (and are advertised) as nonfiction; thus, works on the margin of genre are included. Not fully reliable, but includes many titles missed by others. Only three hundred copies printed.

Bunting, Josiah. "The Military Novel." *Naval War College Review* 26 (November/December, 1973): 30-37.
The author of *The Lionheads* asserts that successful war fiction reveals "basic human 'truths' as they are exposed in that most demanding of circumstances—combat." He reviews the "typology of characters" in military fiction and illustrates the four types by reference to many works of World Wars I and II. Bunting claims: "I do not think Vietnam will produce any significant military fiction" because those who might have written it "were passed over by an inequitable draft system."

Carter, Susanne. "Variations on Vietnam: Women's Innovative Interpretations of the Vietnam War Experience." *Extrapolation* 32, no. 2 (Summer, 1991): 170-183.
Carter sorts out those who write in the realist tradition and those whose works are more experimental while discovering a common theme: "the victimization of women during war, whether or not they are direct participants." She discusses works by key innovators: Jayne Anne Phillips' *Machine Dreams*, Elizabeth Scarborough's *The Healer's War*, Ursula Le Guin's *The Word for World Is Forest*, and short stories by Karen Joy Fowler, Susan Casper, and Kate Wilhelm.

_____. "Vietnam War." In her *War and Peace Through Women's Eyes: A Selective Bibliography of Twentieth-Century American Women's Fiction.* New York: Greenwood Press, 1992.
After a useful introduction that characterizes the contribution of women writers to Vietnam War literature, Carter provides unusually detailed annotations (in some cases, miniature critical essays) on the major novels and appropriately briefer ones on the short fiction. Seven novels and more than forty stories are included; many of the latter are important discoveries for scholars in this field. Carter also provides a checklist of criticism and bibliographic sources.

_____. "Women Novelists: Sculptors of the Vietnam Experience." *Hurricane Alice: A Feminist Quarterly* 7, no. 3 (Fall, 1990): 8-9.
This survey comments briefly on the following: Corinne Brown's *Body Shop*, Bobbie Ann Mason's *In Country*, Jayne Anne Phillips' *Machine Dreams*, Elizabeth Scarborough's *The Healer's War*, Susan Fromberg Schaeffer's *Buffalo Afternoon*, and Patricia L. Walsh's *Forever Sad the Hearts*. "These novels represent a significant contribution to a body of literature which refutes the traditional idea that the experience of war is exclusively male and validates the effects of war felt on the homefront as well."

Christie, Clive. *"The Quiet American" and "The Ugly American": Western Literary Perspectives on Indo-China in a Decade of Transition, 1950-1960.* Occasional

Paper 10. Canterbury, England: University of Kent Centre of South-East Asian Studies, 1989.
Christie provides a broad overview of how the Western literary imagination dealt with Indochina during the 1950s. Before examining the title works, he surveys the French literature of the period, which stresses "the theme of prestige and its loss." Central to this discussion is Jean Larteguy's novel *Yellow Fever*. Christie then treats Greene's novel and the Lederer-Burdick work in separate chapters before going on to compare the French and American visions of Indochina and national destinies. He also comments usefully on Robert Shaplen's *A Forest of Tigers*. There is an appendix on the film versions of the two main novels.

Christopher, Renny. "Fiction: The Romance of Vietnam." *Vietnam Generation Newsletter* 3, no. 3 (November, 1991): 24-25.
While centering her remarks on Danielle Steel's *Message from Nam*, Christopher comments on the domestication of the Vietnam War by its incorporation into romance literature. Christopher compares Steel's book favorably to Christie Dickason's *Indochine* and unfavorably to Anthony Grey's *Saigon*. In spite of its inaccuracies of detail, *Message from Nam* manages to capture current American attitudes toward the Vietnam War. Its limitation is seeing Vietnam only as a place where the United States fought a war. Grey and Dickason provide broader perspectives.

_____. "Fiction: Vietnamese Exile Writers." *Vietnam Generation Newsletter* 3, no. 4 (December/January, 1991/1992): 15-17.
Christopher introduces the growing body of war-related fiction in English by Vietnamese who have settled in America and elsewhere. She comments on Tran Van Dinh's *Blue Dragon, White Tiger: A Tet Story*, Minh Duc Hoai Trinh's *This Side, The Other Side*, and short stories by Vo Phien and Elizabeth Gordon.

Clark, Michael. "Remembering Vietnam." *Cultural Critique*, no. 3 (Spring, 1986): 46-78. Reprinted in *The Vietnam War and American Culture*, edited by John Carlos Rowe and Rick Berg. New York: Columbia University Press, 1991.
Clark is concerned about the way in which television, film, and literature represent the veteran's memory of the war. Of special interest is his treatment of "works that take the memory of Vietnam as their central thematic focus." These include Stone's *A Flag for Sunrise* and two of Caputo's novels: *Horn of Africa* and *Del Corso's Gallery*. Clark also comments on Jayne Anne Phillips' *Machine Dreams* and Bobbie Ann Mason's *In Country*.

Cobley, Evelyn. "Description in Realist Discourse: The War Novel." *Style* 20, no. 3 (Fall, 1986): 395-410.
Though Cobley's primary interest is in theoretical problems of how description is integrated into narrative dynamics, her choice of examples—war novels

emphasizing material conditions— allows for some intriguing remarks on Del Vecchio's *The 13th Valley* and Herr's *Dispatches*.

Couch, William, Jr. "The Image of the Black Soldier in Selected American Novels." *CLA Journal* 20, no. 2 (December, 1976): 176-184.
Although blacks participated notably in America's wars, only their absence is notable in our major war fiction. Couch attempts to explain this absence, then reviews some of the fleeting glimpses of the black soldier's experience that he has discovered. He concludes that white authors have generally abstained from treating black soldiers. Though a useful preamble to the many portrayals of black servicemen in later Vietnam War fiction, Couch's work is undermined by ignoring such black characters as Captain William Redfern in Halberstam's *One Very Hot Day*. See also the annotation under Norman Harris, below.

Dann, Jeanne Van Buren, and Jack Dann. Introduction to *In the Field of Fire*. New York: Tor/Tom Doherty Associates, 1987.
The editors comment on the high rate of post-traumatic stress disorder among veterans, addressing some of its causes and symptoms. Connecting veterans' dreams to the "waking dream" that is fiction, they argue that "science fiction and fantasy . . . bring another level of meaning and truth to the war" in part because they share the unconscious dreamscape of the Vietnam experience.

Durham, Marilyn. "Narrative Strategies in Recent Vietnam War Fiction." In *America Rediscovered: Critical Essays on Literature and Film of the Vietnam War*, edited by Owen W. Gilman, Jr., and Lorrie Smith. New York: Garland, 1990.
Narrative point of view can invite or block the reader's imaginative participation. The narrative strategies of Heinemann's *Paco's Story* and Mason's *In Country* find various ways of creating an intimacy between reader and narrator. Caputo's *Indian Country*, on the other hand, involves "the sweep of the camera's eye rather than the passion of a participant." Point of view undergoes a series of shifts that "diminishes our ability to absorb the persona of the teller."

Franklin, H. Bruce. "The Vietnam War as American Science Fiction and Fantasy." *Science Fiction Studies* 17, no. 3 (November, 1990): 341-359.
In this crucial article, Franklin demonstrates how "American SF helped engineer and shape America's war in Indochina, which then profoundly reshaped American SF." Both sides of the issue are examined in detail. Franklin treats Robert Heinlein's *Glory Road*, Ursula Le Guin's *The Word for War Is Forest*, Joe Haldeman's *The Forever War*, and numerous short stories including Kate Wilhelm's "The Village" and Norman Spinrad's "The Big Flash."

Frazier, J. Terry. "Vietnam War Stories: Looking at the Heart of Darkness."
    Studies in Popular Culture 5 (1982): 1-6.
    After praising Halberstam's *One Very Hot Day*, Haldeman's *War Year*,
    Huggett's *Body Count*, Ford's *Incident at Muc Wa*, and other works for their
    various kinds of verisimilitude, Frazier worries that some element of the war
    experience is still missing. He seeks representations of the gradual accretion of
    guilt and the consequences of this guilt on the soldier's later life. Few probe the
    horror of finding one's self capable of killing and the greater horror of being
    attracted to it.

Gilman, Owen W., Jr. "Vietnam Fiction and the Paradoxical Paradigm of
    Nomenclature." In *Search and Clear: Critical Responses to Selected Literature
    and Films of the Vietnam War*, edited by William J. Searle. Bowling Green,
    Ohio: Bowling Green State University Popular Press, 1988.
    While exploring whether or not there is a viable genre category of "the Vietnam
    War novel," Gilman makes important connections with another category defined
    primarily by subject: science fiction. Both categories are distinguished by
    peculiarities in language (nomenclature) that form the basis for stylistic
    similarities. While science fiction nomenclature is largely invented, however,
    Vietnam War fiction is "told in its own language." Wright's *Meditations in
    Green* gets particular attention.

Harris, Norman. "Novels of the Vietnam War." In his *Connecting Times: The
    Sixties in Afro-American Fiction*. Jackson: University Press of Mississippi, 1988.
    After providing an overview of black perspectives on Vietnam by references to
    fictional and journalistic work, Harris examines John A. Williams' *Captain
    Blackman*, George Davis' *Coming Home*, and Wesley Brown's *Tragic Magic*.
    These and other works show that black soldiers who were historically literate
    were less damaged by their Vietnam experience than those without such literacy.
    The novels also reflect changing attitudes toward fraternization among black
    soldiers. A much abbreviated version appears as "Blacks in Vietnam: A Holistic
    Perspective Through Fiction and Journalism." *Western Journal of Black Studies*
    10, no. 3 (Fall, 1986): 121-131.

Heberle, Mark A. "Correspondent Visions of Vietnam." *War, Literature, and the
    Arts* 1, no. 1 (Spring, 1989): 4-18.
    Reviews "that small but extremely significant body of semifictional works that
    combine journalism with storytelling." Heberle examines the mixture of
    objective reporting and subjective judgment found in the works of journalists
    turned fictioneers whose protagonists are reporters. These include Greene's *The
    Quiet American*, Moore's *The Green Berets*, Kaiko's *Into a Black Sun*, Herr's
    Dispatches, and Hasford's *The Short-Timers*.

Holbling, Walter W. "The Impact of the Vietnam War on U.S. Fiction: 1960s to 1980s." In *Literature and War*, edited by David Bevan. Amsterdam: Rodopi, 1990.
Holbling is concerned with how recent American fiction both acknowledges the uniqueness of the Vietnam experience and aligns it with other literary and cultural trends. He observes, for example, the theme of "gratuitous destruction" in literature and other cultural representations that have no direct link with the war. Of the war novels, Holbling gives special attention to Mailer's *Why Are We in Vietnam?* and O'Brien's *Going After Cacciato*. He concludes by noting the metaphorical power of the war as a vehicle for expressing American societal problems.

——————. "Literary Sense-Making: American Vietnam Fiction." In *Vietnam Images: War and Representation*, edited by Jeffrey Walsh and James Aulich. New York: St. Martin's Press, 1989.
Holbling divides Vietnam War novels into two categories. The first type uses conventional narrative techniques that reveal the meaning of the historical sequence of events. The second type seeks not "the representation of familiar facts" but "the creation of (literary) answers in response to, not in imitation of, events of national historical importance." These latter works are dominated by "the meta-fictional dimension." Key works in each category are briefly treated.

——————. "U.S. Fiction About Vietnam: The Discourse of Contradiction." In *The Vietnam Era: Media and Popular Culture in the U.S. and Vietnam*, edited by Michael Klein. London: Pluto Press, 1990.
Essentially a repackaging of materials and ideas found in his essay listed immediately above, but certain works are treated in greater detail; namely *The Green Berets*, *The 13th Valley*, and *Going After Cacciato*. Holbling stresses the power of personal narratives and includes references to novels and critical works not yet in print when he prepared the earlier article. A sound overview of the major categories and major titles.

Jason, Philip K. "Sexism and Racism in Vietnam War Fiction." *Mosaic* 23, no. 3 (Summer, 1990): 125-137.
The sexist behavior rampant in representative Vietnam War novels renders problematic the successes of the woman's liberation movement. These novels reveal a deep-rooted hostility toward, and fear of, the feminine. Many of them employ metaphors that equate women not only with the enemy, but also with weaponry. The essay makes use of feminist criticism and the ideas of the psychoanalytic pioneer Otto Rank. Extended treatment of Heinemann's *Close Quarters* with lesser attention to Webb's *Fields of Fire*, Huggett's *Body Count*, and Hasford's *The Short-Timers*.

_____. "Vision and Tradition in Vietnam War Fiction." In *America Rediscovered: Critical Essays on Literature and Film of the Vietnam War*, edited by Owen W. Gilman, Jr., and Lorrie Smith. New York: Garland, 1990.

Traditional fictions (*The 13th Valley*, *Fields of Fire*, *Body Count*) are generally third-person narratives representing the experience of the fighting unit while handling time, place, action, and causality according to the conventions of realism. Visionary fictions (*The Short-Timers*, *Close Quarters*, *Going After Cacciato*) tend to a narrower focus with "lyrical, surreal description[s] that create distortions of time, place, and action." These fictions undermine easy cause-and-effect understandings in representing the war's absurd nature.

Jeffords, Susan. "'Things Worth Dying For': Gender and the Ideology of Collectivity in Vietnam Representation." *Cultural Critique*, no. 8 (Winter, 1987/1988): 79-104.

Jeffords argues that the "collective consciousness of America" motif prominent in Vietnam narratives and films is actually gender defined. It is finally an exclusively masculine construct; thus, "Vietnam narratives . . . restabilize a patriarchal structure for social relations." Jeffords examines Del Vecchio's *The 13th Valley*, Heinemann's *Body Count*, and Eastlake's *The Bamboo Bed*. Contains material incorporated into her *The Remasculinization of America*.

Jones, Peter G. *War and the Novelist: Appraising the American War Novel*. Columbia: University of Missouri Press, 1976.

Jones discusses novels of World War II, Korea, and Vietnam (though treatment here is preliminary and sketchy). He offers thematic chapters on "The War Novel as *Bildungsroman*," "The Literature of Command," "Sexuality and Violence in the War Novel," "The Psychology of Combat," and "At War with Technology" (on Kurt Vonnegut, Jr.). Includes brief but useful overviews of David Halberstam's *One Very Hot Day* and John Sack's *M* (usually classified as nonfiction).

Kakutani, Michiko. "Novelists and Vietnam: The War Goes On." *The New York Times Book Review*, April 15, 1984, pp. 1, 39-41.

While praising some aspects of individual novels, Kakutani is concerned with their "myopic focus." She feels that despite its potential, the Vietnam experience has not been fashioned into the most significant literary art—and that perhaps the peculiar nature of the war itself has something to do with this failure. She awaits those works that will go beyond being "reflections of individual experience" and encompass "the military and political complexities of the war, its consequences in public and private lives, as well as its reverberations at home."

Karl, Frederick R. "Vietnam as a Metaphor for Life." In his *American Fictions,1940-1980*. New York: Harper & Row, 1983.

Karl notes the disembodied quality of Vietnam War narratives in contrast to the texture of time and place of World War II narratives. He examines O'Brien's *Going After Cacciato*, asserting influences and precedents and commenting and O'Brien's style. The *Heart of Darkness* echoes in Stone's *Dog Soldiers* are explored, as is the way in which the shadow of Vietnam hangs over the characters and moral vision of Stone's *A Flag for Sunrise*.

Klinkowitz, Jerome. "Vietnam." In his *The American 1960s: Imaginative Acts in a Decade of Change*. Ames: Iowa State University Press, 1980.
Klinkowitz surveys the early novelistic attempts to meet the challenge of fashioning works that would reflect "the radically different nature of this war" for which "conventional modes of understanding were discarded by many as obsolete." He includes comments on Halberstam's *One Very Hot Day*, Pelfrey's *The Big V*, Eastlake's *The Bamboo Bed*, and Bunting's *The Lionheads*. Parallels introduction to Klinkowitz and Somer's *Writing Under Fire* anthology, below.

Klinkowitz, Jerome, and John Somer. Introduction to *Writing Under Fire: Stories of the Vietnam War*, edited by Jerome Klinkowitz and John Somer. New York: Delta: 1978.
This early assessment of Vietnam War fiction makes reference to Andre Malraux's *The Royal Way* (the first Western novel about Vietnam) before going on to underscore the achievement of Graham Greene, Robin Moore, David Halberstam, and others. Special attention is given to Tom Mayer's short-story collection *The Weary Falcon*. Klinkowitz and Somer consider James Park Sloan's *War Games* and William Crawford Woods's *The Killing Zone* to be "the two best to come out of the Vietnam War." Updated as "Writing Under Fire: Postmodern Fiction and the Vietnam War" in Larry McCaffery's *Postmodern Fiction: A Bio-Bibliographical Guide*.

Leepson, Marc. "The Vietnam Novel: Out of the Jungle?" *Veteran* 10, no. 6 (June, 1990): 17-19.
Contrary to Robert Stone's prophesy and example, many of the most recent Vietnam novels are not "second wave" material about how Vietnam shaped American lives and society beyond the war itself, but rather works that remain in the jungle. Leepson notes the appearance of such new "first wave" titles as O'Brien's *The Things They Carried*, Del Vecchio's *For the Sake of All Living Things*, and Michael Peterson's *A Time of War* as well as second wave works like Karlin's *Lost Armies*. He posits the "third wave" category: works set in Vietnam but not in the combat zone. This category would include David Willson's *REMF Diary* and Tim Mahoney's *We're Not Here*. Leepson's overview nets a great number of titles, new and old.

Limon, John. "War and Play: A Theory of the Vietnam Sports Novel." *Arizona Quarterly* 46, no. 3 (Autumn, 1990): 65-90.
Many sports novels of the 1960s allude to Vietnam "by indirection or misdirection." Limon argues: "The sports novel was perfectly poised either to mask the violence of Vietnam or to make the image of Vietnam appear where all had been peace and innocence." His demonstration is strained as he pulls out of hats Vietnam rabbits such as Updike's *Rabbit Redux*, Lawrence Shainberg's *One on One*, and even Don DeLillo's *End Zone*. The game is up when Mailer's *Why Are We in Vietnam?* is treated as a football novel. Someone is joking?

McCaffery, Larry, ed. *Postmodern Fiction: A Bio-Bibliographical Guide*. New York: Greenwood Press, 1986.
Several authors whose works touch the Vietnam War receive brief treatment in this reference work. These include Joan Didion, William Eastlake, Maxine Hong Kingston, Tim O'Brien, and Robert Stone. There is also an entry on one important critic of Vietnam War literature, Jerome Klinkowitz, as well as an updating of Klinkowitz's introduction to the *Writing Under Fire* anthology (above), now called "Writing Under Fire: Postmodern Fiction and the Vietnam War."

Marin, Pilar. "Alienation and Environment in the Fiction of Vietnam." *Revista Canaria de Estudios Ingleses* 15, (November, 1987): 25-34.
Marin discusses how such features of the war as a combatant's sudden entrance and departure, the impenetrability of the jungles, and the lack of clear-cut objectives are reflected in the handling of mood, setting, and structure of key Vietnam War novels. Halberstam's *One Very Hot Day*, Del Vecchio's *The 13th Valley*, and Heinemann's *Close Quarters* are among those works briefly explored. Marin uses Caputo's *A Rumor of War* sometimes as a nonfiction reference and sometimes as if it were another novel.

Miller, Wayne Charles. *An Armed America: Its Face in Fiction*. New York: New York University Press, 1970.
Subtitled "A Study of the American Military Novel," Miller's book begins with novels of the American Revolution and takes the reader through novels written while the Vietnam War was in progress. Though Miller includes no Vietnam War fiction, he does give detailed attention to "The Military Novel in the Nuclear Age" and to other aspects of technological warfare as reflected in fiction. He traces the changing nature of the military hero in ways that form a useful preamble to the study of Vietnam War literature.

Myers, Thomas. "Dispatches from Ghost Country: The Vietnam Veteran in Recent American Fiction." *Genre* 21, no. 4 (Winter, 1988): 409-428.
While consistency is hard to find in the popular and literary representations of

the Vietnam veteran, there is agreement "that the Vietnam vet is different from the veterans of other wars." He often figures as "a bearer of great cultural news internalized by his nation's inability to hear." Treats Heinemann's *Paco's Story*, John Nichols' *American Blood*, Bobbie Ann Mason's *In Country*, and Caputo's *Indian Country*. A less ambitious treatment of this material is the "Afterword" to Myers' book, *Walking Point*.

Naparsteck, Martin J. "The Vietnam War Novel." *Humanist* 39, no. 4 (July/ August, 1979): 37-39.
Writing before Vietnam War novels were receiving much attention, Naparsteck insists that a substantial body of work had already appeared. He comments on O'Brien's *Going After Cacciato*, Joe Haldeman's *War Year*, Halberstam's *One Very Hot Day*, and James Whitfield Ellison's *The Summer After the War*. Naparsteck lists other noteworthy novels and anticipates a large body of significant work: "The Vietnam war is ripe for literary pickings."

Palm, Edward F. "Novels of the Vietnam War and the Uses of Literature." *Marine Corps Gazette*, November, 1986, 92-94, 98-99.
Palm gives special praise to the stylistic innovations of *Going After Cacciato* and applauds the moral vision of *Fields of Fire* while remembering the theme of commitment in *The Quiet American*. He worries that more recent novels, such as Wright's *Meditations in Green* and Rob Riggan's *Free Fire Zone*, with their focus on maladjusted veterans, will skew the way in which the war is remembered, leading readers to take a part for the whole.

Powers, Thomas. "Vietnam in Fiction." *Commonweal*, March 15, 1974, 39-41.
Powers finds Robert Roth's *Sand in the Wind*, William Turner Huggett's *Body Count*, and James Trowbridge's *Easy Victories* worthy of praise, though he reserves his highest praise for the latter, least-known of these novels. While sections of Roth and Huggett are interchangeable, Trowbridge's is unique in its vision and has greater technical sophistication than the others.

Pratt, John Clark. "Bibliographic Commentary: From the Fiction, Some Truths." In *"Reading the Wind": The Literature of the Vietnam War*, by Timothy J. Lomperis. Durham, N.C.: Duke University Press, 1987.
After some salient introductory comments on the sweep of Vietnam War literature, Pratt provides a bibliographic essay divided into a prologue, five acts, and an epilogue, each division concerned with a segment of the war itself. The novels that are responsive to these different stages (whenever written or published) are then treated together and assessed against one another. Though outdated by the mass of novels published in recent years, Pratt's treatment remains the best brief introduction to the field.

_____. "The Lost Frontier: American Myth in the Literature of the Vietnam War." In *The Frontier Experience and the American Dream: Essays on American Literature*, edited by David Mogen, Mark Busby, and Paul Bryant. College Station: Texas A & M Press, 1989.
Pratt surveys a wide range of well-known and relatively obscure works to demonstrate how most "Vietnam War writings show that Americans have . . . misunderstood their own myths and have applied them misguidedly." After summarizing the key critical discussions (by Beidler, Hellmann, and Margaret Stewart) of the relationships of frontier myth to Vietnam writings, Pratt pays special attention to Crumley's *One to Count Cadence*, Moore's *The Green Berets*, Halberstam's *One Very Hot Day*, and Kaiko's *Into a Black Sun*. A lucid, concise exploration.

_____. "Yossarian's Legacy: *Catch-22* and the Vietnam War." In *Fourteen Landing Zones: Approaches to Vietnam War Literature*, edited by Philip K. Jason. Iowa City: University of Iowa Press, 1991.
Pratt explores the direct and indirect influence of Heller's classic on Vietnam War fiction, first noting the features of *Catch-22* that seemed prophetic of the Vietnam experience. In Vietnam War fiction, *Catch-22* is invoked "by direct reference, analogy, echo, and a few instances, parody." The endings of many of the Vietnam novels, however, signal a different vision in which escape and sanctuary are not possible. Pratt treats more than a dozen novels, some obscure but all important to the student of Vietnam War literature.

Puhr, Kathleen M. "Four Fictional Faces of the Vietnam War." *Modern Fiction Studies* 30, no. 1 (Spring, 1984): 99-117.
The novels of the Vietnam experience represent a wide range of fictional modes and use the full gamut of literary techniques. John Briley's *The Traitors* represents the propagandistic novel, James Webb's *Fields of Fire* is the tradition of realism, Charles Durden's *No Bugles, No Drums* blends realism and absurdism, Gustav Hasford's *The Short-Timers* provides "unrelenting absurdism," and John Clark Pratt's *The Laotian Fragments* employs documentary strategies.

_____. "Women in Vietnam War Novels." In *Search and Clear: Critical Responses to Selected Literature and Films of the Vietnam War*, edited by William J. Searle. Bowling Green, Ohio: Bowling Green State University Popular Press, 1988.
After considering the various possibilities suggested by her umbrella title, Puhr focuses on American women, nurses in particular, as the are represented in the fiction. Evelyn Hawkins' *Vietnam Nurse*, Leonard B. Scott's *Charlie Mike*, and Patricia Walsh's *Forever Sad the Hearts* are explored for their various

representations of the woman's role in war. Includes references to Lynda Van Devanter's memoir *Home Before Morning*.

Ringnalda, Donald. "Fighting and Writing: America's Vietnam War Literature." *Journal of American Studies* 22 (April, 1988): 25-42.
Most Vietnam novels, such as Del Vecchio's *The 13th Valley*, are rooted in the realist tradition and "emulate the military operation" by believing in maps, treating time in a linear fashion, overestimating technology, and displaying cultural narcissism. The best Vietnam writers "eschew . . . the entire inheritance of literary realism." Their works emulate the way in which the Vietcong fought, "in the jungle, off the main, well-traveled roads." Praises the achievement of Eastlake, Pratt, Herr, O'Brien, Just, Sloan, Heinemann, Hasford, and Wright.

Rutherford, Andrew. "Realism and the Heroic: Some Reflections on War Novels." *Yearbook of English Studies* 12 (1982): 194-207.
A thoughtful analysis of the demands placed on war novelists by changes in war technology and in presentational matters: "The accumulation of realistic detail, for example, which once seemed a sufficient antidote to romantic idealism, can establish its own film of familiarity." Most of the examples come from the literature of World War II and earlier, though there are some penetrating comments on Webb's *Fields of Fire*.

Sanders, Clinton R. "The Portrayal of War and the Fighting Man in Novels of the Vietnam War." *Journal of Popular Culture* 3, no. 3 (Winter, 1969): 553-564.
The early critical perspective finds novels written between 1965 and 1968 easily categorized as having either patterns of despair or patterns of affirmation. All the novels, however, seem critical of the military managers. Sanders treats John Sack's *M*, Gene D. Moore's *The Killing at Ngo Tho*, Daniel Ford's *Incident at Muc Wa*, William Wilson's *The LBJ Brigade*, David Halberstam's *One Very Hot Day*, and Robin Moore's *The Green Berets*. Most of the works reveal the unconventional nature of the war "in which all supposed allies are potential enemies."

Searle, William J. "The Vietnam War Novel and the Reviewers." *Journal of American Culture* 4, no. 2 (Summer, 1981): 83-94.
Too often "the reviewers' indignation or their assumed familiarity with the war caused them to overlook the flaws and attributes of the fiction itself, particularly in the depiction of combat soldiers." Searle surveys the responses to the more-popular Vietnam War novels, sorting out the political and aesthetic sides of verisimilitude and offering additional critical comments on key works.

_____. "Walking Wounded: Vietnam War Novels of Return." In *Search and Clear: Critical Responses to Selected Literature and Films of the Vietnam*

War, edited by William J. Searle. Bowling Green, Ohio: Bowling Green State University Popular Press, 1988.

Searle first discusses prevailing attitudes toward returning veterans and then treats three representative novels: Charles Colman's *Sergeant Back Again*, Robert Bausch's *On the Way Home*, and Stephen Wright's *Meditations in Green*. Each novel in its own way focuses on disillusionment and its consequences for the returning veteran. By succumbing to the "sick vet" image, these writers foster an unfortunate stereotyping of all Vietnam War veterans.

Smetak, Jacqueline R. "The (Hidden) Anti-War Activist in Vietnam War Fiction." In *Fourteen Landing Zones: Approaches to Vietnam War Literature*, edited by Philip K. Jason. Iowa City: University of Iowa Press, 1991.

Smetak unveils the sublimated or disguised antiwar perspective in a series of major Vietnam novels. These include Webb's *Fields of Fire*, Caputo's *Indian Country*, O'Brien's *Going After Cacciato*, and Fuller's *Fragments*. The analyses are backgrounded by a review of protest literature. Smetak concludes that the hidden antiwar activist dimension in the fiction helps us see "that we who opposed the war were not fundamentally different from those who fought it."

Smith, Myron J., Jr. *War Story Guide: An Annotated Bibliography of Military Fiction*. Metuchen, N.J.: Scarecrow Press, 1980.

In a thirty-page section called "The Years of Cold War and Hot Police Actions, 1945-1978," Smith lists and briefly annotates a range of military novels and story collections including many of the earlier Vietnam War titles.

Spark, Alasdair. "Vietnam: The War in Science Fiction." In *Science Fiction, Social Conflict, and War*, edited by Philip John Davies. Manchester, England: Manchester University Press, 1990.

The Vietnam War frustrated science-fiction writers by perverting technology and placing the technoarmy in a losing position. Science fiction, however, absorbed and reflected these conditions as well as "the authority of the enemy" and sympathetic attitudes toward aliens. Spark reviews many works including titles by Le Guin, Haldeman, Shepard, and Spinrad. Science fiction's status as a predictive medium was upset by Vietnam.

Stewart, Margaret E. *Ambiguous Violence: Myths of Regeneration and Proficiency in U.S. Novels of the Vietnam War*. Madison, Wis.: Center for Southeast Asian Studies, 1986.

This pamphlet examines those novels "that focus on the socially inherited myths" that shape America's vision of the past, present, and future. Gene Moore's *The Killing at Ngo Tho* and John Briley's *The Traitors* offer different versions of "the defense-of-civilization construct." David Halberstam's *One Very Hot Day* and Daniel Ford's *Incident at Muc Wa* examine "the myth of performance as its own reward." The myths that these novels incorporate or expose show that "instability characterizes the structures that shape our cultural imagination."

Suther, Judith D. "French Novelistic Views of America and the Vietnam War." In *Explorations: Essays in Comparative Literature*, edited by Makoto Ueda. Lanham, Md.: University Press of America, 1986.
Suther's brief survey finds that these novels generally "rest comfortably on the tradition of French anti-Americanism" though they range widely as to subgenre. They also reflect France's long involvement in Southeast Asia and "the residue of experience, military and other, that forms part of the novelists' culture." Most attention is given to Jean Anglade's *Le Point de suspension*, Pierre Boulle's *Les Oreilles de jungle*, and Olivier Todd's *Les Canards de Ca Mao*. Many other works are noted briefly.

Tal, Kali. "The Mind at War: Images of Women in Vietnam Novels by Combat Veterans." *Contemporary Literature* 31, no. 1 (Spring, 1990): 76-96.
The combat veteran writer "generates female characters that represent the level of his own alienation." While women are generally turned into objects in these novels, Asian women receive the most extreme objectification. Tal exemplifies her point through references to major Vietnam War fictions by O'Brien, Eastlake, Heinemann, Huggett, and Webb as well as to such lesser known works as Donald McQuinn's *Targets* and Ed Dodge's *Dau*. In some of these novels female characters "play a therapeutic role—the alter ego who insists that the accumulated 'masculinities' of the soldier are a trap the protagonist must escape."

Tetlow, Joseph A. "The Vietnam War Novel." *America*, July 19-26, 1980, 32-36.
Tetlow, having surveyed forty novels, discerns four broad categories: "guerrilla picaresque" novels of personal experience, realistic novels about one unit or operation, "big war novels of synoptic vision," and "fables and fabulous tales." The major works as of early 1980 are fit into this scheme. Those by O'Brien, Kolpacoff, Hasford, Webb, and Loyd Little are given special praise.

Wiedemann, Barbara. "American War Novels: Strategies for Survival." In *War and Peace: Perspectives in the Nuclear Age*, edited by Ulrich Goebel and Otto Nelson. Lubbock: Texas Tech University Press, 1988.
This derivative overview of American war fiction observes the shift from realism to fantasy in the successive waves of novels that followed both World War II and Vietnam. Wiedemann notes how O'Brien's *Going After Cacciato* portrays various options for escaping from the war while making Berlin's escape through fantasy the most acceptable and successful one.

Wilson, James C. "American Novels of the Vietnam War: A Bibliography."
American Notes and Queries 20, no. 5/6 (January/February, 1982): 80-82.
  Wilson gives a brief account of the history of Vietnam War fiction, arguing that
  there have been few popular and critical successes because of the unpopularity
  of the war itself. A handful of works, he asserts, deserve acclaim. His list has
  forty-three entries.

Poetry

Balaban, John. "Poetry and Politics in Vietnam." In *The Vietnam Era: Media and
Popular Culture in the U.S. and Vietnam*, edited by Michael Klein. London:
Pluto Press, 1990.
  Balaban reviews the two major strands of Vietnamese poetry: the native oral
  tradition and the Chinese literary tradition. After a capsule history, he discusses
  the relationship of poetry to the common people and ends with some brief
  comments on poems by Vietnamese soldiers, two of which he presents in
  translation. Would it have made a difference, Balaban wonders, to know how
  deeply poetry reaches "into the minds of the Vietnamese at all levels of
  society?"

Coupe, Laurence. "'Tell Me Lies About Vietnam': English Poetry and the
American War." In *Tell Me Lies About Vietnam: Cultural Battles for the
Meaning of the War*, edited by Alf Louvre and Jeffrey Walsh. Philadelphia:
Open University Press, 1988.
  English poets challenged their government's prevailing orthodoxy about
  America's Vietnam policy. Coupe discusses the work of Adrian Mitchell, D. J.
  Enright, and James Fenton, making frequent comparisons between these British
  poets and their American counterparts. He also considers the ideas of activist-
  anthologist Michael Horovitz (*Children of Albion: Poetry of the 'Underground'
  in Britain*).

Ehrhart, W. D. "Soldier-Poets of the Vietnam War." *Virginia Quarterly Review*
63, no. 2 (Spring, 1987): 246-265.
  This essay, which also appears in *Tell Me Lies About Vietnam*, edited by Alf
  Louvre and Jeffrey Walsh (see Coupe, above), is an earlier version of the essay
  by the same name that appears in Gilman and Smith's *America Rediscovered*
  (see entry, below). Like Ehrhart's "Introduction" to his *Unaccustomed Mercy*
  poetry anthology, it stresses the early publication history of poetry by Vietnam
  veterans.

_____. "Soldier-Poets of the Vietnam War." In *America Rediscovered:
Critical Essays on Literature and Film of the Vietnam War*, edited by Owen W.

Gilman, Jr., and Lorrie Smith. New York: Garland, 1990.
Ehrhart traces the history of war poetry by Vietnam veterans, beginning with the anthology *Winning Hearts and Minds* (1972) through volumes of the late 1980s by Bruce Weigl and Walter McDonald. He also briefly characterizes the work of Basil T. Paquet, Michael Casey, D. C. Berry, John Balaban, Bryan Alec Floyd, D. F. Brown, and others while arguing why the particular nature of the Vietnam War and the conditions of return led "so many former soldiers . . . to the solitude of pen and paper."

Felstiner, John. "Bearing the War in Mind." *Parnassus: Poetry in Review* 6, no. 2 (Spring/Summer, 1978): 30-37.
An important review of an important anthology: *Demilitarized Zones: Veterans After Vietnam*, edited by Jan Barry and W. D. Ehrhart. Felstiner illustrates the ways in which the poems collected here expose "a state of mind caught between an intolerable past and an inhospitable present." He notes that the dominant tone of the most effective poems "is not sentimental or poeticized, but understated, flat, stripped." Other related poetry volumes are also discussed.

Gitlin, Tod. "Notes on War Poetry." *Confrontation* 8 (Spring, 1974): 145-147.
"The best Vietnam war poetry by Americans differed from World War I poetry in its acerbity, bitterness, and precision." Gitlin comments very briefly on Levertov, Bly, Kinnell, and Rich. He finds most significant those poems that draw a relationship between victims and executioners.

Hidalgo, Stephen P. "A Selected Bibliography of Vietnam War Poetry." *Bulletin of Bibliography* 48, no. 1 (March, 1991): 12-24.
Hildalgo lists collections of poems dominated by Vietnam War material as well as individual poems about the war found in more miscellaneous collections. The entries are grouped by year of publication beginning in 1965 and running through 1990. A brief survey of secondary sources (criticism and reviews) not listed in earlier bibliographies appears in a single alphabet.

Johnson, Mark. "'History, the Body's Prison': American Poetry During and After Vietnam." *Publications of the Missouri Philological Association* 8 (1985): 25-30.
The impact of the Vietnam War on the American consciousness is reflected in four long poems that exemplify "a cultural and literary shift from polarization to fragmentation." This shift echoes that uncovered in Godfrey Hodgson's analysis of the American political climate, *America in Our Time* (1978). The works are Robert Kelly's *The Common Shore*, Allen Ginsberg's *The Fall of America*, Robert Pinsky's *An Explanation of America*, and Daniel Hoffman's *Brotherly Love*.

McCarthy, Eugene J. "Poetry and War." *Confrontation* 8 (Spring, 1974): 131-136.
The former senator and presidential candidate gives his 'greatest hits' of war
poetry that includes Vietnam War favorites. The poetry of Vietnam veterans is
"not much good" and is characterized by "a laying bare of self by way of
purification."

Mersmann, James F. *Out of the Vietnam Vortex: A Study of Poets and Poetry
Against the War*. Lawrence: University of Kansas Press, 1974.
Mersmann gives an overview of the protest movement during the Vietnam War
era and places the antiwar poetry in this context as well as in the larger context
of war poetry. In separate chapters, he treats relevant works by Allen Ginsberg,
Denise Levertov, Robert Bly, and Robert Duncan. Mersmann sees less an
indictment of this particular war and more a turning away from militarism.
Written before their works were easily available, this book pays no attention to
the protest poems by Vietnam veterans.

Nelson, Cary. "Whitman in Vietnam: Poetry and History in Contemporary
America." In his *Our Last First Poets: Vision and History in Contemporary
American Poetry*. Urbana: University of Illinois Press, 1981.
Nelson argues that "what above all undoes most Vietnam poems . . . is an
apparent ignorance of how history has usurped both their language and their
form." He can say that because he is speaking of the older, nonveteran
generation of protest poets. Nelson comments on Levertov, Wright, Merwin,
Ginsberg, and Rich—whom he finds most successful. This essay first appeared
in *Massachusetts Review* 16 (Winter, 1975): 55-71. (Other essays in this book
touch upon these and other poets as they confronted the history of the 1960s.)

Pratt, John Clark. Preface to *Unaccustomed Mercy: Soldier-Poets of the Vietnam
War*, edited by W. D. Ehrhart. Lubbock: Texas Tech University Press, 1989.
The overview to Ehrhart's anthology discusses the ways in which the poetry of
this war differs from previous war poetry: "Overall, a reader senses that each
of these poets feels used, hardly a cog in a mighty machine but rather a misfit,
one who understands what no other American can." Pratt includes brief critical-
biographical comments on the twelve poets represented: John Balaban, Jan
Barry, D. F. Brown, Michael Casey, Horace Coleman, Ehrhart, Bryan Alec
Floyd, Yusef Komunyakaa, Gerald McCarthy, Walter McDonald, Basil T.
Paquet, and Bruce Weigl. The book includes a selected bibliography of further
readings about the war also by Pratt.

Shaw, Robert B. "The Poetry of Protest." In his *American Poetry Since 1960:
Some Critical Perspectives*. Cheadle, Cheshire, England: Carcanet, 1973.
Shaw recaptures the mood of the mid-1960s when poetry read-ins and protest
anthologies revealed a politically active community of poets. He classifies the

antiwar poetry into three categories: "diatribe and documentary," "autobiographies," and "apocalyptic and satire." Shaw offers brief glances at work by Denise Levertov, Robert Lowell, Robert Bly, Adrienne Rich, and Robert Duncan.

Smith, Lorrie. "'After Our War': Poets of the Vietnam Generation." *Poetry Wales* 25, no. 1 (June, 1989): 7-11.
This short but informative overview stresses the subversive nature of poetry by Vietnam veterans and comments on the key anthologies and most significant collections by individual poets. Smith briefly comments on W. D. Ehrhart, Walter McDonald, D. F. Brown, Bruce Weigl, John Balaban, and Yusef Komunyakaa. *Shallow Graves* by Wendy Wilder Larsen and Tran Thi Nga also gets attention.

_____. "Resistance and Revision in Poetry by Vietnam War Veterans." In *Fourteen Landing Zones: Approaches to Vietnam War Literature*, edited by Philip K. Jason. Iowa City: University of Iowa Press, 1991.
Smith argues that poetry is "inherently more subversive than narrative" and thus better suited to "a literary project which seeks to disrupt and re-imagine cultural myths rather than reproduce the status quo." She examines works by W. D. Ehrhart, John Balaban, Bruce Weigl, and D. F. Brown, who is treated at length. Smith believes that these veteran poets tend to resist the cultural codes and literary conventions that homogenize perceptions of war, thus reawakening the reader to war's horror.

_____. "A Sense-Making Perspective in Recent Poetry by Vietnam Veterans." *American Poetry Review* 15, no. 6 (November/December, 1986): 13-18.
The poetry of Vietnam veterans is not only a poetry of record and testimony but also one that involves retrospective evaluation and "heuristic vision." Much of the veterans' poetry "is an anti-poetry stripped of transfiguring metaphor but enriched by the accuracy of a witnessing moral vision." Smith pays special attention to the work of W. D. Ehrhart and Bruce Weigl while mentioning other poets in passing.

True, Michael. "War and Poetry." *Confrontation* 8 (Spring, 1974): 137-144.
True develops the thesis that "the only good war poems are anti-war poems" by reference to World Wars I and II and, finally, to Vietnam War poetry. He mentions the *Winning Hearts and Minds* anthology (Larry Rottman's poems in particular) and Michael Casey's *Obscenities*. Vietnam poetry has a new consciousness, a loss of innocence more profound than that of earlier wars.

Tuso, Joseph F. *Singing the Vietnam Blues: Songs of the Air Force in Southeast Asia*. College Station: Texas A & M Press, 1990.
Tuso has collected 148 songs that were written or sung by combat flyers during the Vietnam War. Each is about the war in some way. Tuso provides a historical context for each song and also explains whatever would otherwise remain obscure about the task, mission, or military references. While the collection itself is a fascinating primary source, Tuso's commentaries, especially those on military culture, make this book a valuable critical endeavor. Glossary included.

Von Hallberg, Robert. "Politics." In his *American Poetry and Culture, 1945-1980*. Cambridge, Mass.: Harvard University Press, 1985.
Vietnam War protest poetry may be usefully seen in the larger context of political poetry that questioned U.S. "aspirations to empire" as well as attitudes and policies regarding socioeconomic class. Many of the protest poets were first and finally political in these wider arenas. Von Hallberg discusses Robert Bly, James Wright, Robert Duncan, Adrienne Rich, and other poets of political conscience.

Wimmer, Adi. "The American Idea of National Identity: Patriotism and Poetic Sensibility Before and After Vietnam." In *Cultural Legacies of Vietnam: Uses of the Past in the Present*, edited by Richard Morris and Peter Ehrenhaus. Norwood, N.J.: Ablex, 1990.
Wimmer recounts the destruction of the myth of America's "redemptive vision" and how America's "arrogant generosity" is anatomized in memoirs by Caputo, O'Brien, and Ehrhart. Noting that established poets were the first voices of fierce opposition, Wimmer then comments on works by Allen Ginsberg, Charles Olson, Robert Bly, Robert Duncan, and others. After Vietnam, veteran poets continued the attack, among them Ehrhart and John Balaban. In their most recent work, these poets seek a new American mythology.

Drama

Asahina, Robert. "The Basic Training of American Playwrights: Theater and the Vietnam War." *Theater* 9, no. 2 (Spring, 1978): 30-37.
The earliest overview of Vietnam War drama. Asahina comments on Megan Terry's *Viet Rock*, John Guare's *Muzeeka*, Ron Cowen's *Summertree*, Arthur Kopit's *Indians*, and David Rabe's "Vietnam Trilogy." Many of these plays, Asahina feels, are too tightly tied to the 1960s or too weighed down by documentary facts. Rabe is singled out as an important voice, "the only [Vietnam] playwright really concerned with the art of the theater rather than with the form or the content of the media." This issue of *Theater* includes the text of Adrienne Kennedy's *An Evening with Dead Essex*.

Carpenter, Charles A. *Modern Drama Scholarship and Criticism, 1966-1980: An International Bibliography*. Toronto: University of Toronto Press, 1986.
If more specialized bibliographies are not available, this wide-ranging reference work is a place to begin. Carpenter has brief listings on Kennedy, Kopit, Rabe, Terry, Valdez, and others.

Coven, Brenda. *American Women Dramatists of the Twentieth Century: A Bibliography*. Metuchen, N.J.: Scarecrow Press, 1982.
Coven covers a huge number of playwrights, many quite briefly. Among these are Adrienne Kennedy and Megan Terry. Primary and secondary materials are listed.

DeRose, David J. "A Dual Perspective: First-Person Narrative in Vietnam Film and Drama." In *America Rediscovered: Critical Essays on Literature and Film of the Vietnam War*, edited by Owen W. Gilman, Jr., and Lorrie Smith. New York: Garland, 1990.
Though mostly concerned with voice-over narrations and their function in the films of the war, DeRose also briefly explores narrational elements in Gray's *How I Got That Story* and DiFusco's *Tracers*. The retrospective narrative voice complicates the ongoing present of the film or drama by enabling "the veteran artist to communicate his war experiences via his eventual grasp of their significance and consequences." Several references to Rabe's Vietnam plays.

_____. "Soldados Razos: Issues of Race in Vietnam War Drama." *Vietnam Generation* 1, no. 2 (Spring, 1989): 38-55.
Among the plays reflecting minority experiences are Ruben Sierra's *Manolo*, Luis Valdez's *Vietnam Campesino* and *Soldado Razo*, Jaime Carrero's *Flag Inside*, Melvyn Escueta's *Honey Bucket*, Fred Gamel's *Wasted*, Charles Michael Moore's *The Hooch*, Jamal's *LBJ*, Adrienne Kennedy's *An Evening with Dead Essex*, Stephen Mack Jones's *Back in the World*, and Tom Cole's *Medal of Honor Rag*. DeRose links the themes and techniques of these and other plays.

_____. "The Speed of Darkness and 'Crazed Vets on the Doorstep' Drama." *Vietnam Generation Newsletter* 3, no. 3 (November, 1991): 40-42.
Steve Tesich's *The Speed of Darkness* is only the latest in a series of plays that employ the crazed-vet motif. DeRose sorts out the responsible and irresponsible handlings of this motif, commenting briefly on Lyle Kessler's *The Watering Place*, Stephan Metcalfe's *Strange Snow*, James Duff's *Home Front*, and a number of other plays both well-known and obscure. He treats Tesich's play in detail, praising its "raw emotional power."

Durham, Weldon B. "Gone to Flowers: Theatre and Drama of the Vietnam War." In *America Rediscovered: Critical Essays on Literature and Film of the Vietnam*

War, edited by Owen W. Gilman, Jr., and Lorrie Smith. New York: Garland, 1990.
This chronological overview begins with Megan Terry's *Viet Rock* (1966) and provides from a paragraph to two pages of commentary on each of the major and minor plays responding to the war through James Duff's *Home Front* (1985). Durham is especially useful on such less-well-known plays as Stephen Metcalfe's *Strange Snow* (1982) and Larry Kerton's *Asian Shade* (1983). He links plays by pointing out their thematic and theatrical continuities as well as their relationships to contemporary trends.

Fenn, Jeffery. "Vietnam: The Dramatic Response." In *Tell Me Lies About Vietnam: Cultural Battles for the Meaning of the War*, edited by Alf Louvre and Jeffrey Walsh. Philadelphia: Open University Press, 1988.
Vietnam War drama underwent "significant evolution in style and attitude." The first dramatic responses were short protest plays staged by radical theater groups. Later, as the returning veterans made Vietnam a more significant issue for the general public, more thoughtful full-length plays (some of them productions of the commercial theater) "examined the nature of American society and the effects of cultural conditioning." Metaphors of fragmentation and disintegration dominate the plays about the Vietnam era.

Reston, James, Jr. Introduction to *Coming to Terms: American Plays and the Vietnam War*. New York: Theatre Communications Group, 1985.
This brief overview finds the Vietnam War "a national experience that is still denied and repressed," but Reston insists that the artist's vision gives us "the most accurate, most profound memory of Vietnam." He comments hastily on the plays in this collection: Rabe's *Streamers*, Mann's *Still Life*, Gray's *How I Got That Story*, Tom Cole's *Medal of Honor Rag*, Michael Weller's *Moonchildren*, Stephen Metcalfe's *Strange Snow*, and Terrence McNally's *Botticelli*.

Ringnalda, Donald. "Doing It Wrong Is Getting It Right: America's Vietnam War Drama." In *Fourteen Landing Zones: Approaches to Vietnam War Literature*, edited by Philip K. Jason. Iowa City: University of Iowa Press, 1991.
Drama is the genre best equipped for grappling with the Vietnam War because it is least equipped. Narrative forms do not permit the expression of radical consciousness. The strategies of indirection characteristic of Vietnam War drama pay less attention to combat mimesis and more to the subtexts of the war: the duplicity and complicity of Americans and American culture. Ringnalda treats Mann's *Still Life*, Rabe's Vietnam plays, and Gray's *How I Got That Story* in significant detail.

Savran, David. *In Their Own Words: Contemporary American Playwrights*. New York: Theatre Communications Group, 1988.

This important series of interviews includes many of the playwrights whose works are dramatic responses to the Vietnam War. Each interview is prefaced by a brief career biography. We learn that Chekhov was an early influence on Megan Terry, Brecht on Valdez. Also included are interviews with David Rabe and Emily Mann (listed under those authors in the section "Authors and Works").

Scharine, Richard G. "Vietnam—Theatre as a Mirror to National Institutions." In his *From Class to Caste in American Drama: Political and Social Themes Since the 1930s*. New York: Greenwood Press, 1991.
Scharine gives more attention to the political background of the drama than to the drama itself, and as much to films as to stage plays. He offers sketchy references to a few of the key plays, more extended treatments of Rabe's *Sticks and Bones* and (the marginally relevant) *The Trial of the Catonsville Nine* by Daniel Berrigan.

Zinman, Toby Silverman. "Search and Destroy: The Drama of the Vietnam War." *Theater Journal* 42, no. 1 (March, 1990): 5-26.
The "search and destroy" metaphor refers to "the loss of access to substantive meanings as well as to an aesthetically satisfying form" in representative American plays about the war. Zinman divides her discussion into two parts, finding that the content and tone of the plays by veterans (John DiFusco's *Tracers*, H. Wesley Balk's *The Dramatization of 365 Days*, Gray's *How I Got That Story*, and several pieces by Rabe) differs from those by civilians (Cole's *Medal of Honor Rag*, Kennedy's *An Evening with Dead Essex*, Mann's *Still Life*, Kopit's *Indians*, McNally's *Botticelli*, Weller's *Moonchildren*, and Terry's *Viet Rock*). Zinman views most of these plays as moral and aesthetic failures.

Film

Adair, Gilbert. *Vietnam on Film: From "The Green Berets" to "Apocalypse Now."* New York: Proteus, 1981.
Adair first links movies of the Vietnam War to the war movie and war story traditions and then surveys the peculiarities of the genre. He explores many relatively obscure movies that treat the draft, draft dodging and desertion, and the returning veteran. Many of these, Adair claims, are worthy of renewed attention. He also treats the major productions of the late 1970s. Appended is a detailed "Filmography."

Anderegg, Michael, ed. *Inventing Vietnam: The War in Film and Television*. Philadelphia: Temple University Press, 1991.
In his introduction, Anderegg argues that film representations "have supplanted

even so-called factual analyses as the discourse of the war, as the place where some kind of reckoning will need to be made and tested." The essays are arranged to reflect the chronology of the films (or television series) that they discuss. Most of the major and many of the minor Vietnam War films find capable analysis in the hands of Cynthia J. Fuchs, John Hellmann, Tony Williams, Judy Lee Kinney, Susan White, Owen W. Gilman, Jr., Thomas Doherty, and others. Includes a "Selected Bibliography" and a "Selected Filmography and Videography."

Auster, Albert, and Leonard Quart. *How the War Was Remembered: Hollywood and Vietnam*. New York: Praeger, 1988.
Taking a flexible, typological approach to the history of films directly or indirectly about the Vietnam War, this study stresses "the social, political, and cultural meaning and value of these films" without neglecting aesthetic dimensions. Among the mythic character types explored are the superman, the hunter-hero, and the survivor. The films are examined as means of shaping the national memory of the war.

Dittmar, Linda, and Gene Michaud, eds. *From Hanoi to Hollywood: The Vietnam War in American Film*. New Brunswick, N.J.: Rutgers University Press, 1990.
Offering a wide range of perspectives on a wide range of issues, this collection is much more dynamic than the single-author books on the Vietnam War and film. Essays are concerned with how the genre remakes history, how particular films represent the war, societal and psychological dimensions of the films, and the realm of documentaries on the war. The editors provide an effective introduction and useful appendices: a chronology and a filmography.

Rowe, John Carlos. "'Bringing It All Back Home': American Recyclings of the Vietnam War." In *The Violence of Representation: Literature and the History of Violence*, edited by Nancy Armstrong and Leonard Tennenhouse. New York: Routledge, 1989.
Rowe's study leans primarily on film but also includes references to television programs, oral histories, and other responses to the war. He argues that "counter-culture or counter-hegemonic" efforts at odds with dominant ideology are absorbed into "an enveloping rhetorical system designed to maintain traditional order and values." This discussion makes use of, and synthesizes, various contemporary critical perspectives.

Smith, Julian. *Looking Away: Hollywood and Vietnam*. New York: Charles Scribner's Sons, 1975.
This intriguing study in American popular culture examines the peculiar way in which the movie industry ignored meeting Vietnam head-on during the war years. Smith explores the oblique ways in which such movies as *The Sand*

Pebbles, *The French Connection*, *Little Big Man*, *Soldier Blue*, and *Straw Dogs* reflect attitudes toward the war. Other works discussed include *China Gate*, *The Quiet American*, *The Green Berets*, and *A Yank in Viet-Nam*.

AUTHORS AND WORKS

Asa Baber

Land of a Million Elephants

Quivey, James. "When Buffalos Fight It Is the Grass That Suffers: Narrative Distance in Asa Baber's *Land of a Million Elephants.*" In *Search and Clear: Critical Responses to Selected Literature and Films of the Vietnam War*, edited by William J. Searle. Bowling Green, Ohio: Bowling Green State University Popular Press, 1988.
Because their authors were overwhelmed by experience, most of the early novels of the war maintain little narrative distance. An exception is Baber's novel, which "seems more a product of post-war reflection than mid-conflict intensity." The dramatic-objective point of view, the absence of time-conscious strategies, and the absence of conventional heros or villains all contribute to the distancing effect. Baber even minimizes the significance of death by folding it into a larger vision.

John Balaban

Beidler, Philip D. *American Literature and the Experience of Vietnam*, pp. 129-136. Athens: University of Georgia Press, 1982.
Balaban's cultured style and evocation of cultural context is reminiscent of Eliot and Pound. His technical skills, allusiveness, and borrowings "constitute affirmations of grand purpose." Through the poems, the reader comes to share Balaban's discovery that this war— "our war"—while never forsaking its own particularity, "is also in some degree all wars." Beidler provides partial explications of key passages in various poems.

_____. *Re-writing America: Vietnam Authors in Their Generation*, pp. 147-157. Athens: University of Georgia Press, 1991.
Beidler gives special emphasis to the "range and eclecticism" of Balaban's literary career (as poet, novelist, translator, children's author) before examining the poems by which he supports his argument that Balaban is a "poetic and cultural mythmaker." Beidler pays special attention to Balaban's second collection, *Blue Mountain*, which furthers the project of reconstitution of self as "poet after our war" by manifesting a doubled vision of "there" and "here" that is subsumed in "a single terrain of poetic mythography."

Stephens, Michael G. *The Dramaturgy of Style: Voice in Short Fiction*, pp. 144-148. Carbondale: Southern Illinois University Press, 1986.
Balaban is characterized as "quite skillful, a Poundian sort of technician, so that his voice emerges layered, even tropical, and allusive." Balaban effectively combines "the ornamental and the elemental."

Walsh, Jeffrey. "'After Our War': John Balaban's Poetic Images of Vietnam." In *Vietnam Images: War and Representation*, edited by Jeffrey Walsh and James Aulich. New York: St. Martin's Press, 1989.
John Balaban's poetry of the Vietnam War differs from the work of others in that it presents "a sense of history and an awareness of Vietnamese culture." To Walsh, the "larger human meaning" of this war demands such an awareness. Examination of individual poems shows Balaban's "instinct for witnessing the casual and the normal" in a unique way that escapes the predominant "ethnocentric narrowness of perspective." Balaban's work also traces the war's impact on the American spirit and culture.

Remembering Heaven's Face: A Moral Witness in Vietnam

Jason, Philip K. "Remembering Heaven's Face: A Moral Witness in Vietnam." In *Magill's Literary Annual, 1992*. Pasadena, Calif.: Salem Press, 1992.
The unique vision of Balaban's Vietnam War poetry is explained and extended in this memoir of his years of alternative service with relief organizations. Because Balaban was able to get close to the Vietnamese people and because he became a student of their language and culture, his perspective on U.S. involvement there is an extraordinary counterbalance to the memoirs (and fictions) of those who served in the military or as correspondents. Balaban's book is a revelation in which American and Vietnamese cultures and conflict are subsumed into a larger harmony among individuals in the human community.

Robert Bausch

On the Way Home

Calloway, Catherine. "Robert Bausch's *On the Way Home*: Echoes of William Faulkner's *Soldier's Pay*." *Publications of the Arkansas Philological Association* 12 (Spring, 1986): 15-26.
As one of the first significant novels of return by a Vietnam veteran, Bausch's work avoids the heart-of-darkness motif and provides us with a probing psychological examination of the war's effects on a soldier and his family. Comparison to Faulkner's early novel of World War I reveals many parallels,

including the universality of such themes as post-traumatic stress and difficulty in adjusting to civilian life. Calloway, who praises Bausch's delineation of the protagonist's mother, finds his first novel far more sophisticated than Faulkner's apprentice work.

D. C. Berry

saigon cemetery

Beidler, Philip D. *American Literature and the Experience of Vietnam*, pp. 122-129. Athens: University of Georgia Press, 1982.
Berry strives for a poetic style that expresses "experiential memory." That style is characterized by "the jumpy spacing, the short metrical phrases, the elliptical syntax, the erratic and nervous shifting from line to line and margin to margin." Berry seems to be influenced by E. E. Cummings. The book attempts to merge the true nature of a soldier's experience in Vietnam with "larger dimensions of art and collective myth."

Alain Boublil, Richard Maltby, Jr., and Claude-Michel Schonberg

Miss Saigon

Behr, Edward, and Mark Steyn. *The Story of "Miss Saigon."* New York: Arcade, 1991.
Provides notes on the historical basis for the play, the Asian influence on Western art, the "Madame Butterfly" motif, and the development of the London and New York productions. Interviews with the authors, producer Cameron Mackintosh, and other members of the production team provide information on the creation of the play. Intriguing backstage drama with useful insights into the play's cultural daring and achievement.

DeRose, David J. "The Saigon Miss-Tique." *Vietnam Generation Newsletter* 3, no. 1 (February, 1991): 8-9.
DeRose reviews the recasting dilemma for the American production and comments on the issues of racism in both the casting history and the play's own stereotyping of characters. The formulaic nature of musical theater demands the kinds of simplification that do a disservice to those who suffered in the war, though there is some truth in the basic story line "as a romantic metaphor for the U.S. presence in Vietnam."

Chandler Brossard

Raging Joys, Sublime Violations

Beidler, Philip D. *"Raging Joys, Sublime Violations*: The Vietnam War in the Fiction of Chandler Brossard.*" Review of Contemporary Fiction* 7, no. 1 (Spring, 1987): 166-175.
This novel functions "as a comprehensive literary inquiry into the experience of the Vietnam War." It shows that the United States succumbed "to the old American habit of allowing sexuality, arising out of a whole psychic history of suppressions, evasions, exclusions, and, yes, sublimations, to transmute itself into an endless nightmare of aggression and destruction."

D. F. Brown

Smith, Lorrie. "Resistance and Revision in Poetry by Vietnam Veterans," pp. 58-65. In *Fourteen Landing Zones: Approaches to Vietnam War Literature*, edited by Philip K. Jason. Iowa City: University of Iowa Press, 1991.
Smith demonstrates how "Brown goes further than any other veteran poet towards formal dissolution in order to deconstruct the very modes of thought and speech which permitted our involvement in Vietnam and which perpetuate war's mystique." She examines Brown's "elliptical, anorexic lines, abrupt cuts and jumps in time, shifting perspectives and tenses, and radical dislocations of syntax" in the *Returning Fire* volume and in more recent poems.

C. D. B. Bryan

Friendly Fire

Beidler, Philip D. *American Literature and the Experience of Vietnam*, pp. 150-153. Athens: University of Georgia Press, 1982.
Bryan, as narrator of official and personal versions of the events about which he writes, demonstrates his own growth of consciousness in the search for a proper "perspective and mode of articulation to come to terms with an Iowa family's loss of a son, killed by his own artillery." His work strives to make sense of a society that uses language in such a way that such euphemisms as "friendly fire" are not only possible but predictable. Michael Mullen's accidental death, the attempt to conceal it, and the effect of his death on others become a microcosmic version of America's Vietnam experience. Bryan's quest for an unattainable objectivity allows the narrative to end, though the search can never be finished.

Johnson, Diane. "The Loss of Patriotic Faith in C. D. B. Bryan's *Friendly Fire.*"
In her *Terrorists and Novelists*. New York: Alfred A. Knopf, 1982.
After summarizing Bryan's account, Johnson wonders about her dissatisfaction
with the work. Partly, it has to do with Bryan's turning on the Mullens,
transforming himself "from a careful investigative journalist to something like
an unreliable narrator, inviting scrutiny of his own motives and character."
Perhaps this quality is in the nature of the "new journalism." Johnson is also
unhappy with Bryan's quick acceptance of military procedure.

Weber, Ronald. *The Literature of Fact: Literary Nonfiction in American Writing*,
pp. 156-165. Athens: Ohio University Press, 1980.
Weber summarizes the story of the Mullens' lives, as Bryan has detailed it, and
then goes on to examine the ways in which Bryan "turns the book's focus on
himself and his relation to the Mullens." The story of the Mullens' loss and
interpretation of events and the story of what actually happened to their son (as
Bryan came to understand it and as he related it in his final chapter) are two
distinct tragedies. The reader is left to choose.

Williams, Mary C. *"Friendly Fire."* In *Magill's Literary Annual, 1977*. Englewood
Cliffs, N.J.: Salem Press, 1977.
Bryan's prefatory claims to authenticity are needed because the book reads like
fictionalized history or biography. It is filled with novelistic devices, though the
style remains journalistic. Bryan's relationship to his subjects seems ambivalent:
"He questions their motives as well as his own." While the book maintains the
assumption "that the Vietnam war was a costly mistake," other assumptions
about the central figures undergo change. Ironies and shifting perspectives make
ultimate truths unknowable.

Robert Olen Butler

Beidler, Philip D. *Re-writing America: Vietnam Authors in Their Generation*, pp.
52-63. Athens: University of Georgia Press, 1991.
Of Butler's six major novels, three involve "the linkage of [major Vietnam
themes] with a distinctive major innovation of technique." In *The Alleys of Eden*,
Son Dogs, and *On Distant Ground*, Butler "has developed the figure of the
recurring memory of Vietnam as a national dream-nightmare into the basis of
what might be called a major Vietnam cycle of fiction, with major recurring
characters, incidents, scenes, and master symbologies." Beidler summarizes the
workings of what he calls Butler's Vietnam trilogy. He also treats the non-
Vietnam works.

On Distant Ground

Johnson, Ronald L. *"On Distant Ground."* In *Magill's Literary Annual, 1986.* Englewood Cliffs, N.J.: Salem Press, 1986.

The novel's "sharp, dramatic focus and crisp, character-revealing dialogue" show Butler's training as a playwright. He has a clean style and tight focus in which all the facts are right, but the novel is mainly concerned with "the relationships between an individual's sense of his own identity and the cultural surroundings in which he lives" and with "the clash of specific cultures." Butler's value here and in his other work lies in exploring the moral ambiguities of the action that he sets in motion. Johnson refers to other novels in Butler's loose trilogy and provides an excellent plot summary.

Philip Caputo

Beidler, Philip D. *Re-writing America: Vietnam Authors in Their Generation*, pp. 37-52. Athens: University of Georgia Press, 1991.

Beidler traces Caputo's career from *A Rumor of War* through the subsequent fictions of *Horn of Africa, Del Corso's Gallery*, and *Indian Country*. Caputo is characterized as a Hemingwayesque neotraditionalist caught up somewhat in a "myth of literary personality." Beidler finds a "literary project of historical-mythic inscription" as "the obsessive center of both of Caputo's first two novels" through explicit echoes of Joseph Conrad and Graham Greene.

Bonetti, Kay. *Philip Caputo: Interview with Kay Bonetti*. Sound recording. Columbia, Mo.: American Audio Prose Library, 1988.

Caputo discusses his eight-year struggle to write *A Rumor of War* as well as the dominant themes in that work and his subsequent novels. How do honorable people behave in extreme circumstances?

Indian Country

Beidler, Philip D. *Re-writing America: Vietnam Authors in Their Generation*, pp. 48-52. Athens: University of Georgia Press, 1991.

The novel is "an odyssey of recuperation and ritual atonement for an old memory of horror endlessly revisited." Beidler examines the interplay between the main story line of Chris Starkmann's expiation and the sequence of chapters that describes the "passage toward healing" of Wawiekumig (Old Louis), the Indian shaman and fishing guide. Starkmann is one in a series of "survivor returnees" in Caputo's post-Vietnam fictions.

Bonn, Maria S. "A Different World: The Vietnam Veteran Novel Comes Home."
In *Fourteen Landing Zones: Approaches to Vietnam War Literature*, edited by
Philip K. Jason. Iowa City: University of Iowa Press, 1991.
Heinemann's *Paco's Story* is the linchpin in Bonn's analysis of how veterans'
fictions reflect the unusual conditions of return for participants in this unpopular
war. Bonn compares Paco's situation to that of Heinemann's Philip Dosier of
Close Quarters and to Chris Starkmann of Philip Caputo's *Indian Country*,
which gets the most detailed treatment. She explores how these novels treat the
limits and terms of reintegration, describing how Starkmann's embrace of an
alternate mythology paves the way for his uniquely successful reconciliation.

Myers, Thomas. *Walking Point: American Narratives of Vietnam*, pp. 224-227.
New York: Oxford University Press, 1988.
Myers compares *Indian Country* to Mason's *In Country* in that both have
"themes of confrontation and forgiveness." In dealing with the issues of guilt
and expiation, Caputo self-consciously taps American traditions, moving Chris
Starkmann through a "ritualized forest" that shares the spiritual terrain walked
by James Fenimore Cooper's Natty Bumppo and Hemingway's Nick Adams.

A Rumor of War

Beidler, Philip D. *American Literature and the Experience of Vietnam*, pp. 153-
158. Athens: University of Georgia Press, 1982.
Like Ron Kovic in his *Born on the Fourth of July*, Caputo sees himself "as
bearing witness to the experience of the war in the dimension of personal
memory" while presenting himself as the main character in a work of "complex
literary invention." Caputo's writing is about the evolution of his own
consciousness about the war, "an attempt to trace the everchanging nature of
balance between event and vision, phenomenon and perspective, growth of
experience and growth of mind." At the end, the younger Caputo who is the
main figure is much like the older one who tells the story.

Cronin, Cornelius A. "From the DMZ to No Man's Land: Philip Caputo's *A
Rumor of War* and Its Antecedents." In *Search and Clear: Critical Responses
to Selected Literature and Films of the Vietnam War*, edited by William J.
Searle. Bowling Green, Ohio: Bowling Green State University Popular Press,
1988.
Caputo's work consciously looks backward to earlier combat literature,
especially through the epigraphs that invoke such World War I writers as
Wilfred Owen and Siegfried Sassoon. Moreover, the memoir's structure parallels
that of British World War I officer memoirs. The references to antecedents are
finally used to underscore the differences, one of which is the World War I

writers' sense of combat as a group experience versus the Vietnam War writers' sense of it being an individual one.

Melling, Philip H. *Vietnam in American Literature*, pp. 60-64. Boston: Twayne, 1990.
This brief discussion views Caputo as a representative autobiographer who "sees himself as the first generation of a new condition of modernity in American life," as a bridge between the past and the future. In contrast to the verbal insufficiencies of the Puritan narratives, Caputo's "text suffers from a surfeit of literacy, a desire to compensate for a personal, monumental sense of sin." By insisting on how exceptional Vietnam was, Caputo limits his capacity for a convincing realism.

Myers, Thomas. *Walking Point: American Narratives of Vietnam*, pp. 89-104. New York: Oxford University Press, 1988.
"Both a true work of the imagination and a valuable compensatory history, a memoir whose very literariness—its crafted, minute rendering of its speaker's rite of passage—is the pathway to its historical significance." Myers examines Caputo's handling of narrative voice and the stages of his development from "romantic adventurer" infected by the warrior ethos to a disengaged, chastened nonhero whose "retrospective voice" asserts "human value and the demand for honesty amid the debris of exploded myth."

Solotaroff, Ted. "A Witness of Vietnam." In his *A Few Good Voices in My Head*. New York: Harper & Row, 1987.
An accessible treatment of the moral issues of *Rumor* that observes the tension between the distancing effect of the title and the "relentless immediacy" of Caputo's descriptions. Solotaroff summarizes how "the course and character and damage of America's involvement was registered on [Caputo's] altered body, mind, nerves, and spirit." Caputo's vision forces personal and public responsibility to merge.

Styron, William. "A Farewell to Arms." In his *This Quiet Dust and Other Writings*. New York: Random House, 1982.
Styron shares memories of his own Marine Corps experience as he responds to Caputo's narrative. "Some of Caputo's troubled, searching meditations on the love and hate of war, on fear, and the ambivalent discord that warfare can create in the hearts of decent men, are among the most eloquent I have read in modern literature." This detailed appreciation first appeared in *The New York Review of Books*, June 23, 1977.

Wilson, James C. *Vietnam in Prose and Film*, pp. 62-64. Jefferson, N.C.: McFarland, 1982.

Caputo "provides the most detailed dismissal of the many moral objections to the war" by finding ways to rationalize his participation. In various ways, Caputo tries to justify his behavior by describing himself as caught up in the very nature of the war itself, "as if an immoral war excuses immoral individual conduct." For Wilson, *A Rumor of War* is an elegantly written excuse for inexcusable behavior: "If individuals cannot be held accountable for their own actions, then who can?"

Michael Casey

Obscenities

Beidler, Philip D. *American Literature and the Experience of Vietnam*, pp. 78-82. Athens: University of Georgia Press, 1982.
In *Obscenities*, Casey's diction rests on "the concrete and the quotidian." His matter-of-fact style gives credibility and sometimes an offbeat humor to the strange and ludicrous events that it records. Casey's juxtapositions convey "utter literal truthfulness" while releasing "an immense power of imaginative suggestion as well." Beidler pays special attention to "A Bummer" and "Hoa Binh," which share "a similar inevitability of poetic statement."

Kunitz, Stanley. Foreword to *Obscenities*, by Michael Casey. New Haven, Conn.: Yale University Press, 1972.
Kunitz praises *Obscenities* as the first significant American book of poems to come out of the Vietnam War. After setting Casey's work in the context of earlier war poetry, Kunitz discusses the narrative dimension of Casey's art. He insists that this is no mere random collection and that the book should be read straight through like a novel or a play so that the reader can grasp "a progress of awareness" that Casey develops.

James Crumley

One to Count Cadence

Beidler, Philip D. *American Literature and the Experience of Vietnam*, pp. 55-58. Athens: University of Georgia Press, 1982.
In *One to Count Cadence*, Crumley's hero and narrator, Slag Krummel, treats himself both as an individual and as an "image of his culture as a whole." His war is less a confrontation with the enemy and more a struggle with "the warrior mythos that has spawned him." Krummel is infected by the "aimless spirit of the killing itself." He has become one with it and with what he says about Joe

Morning: "Even if he isn't dead . . . he is lost." Crumley simultaneously evokes and undercuts the glamour of the American warrior tradition. Effective mixture of realistic depiction and surreal fantasy.

Richard Currey

Bonetti, Kay. *Richard Currey: Interview with Kay Bonetti.* Sound recording. Columbia, Mo.: American Audio Prose Library, 1991.
Currey discusses the relationship between his own West Virginia summers and how this part of his background as well as his experience in Vietnam is transformed in his novel *Fatal Light.* He strives to merge the intensity of poetry with the satisfaction afforded by narrative fiction.

George Davis

Coming Home

Mitchell, Verner D. "I, Too, Sing America: Vietnam as Metaphor in *Coming Home.*" *Vietnam Generation* 1, no. 2 (Spring, 1989): 118-124.
Davis turns the Vietnam War into a metaphor "for dramatizing the black man's struggle for basic human rights in America." He does it without repeating the simplistic stereotypes of blacks, giving instead "an empathetic rendering of black soldiers in human terms," which gives readers some chance of understanding their ambivalent relationship to the military and to the country. Mitchell examines the roles of the main characters, Childress and Ben, as representative black veterans.

John Del Vecchio

The 13th Valley

Conlon, John J. "*The 13th Valley.*" In *Magill's Literary Annual, 1983.* Englewood Cliffs, N.J.: Salem Press, 1983.
Del Vecchio, while telling the gripping tale of a single major battle, underscores the "problems of military personnel during the Vietnam era." The conditions of isolation and disorientation, the limited solace of soldierly camaraderie, racial tensions, the rotation system, and other issues are woven into the plot. Conlon praises Del Vecchio's realism and the way in which his characters both deny meaning and continue to seek it.

Hellmann, John. *American Myth and the Legacy of Vietnam*, pp. 128-134. New York: Columbia University Press, 1986.
"Like *Moby Dick*, *The 13th Valley* is a tragic epic, with Del Vecchio following Melville's strategy of having the commander of the operation see a cosmic significance in the objective." The secondary characters represent various aspects of America's ideal self-concept, and their interaction creates "a moving vision of American democracy." In the end, Cherry (the initiate) must see the human representatives of America's mythic traits "lost in the furious meaning-lessness of Vietnam."

Jeffords, Susan. *The Remasculinization of America: Gender and the Vietnam War*, pp. 67-68, 71-72. Bloomington: Indiana University Press, 1989.
When James Chelini comes to Vietnam, his comrades name him Cherry. His inexperience of war is equated with sexual inexperience and by extension with femininity rather than masculinity. In his transformation from virgin to God, "Cherry's immaculate conception depends . . . on the difference that gender proclaims." The deification is a result of male bonding and an acquired taste for violence. The portrait of Lt. Brooks reveals the connection between sexual relations and violence. Men are, and, it seems, must be, united against women.

Myers, Thomas. "Diving into the Wreck: Sense Making in *The 13th Valley*." *Modern Fiction Studies* 30, no. 1 (Spring, 1984): 119-134.
This article is the forerunner of Myers' treatment of the same work in his book-length study *Walking Point*, annotated below.

_____. *Walking Point: American Narratives of Vietnam*, pp. 56-69. New York: Oxford University Press, 1988.
Del Vecchio's massive achievement can be compared to Melville's *Moby Dick*; it conveys "the same tensions of man and nature, knowledge and innocence, and history and language that Ahab's vengeful hunt entails." Against his main narrative, Del Vecchio offers other texts: Lt. Brooks's dissertation, a glossary, and "official" military reports of the day's activities accompanied by topographic maps. These contrasting texts both intensify and undercut the force of the realistic narrative, helping to project the concluding ambiguities.

Stephens, Michael G. *The Dramaturgy of Style: Voice in Short Fiction*, pp. 171-176. Carbondale: Southern Illinois University Press, 1986.
Del Vecchio's epical impulse works not by voice, "but by factual accretions joined to types and stereotypes in archetypal combat situations." Because he does not develop "a voice that sees and speaks, that seizes the rhythm of experience, [he] allows some of this enormous potential to slip away." Stephens points out that in isolated passages Del Vecchio proves an effective stylist; however, style and narrative voice are constantly undermined by other concerns.

Joan Didion

Felton, Sharon. "Joan Didion: A Writer of Scope and Substance." *Hollins Critic* 26, no. 4 (October, 1989): 1-10.
This brief overview stresses Didion's "proficiency in a variety of genres" and her "maturing and expanding vision." *Democracy* questions "the epistemological natures of fact and fiction" as Didion interacts with her heroine, Inez Victor. Good starting place with useful generalizations about Didion's work.

Olendorf, Donna. "Joan Didion: A Working Checklist, 1955-1980." *Bulletin of Bibliography* 38, no. 1 (January-March, 1981): 32-44.
Includes primary and secondary sources. Although this is a pre-*Democracy* compilation, it is useful for locating biographical materials and studies of Didion's themes and methods.

Democracy

Ching, Stuart. "'A Hard Story to Tell': The Vietnam War in Joan Didion's *Democracy*." In *Fourteen Landing Zones: Approaches to Vietnam War Literature*, edited by Philip K. Jason. Iowa City: University of Iowa Press, 1991.
Images of collapse recur throughout Didion's novel, whose internal drama "is set against the historicity of the Vietnam War." Ching points out the specific connections between events in the chronology of the war and events in the lives of Didion's characters, all the while mapping the pattern of imagery that links the two stories, allowing them to interact thematically. The symbol of the gyre, adopted from Yeats's "The Second Coming," informs Didion's vision of disintegration.

Hanley, Lynne. "Reconstructing Vietnam: Joan Didion and Doris Lessing." In her *Writing War: Fiction, Gender, and Memory*. Amherst: University of Massachusetts Press, 1991.
Set against the standard (and male) "soldier's story"—too often taken as *the* story of Vietnam—are such narratives as Didion's *Democracy*, works that concern themselves with those "who devised and executed the policies that put the American soldier in the mud." Hanley emphasizes how Didion turns our attention to those who profited or hoped to profit from the war and to the war's alienating effect on American women. Lessing's various novels offer "a critique of our representations of war" and of our ability to forget war's essential nature.

Henderson, Katherine Usher. "Joan Didion: The Bond Between Narrator and Heroine in *Democracy*." In *American Women Writing Fiction: Memory, Identity,*

Family, Space, edited by Mickey Pearlman. Lexington: University of Kentucky Press, 1989.

In *Democracy*, Didion offers "an uneasy affirmation of personal meaning in a world where society and politics are defined by artifice and self-seeking." Ironically, she described effective relationships in a violent, chaotic world. Henderson traces Didion's relationship to her heroine, Inez, while pointing out how the fall of Saigon affects all the major characters. Essay followed by extensive primary and secondary bibliography that includes reviews of *Democracy*.

Stout, Janis P. "Joan Didion and the Presence of Absence." In her *Strategies of Reticence: Silence and Meaning in the Works of Jane Austen, Willa Cather, Katherine Anne Porter, and Joan Didion*. Charlottesville: University Press of Virginia, 1990.

Stout argues Didion's curtailed style and aggressive use of blankness throughout her writings. In the section on *Democracy* (pp. 175-187), Stout notes a moderated version of Didion's bare style that is used to protect narrator and reader from "the pressure of emotion" and from the disorder that inhabits and surrounds the characters. This pressure and sense of collapse stem, in part, from the revelation of a hollow American society "epitomized in the fall of Vietnam."

Tager, Michael. "The Political Vision of Joan Didion's *Democracy*." *Critique* 31, no. 3 (Spring, 1990): 173-184.

Democracy explores the U.S. tendency, since World War II, "to curtail democracy to further foreign policy goals." Though primarily concerned with political rhetoric surrounding Vietnam, the novel recognizes the corruption of language in other communist containment operations. Tager examines the plot carefully, especially its juxtapositions of scenes, noting that "Vietnam's own history never enters the novel; it represents a means for Americans to advance their own agendas."

Winchell, Mark Royden. *Joan Didion*. Rev. ed., pp. 125-133. Boston: Twayne, 1989.

Winchell discusses the novel in terms of Didion's satirical treatment of political styles. He compares her main characters to those in her earlier novels, and he provides interesting speculations about why Didion chose Hawaii as her setting. Winchell also notes that "*Democracy* is finally more about Vietnam than Hawaii," though Didion makes no attempt at a definitive statement. He suggests a linkage between this novel and the classic work of the same name by Henry Adams as well as Adams' autobiography.

Robert Duncan

Mackey, Nathaniel. "From Gassire's Lute: Robert Duncan's Vietnam War Poems."
Talisman: A Journal of Contemporary Poetry and Poetics 5 (Fall, 1990): 86-99.
Duncan's Vietnam War poems show him hovering between two poles: He
strenuously decries U.S. involvement in Vietnam and yet he "accepts, even all
but embraces the war as a revelatory, epiphanic event." Duncan appropriates the
ancient legend of Gassire's lute, in which the lute's voice is nourished by blood,
to acknowledge the ambivalent relationship between poetry and war.

Charles Durden

No Bugles, No Drums

Myers, Thomas. *Walking Point: American Narratives of Vietnam*, pp. 126-139.
New York: Oxford University Press, 1988.
The protagonist-narrator is reminiscent of Twain's *Huckleberry Finn*. Jamie
Hawkins' reading of the war "begins in the assertion of pure innocence and ends
in the admission of total complicity." The novel keeps absurdist company with
Heller's *Catch-22* but is more hardboiled. Hawkins is faced with a number of
moral decisions that weigh down the comedy. "His assertion of nonviolence
within violent history is coupled with the demand that the circumstances of his
war speak to him in logical terms."

Wilson, James C. *Vietnam in Prose and Film*, pp. 73-75. Jefferson, N.C.:
McFarland, 1982.
Wilson considers Durden's hero, Jamie Hawkins, a victim of the "throwaway
society" and its exploitative packaging and marketing of the war. Durden's
juxtapositions imply "that the war is a function of advanced consumer
capitalism," a venture that is maintained primarily because it is good for
business. Examining the war in terms of economic incentives sharpens the
narrator's class consciousness. Through Hawkins' growing cynicism, Durden
exposes a society that treats its common soldier as a disposable commodity.

William Eastlake

Lewis, Linda K. "William Eastlake." *Bulletin of Bibliography* 41, no. 1 (March,
1984): 6-11.
Primary sources include a separate listing of "Vietnam Articles." Secondary
sources include biographical references, general criticism, and reviews of
Eastlake's various novels including *The Bamboo Bed*.

McPheron, William. "William Eastlake: A Checklist." *Review of Contemporary Fiction* 3, no. 1 (Spring, 1983): 93-105.
   The three sections on primary sources are books, stories in books and periodicals, and "articles, sketches, and reviews." Secondary sources include "reviews" and "critical and biographical commentary." Useful list of reviews of *The Bamboo Bed*.

O'Brien, John. "Interview with William Eastlake." *Review of Contemporary Fiction* 3, no. 1 (Spring, 1983): 4-17.
   Eastlake discusses writers whom he admires, influences, and personal relationships with other writers. Eastlake's three war novels—*Castle Keep*, *The Bamboo Bed*, and *The Long Naked Descent into Boston*—are contrasted. Also, Eastlake comments on his choice of an impressionistic style. Some career and biographical information.

The Bamboo Bed

Beidler, Philip D. *American Literature and the Experience of Vietnam*, pp. 51-55. Athens: University of Georgia Press, 1982.
   Considered, along with Crumley's *One to Count Cadence* and Halberstam's *One Very Hot Day*, as one of the most significant novels of the early period. Like the others, Eastlake's novel is prophetic of what is to come later. It "makes its meaning by flaunting its own artificiality." As "a model of self-conscious artifice," it suggests that the vision of "art-truth" may be truer than any array of verifiable facts, especially with regard to the experience of this war. *The Bamboo Bed* "is full of pregnant one-line profundity, non-sequitur nonsense that reads like a textbook in the modern absurd."

Fair, Alan. "The Beast in the Jungle: Mailer, Eastlake, and the Narrating of Vietnam." In *Tell Me Lies About Vietnam: Cultural Battles for the Meaning of the War*, edited by Alf Louvre and Jeffrey Walsh. Philadelphia: Open University Press, 1988.
   In their respective novels, Mailer and Eastlake attempt "to render both the war and the psyche that produces and is produced by it. Mailer's critical fiction (*Why Are We in Vietnam?*) develops a meaningful analysis which produces a sense of the national dependency on myth, whereas Eastlake explores the personal effects of those myths." Eastlake also explores "the capacities of the text itself to comprehend/represent the American psyche."

Jeffords, Susan. *The Remasculinization of America: Gender and the Vietnam War*, pp. 35-41. Bloomington: Indiana University Press, 1989.
   Eastlake "links a presentation of the feminine as female body to a thematization

of male aggression, depicting (hetero)sexual intercourse as a means to rise above violence caused by male competitiveness." His novel is one more example of how Vietnam representations repeatedly image the feminine only "as a function of the masculine." *The Bamboo Bed*'s confusion of fact and fiction is finally in the service of a gender ideology, not an aesthetic one. Even Madame Dieudonne's response to her image in the mirror promotes the masculine point of view.

Kazin, Alfred. *Bright Book of Life: American Novelists and Storytellers from Hemingway to Mailer*, pp. 91-93. Boston: Atlantic Monthly Press/Little, Brown, 1973.
The "manic plenitude of American destructiveness" in Vietnam outran the imaginations of most novelists. Even Eastlake's novel "finally seems to elude literary ambition." To Kazin, this work "is an indictment of our historic American ferocity, and finally not about Vietnam but about all of America's wars." Eastlake satirizes Hemingway's style and his version of the hero.

W. D. Ehrhart

Beidler, Philip D. *Re-writing America: Vietnam Authors in Their Generation*, pp. 157-162. Athens: University of Georgia Press, 1991.
This brief overview of Ehrhart's career observes the "GI bluntness as well as [the] Owen-Sassoon-Hemingway precision and control" of Ehrhart's earlier work. Ehrhart is at once polemical and visionary. The bitter tones and blunt ironies that characterize some of his poems are offset by others in which possibilities for redemption and healing are offered.

Stephens, Michael G. *The Dramaturgy of Style: Voice in Short Fiction*, pp. 141-144. Carbondale: Southern Illinois University Press, 1986.
Ehrhart's voice "is a good representation" of "the disenfranchised, antiestablishment patriot." Stephens focus is on *To Those Who Have Come Home Tired: New and Selected Poems*. He feels that in the newer poems Ehrhart's "images are more ironical and humorous."

Gloria Emerson

Beidler, Philip D. *Re-writing America: Vietnam Authors in Their Generation*, pp. 208-221. Athens: University of Georgia Press, 1991.
The "dialectical consciousness" of American culture offered in the title *Winners and Losers* finds abundant opportunities for games of oppression. It is also an ironic, angry title, as the individual episodes show how easily winning and

losing can be mistaken for something else, how the very categories are traps. In *Some American Men*, Emerson's post-Vietnam feminist text sets as a cultural goal going beyond "gender as social construction." Emerson challenges our myths of power in both works.

Winners and Losers

Beidler, Philip D. "The Good Women of Saigon: The Work of Cultural Revision in Gloria Emerson's *Winners and Losers* and Frances FitzGerald's *Fire in the Lake*." *Genre* 24, no. 1 (Winter, 1988): 523-534.
A detailed analysis of two structurally dissimilar works by female journalists, each of which reveals the relationships between language and power. Both works assert their "linguistic and cultural meanings through a radical critique of our fundamental categories of linguistic and cultural assumption." Both reveal the limitations of our "essentially western and male" cultural consciousness in perceiving and responding to the dilemma posed by Vietnam. This material is elaborated in Beidler's *Re-writing America: Vietnam Authors in Their Generation*.

James Fenton

Children in Exile

Dillard, R. H. W. "*Children in Exile*." In *Magill's Literary Annual, 1985*. Englewood Cliffs, N.J.: Salem Press, 1985.
Dillard feels that Fenton's poems of tragedy in Cambodia are part of the larger tragedy of turmoil in Indochina to which Vietnam's ordeal is a parallel. Fenton, though strikingly contemporary in his concerns, is clearly connected to the traditions of British war poetry and to W. H. Auden. "Only William Eastlake's *The Bamboo Bed* . . . rivals Fenton's "Dead Soldiers" as a literary portrait of the complex madness of Indo-Chinese war."

Hulse, Michael. "The Poetry of James Fenton." *Antigonish Review* 58 (Summer, 1984): 83-102.
This friendly overview of Fenton's career as a poet remarks on his fascination with war and with "the process of history and memory that attend upon war." Hulse finds Fenton influenced at different times in his career by Auden and Eliot. The essay includes brief comments on a few of Fenton's poems of conflict in Southeast Asia.

Frances FitzGerald

Beidler, Philip D. *Re-writing America: Vietnam Authors in Their Generation*, pp. 221-237. Athens: University of Georgia Press, 1991.
Fire in the Lake is "an attempt to trace out the tragedy of Vietnam" by "unwriting [the] received dialectical formula of American consciousness, a formula essentially western and essentially male." This feminist text weighs the "depths of tragedy of Vietnam against the backdrop of . . . an orgy of American techno-macho-malewrite and malespeak sublimely unaware of its . . . cultural arrogance." *America Revised* and *Cities on a Hill* bring Fitzgerald's poet-Vietnam insights into the realms of public education and "the myth of national exceptionalism."

Fire in the Lake

Beidler, Philip D. "The Good Women of Saigon: The Work of Cultural Revision in Gloria Emerson's *Winners and Losers* and Frances FitzGerald's *Fire in the Lake*." *Genre* 24, no. 1 (Winter, 1988): 523-534.
See annotation under Gloria Emerson, *Winners and Losers*, above.

Jack Fuller

Fragments

Rohrberger, Mary. "*Fragments*." In *Magill's Literary Annual, 1985*. Englewood Cliffs, N.J.: Salem Press, 1985.
In this detailed review-essay, Rohrberger outlines the plot, comments on the effect of the first-person narration, and examines how the novel presents two contrasting philosophies for explaining the characters' experiences in Vietnam. She also points out how the novel keeps readers in touch with Vietnam's long history as a battleground. In this and other ways, *Fragments* sets the war into contexts that aid understanding.

Ronald J. Glasser

365 Days

Melling, Philip H. *Vietnam in American Literature*, pp. 44-48. Boston: Twayne, 1990.
Glasser's "semifictional autobiography" probes for pathological signs both in the

literal dimension of its medical material and, more importantly, on a moral plane. The diagnostic style, with its absence of emotion, leads to clarification and understanding: "For Glasser, the technique of surgery and the craft of writing are controlled by the pace at which things happen, the use of objects that correlate activity and inhibit misleading speculation."

Styron, William. "The Red Badge of Literature." In his *This Quiet Dust and Other Writings*. New York: Random House, 1982.
Styron praises Glasser's "remarkable miniature portraits of men at war," but especially the hospital scenes "where the force of Glasser's professional concern melts with the compassion and sensibility of a gifted storyteller." This book is valuable because "it shows that in the midst of their most brutish activity there is a nobility in men that war itself cannot extinguish." First appeared in *Washington Monthly*, March, 1972.

Graham Greene

Costa, Richard Hauer. "Graham Greene: A Checklist." *College Literature* 12, no. 1 (1985): 85-94.
Costa first gives a chronological list of fiction and nonfiction books by Greene followed by a list of screenplays and a brief list of miscellaneous pieces in essay collections. Secondary sources include interviews, bibliographies, book-length critical studies, and critical essays in periodicals and anthologies.

The Quiet American

Allott, Miriam. "The Moral Situation in *The Quiet American*." In *Graham Greene*, edited by Harold Bloom. New York: Chelsea House, 1987.
Allott explores the character of Fowler in great detail, examining his relationship toward Phuong and his scenes with Inspector Vigot and with the Catholic priest. Greene's brand of existentialism is called a more feeling, more positive one than that represented in much continental fiction. Allott believes that "what has mattered in Fowler's story is that he is capable of feeling pity and sorrow" for Fowler, not just antipathy. This essay first appeared in *Graham Greene: Some Critical Considerations* (Lexington: University Press of Kentucky, 1963).

Christie, Clive. "Between France and America: Graham Greene and *The Quiet American*." In his *"The Quiet American" and "The Ugly American": Western Literary Perspectives on Indo-China in a Decade of Transition, 1950-1960*. Occasional Paper 10. Canterbury, England: University of Kent Centre of South-East Asian Studies, 1989.

Even though Greene does not admire certain French policies and actions, his novel presents "an essentially French perspective on Indochina to an English-speaking, particularly American, audience." Christie develops a detailed biographical and historical context for his treatment of the novel, one that views it among Greene's other works set in "Third World" countries and that makes use of Greene's Indochina reportage.

Couto, Maria. *Graham Greene: On the Frontier, Politics and Religion in the Novels*, pp. 166-176. New York: St. Martin's Press, 1988.
The Quiet American is illustrative of two propositions: "(i) To be human is to be political, and (ii) the politics of today is inseparable from living, from the essential issues of freedom and dignity basic to life." Couto provides excellent insights into the secondary characters, Phuong and Dominguez. She sets this novel in the context of Greene's other political fictions and links his politics "to the ideals of conservative Liberals in the early years of this century."

DeVitis, A. A. *Graham Greene*. 2d ed., pp. 108-114. Boston: Twayne, 1986.
Greene creates an interiorized drama that depends upon the reader's adjustment to an unreliable narrator. Like many of Greene's earlier novels, it compresses "political issues into the differences that exist between human beings." Also in conflict are the forces of innocence and experience represented respectively by Pyle and Fowler. While Pyle's innocence is suspect because uninformed by experience, Fowler's experience is contaminated by his lack of commitment.

Evans, Robert O. "Existentialism in Greene's *The Quiet American.*" *Modern Fiction Studies* 3, no. 3 (Autumn, 1957): 241-248.
Evans sees in this novel the full flowering of Greene's increasing existentialism. Though Fowler is a lethargic hero, the book is not static because Fowler's decisions (or indecisions) have broad effects. This novel is part of Greene's search for a way of life that will preserve the dignity of the individual in a materialistic society. Without being religious, as many other Greene novels are, *The Quiet American* is highly ethical. Evans believes, however, that one cannot equate Fowler's views with Greene's. The essay appears in a special Graham Greene issue that includes useful but dated bibliographical material.

Frenier, Mariam Darce. "Two *Quiet Americans*: British Literature into American Propaganda." *Vietnam Generation* 1, no. 1 (Winter, 1989): 81-93.
Joseph Mankiewicz's film version of Greene's novel subverts Greene's vision in the same way that the American Cold War mentality misinterpreted the Vietnam conflict and the earlier French experience. Frenier examines several specific ways in which "the movie inverts the novel," offering explanations for how these departures originated. These include refashions of the opening and close as well as the "reversal of Pyle's and Fowler's roles."

Gaston, Georg M. A. *"The Quiet American*: A Secular Prospect.*"* In his *The Pursuit of Salvation: A Critical Guide to the Novels of Graham Greene.* Troy, N.Y.: Whitston, 1984.
Greene wrote this novel when he was at the top of his craft. He follows the format of the detective story, with a particularly complicated version of the convention of confession. Greene's recurrent theme of personal salvation is at the heart of the novel, "concentrated primarily in the character of Fowler." Gaston examines the setting, structure, and philosophical implications of the novel in detail. He finds in Greene a "private and primarily aesthetic" brand of existentialism. An earlier version appears as "Structure of Salvation in *The Quiet American,"* in *Renascence* 31, no. 2 (Winter, 1979): 93-106.

Hughes, R. E. *"The Quiet American*: The Case Reopened.*" Renascence* 12, no. 1 (Autumn, 1959): 41-42, 49.
Hughes focuses on Greene's narrative technique and use of dramatic irony to demonstrate that Fowler is not Greene's alter ego. Hughes argues that "the priest in the blood-speckled soutane" is Greene's symbol "for an adequate participation in humanity," though Fowler does not realize it. Greene's art remains essentially Catholic, even though Fowler's vision is not. (This is a special issue on Greene.)

Larsen, Eric. "Reconsideration: *The Quiet American.*" *The New Republic*, August 7 and 14, 1976, 40-42.
Writing twenty years after its publication, Larsen explains how and why Greene's book "is still the best novel to have come out of the Vietnam war." Even granting Greene's dependence on caricature, Larsen insists that the novel "strikes home, and history, the ruthless arbiter in these matters, has given it the additional grim stamp of truth." *The Quiet American* records a national failure of perception and emotion.

Myers, Thomas. *Walking Point: American Narratives of Vietnam*, pp. 38-42. New York: Oxford University Press, 1988.
Discusses "the shadow cast over the entire American corpus of Vietnam works by Greene's 1955 work," not only because of its uncanny prophetic vision but also because it demonstrated "that re-creation and interpretation are not only unopposed but naturally conjoined processes in the self-conscious historical novel." Myers touches upon how later writers make use of "Greene's model of the historical novel as a variety of realistic parable."

Rudman, Harry W. "Clough and Graham Greene's *The Quiet American.*" *Victorian Newsletter* 19 (Spring, 1961): 14-15.
Rudman provides a brief overview of the novel in order to establish the thematic relevance of two poetry quotations from Byron and Clough used as epigraphs (Rudman supplies the titles) and another quotation (from Clough) used with no

attribution late in the novel. Rudman calls the poetry excerpts "conversational in tone, realistic and practical in point of view, moralistic in intent."

Smith, Grahame. *The Achievement of Graham Greene*, pp. 129-137. Totowa, N.J.: Barnes & Noble Books, 1986.
The novel is "a failure in politics as well as artistry." Greene seems to have substituted antagonism "for a reasoned and also an imaginatively worked out response to a political reality." Smith finds weaknesses in Greene's style and characterizations while recognizing that the book contains the seeds of an important Greene theme to be developed later— that of "the transformation of cynicism into commitment." For Smith, this novel is one of Greene's failures.

Stratford, Philip. *Faith and Fiction: Creative Process in Greene and Mauriac*, pp. 308-316. Notre Dame, Ind.: Notre Dame University Press, 1964.
Stratford discusses the novel in terms of Greene's concern with the problem of commitment. Once the detached Fowler becomes engaged, as fully engaged as Pyle ever was, "the success of his involvement gives him no satisfaction." Greene points out the selfishness of both men and condones neither. The minor characters, Trouin and Vigot, are the more positive figures. The novel's title is misleading because this story is much more Fowler's than Pyle's.

Trilling, Diana, and Philip Rahv. "America and *The Quiet American*." *Commentary* 22, no. 1 (July, 1956): 66-71.
In this exchange of letters, the authors address the state of American liberalism as it is obliquely reflected and provoked by Greene's novel (which Rahv reviewed in the May, 1956, issue). This debate is a fine example of the immediate impact of the novel on America's intellectual community. It reveals Cold War tension in full bloom. At issue: is Greene's apparent anti-Americanism inevitably pro-Communism?

Vargo, Lisa. "*The Quiet American* and 'A Mr. Liebermann.'" *English Language Notes* 21, no. 4 (June, 1984): 63-70.
Vargo examines the textual and other evidence concerning Greene's attempt to capture American idiom in his portraits of Alden Pyle and other American characters. Successive editions show Greene responding to this problem, perhaps motivated by the critical comments of A. J. Liebling, whose *The New Yorker* review (April 7, 1956) made fun of Greene's handling of American speech. Vargo also discusses Greene's use of French. (Liebling's review is included in his *The Most of A. J. Liebling* (New York: Simon & Schuster, 1963).)

Wilson, James C. *Vietnam in Prose and Film*, pp. 8-14. Jefferson, N.C.: McFarland, 1982.
In his chapter called "A First Warning," Wilson applauds Greene's achievement,

calling it "probably the best novel written about the Vietnam War" because of its prescient insights into American character and culture. In Alden Pyle, Greene anticipates American officials sold on their own abstractions and propaganda, unable to make a connection between words and truth. Greene's warning against American involvement and its likely consequences, his own engagement in the issues, parallels the final decision by his cynical character Fowler to take a stand, "to deal himself into history."

Anthony Grey

Saigon

Reynolds, R. C. "Exploding the Myths: One Author's Response to War." *Journal of the American Studies Association of Texas* 16 (1985): 42-48.
Despite an unsympathetic protagonist, overly contrived plotting, and poor character development, Grey's novel is still a significant achievement. Its importance lies in the author's impressive knowledge of Asian history and culture and in his ability to evoke a sense of place. Reynolds examines Grey's allegorical pattern and the way in which he maintains his theme of a democratic rebellion in Vietnam into which the United States accidentally blundered.

Winston Groom

Beidler, Philip D. *Re-writing America: Vietnam Authors in Their Generation*, pp. 79-90. Athens: University of Georgia Press, 1991.
After summarizing Groom's traditional war novel, *Better Times Than These*, which he admires for "its depiction of the noise, panic, and confusion of combat," Beidler examines the more ambitious *As Summers Die*, the even more innovative and successful *Forrest Gump* (which is more properly a Vietnam War novel), and *Gone the Sun*, which also returns "to the experience of Vietnam and its enduring effects upon the lives of those Americans who underwent it." Groom's career unfolds as a southern version of "the novelist as cultural mythmaker."

David Halberstam

One Very Hot Day

Jones, Peter G. *War and the Novelist: Appraising the American War Novel*, pp. 90-94. Columbia: University of Missouri Press, 1976.

Jones praises this work as one of only two significant works on the Vietnam War to have appeared by the time that he made his study. Nonetheless, he considers the characters of Anderson and Redfern to be personified clichés. Halberstam, Jones believes, admires the American fighting man "while denouncing the government that sends him into such complex situations unprepared." Through Captain Beaupre, Halberstam represents changes in America's attitudes and moral perspective regarding war.

Myers, Thomas. *Walking Point: American Narratives of Vietnam*, pp. 42-56. New York: Oxford University Press, 1988.
Like Graham Greene's *The Quiet American*, Halberstam's novel is prophetic of America's future involvement in Vietnam. Focused on the period when our military support was largely advisory, it exposes how "the re-creation of American myth on foreign soil and within a misunderstood culture" is doomed to failure. Central to Halberstam's success is his ability "to connect aspects of American tragedy to the larger Vietnamese one" by creating convincing Vietnamese characters whose concerns are represented. Conflicts between American perspectives and those of America's Vietnamese allies are handled skillfully.

Wilson, James C. *Vietnam in Prose and Film*, pp. 54-56. Jefferson, N.C.: McFarland, 1982.
"Halberstam succeeds in providing a critical perspective with which to interpret the war, setting his novel in a social and historical context that he knew well." Through the focus on a single mission and a single day during the early advisory stage of America's involvement there, Halberstam is able to bring out the futile and corrupt nature of America's presence in Vietnam.

Joe Haldeman

The Forever War

Hall, Peter C. "'The Space Between' in Space: Some Versions of the Bildungs-roman in Science Fiction." *Extrapolation* 29, no. 2 (Summer, 1988): 153-159.
Haldeman's novel not only reflects his experience in Vietnam but also serves as "a rebuttal of Heinlein's *Starship Troopers*" by acting "as a post-Vietnam corrective to Heinlein's Cold War novel." Hall focuses on how protagonist William Mandella's development as an individual is shaped by his reactions against his military training and environment.

Gustav Hasford

The Short-Timers

Gilman, Owen W., Jr. "Vietnam and John Winthrop's Vision of Community." In *Fourteen Landing Zones: Approaches to Vietnam War Literature*, edited by Philip K. Jason. Iowa City: University of Iowa Press, 1991.
The theme of community as established in the Puritan vision of John Winthrop serves as a touchstone for examining the treatment of combat units in Hasford's novel and Tim O'Brien's *Going After Cacciato*. Hasford reveals the pressure exerted by the short-timer mentality upon the togetherness inculcated in basic training. Hasford dramatizes the inverted Christian call that is part of basic indoctrination, the necessity for leadership, and the Lusthog squad's dynamic of individual versus group identity. Against Gustav Hasford's bleak view of the potential for community, O'Brien offers a more hopeful vision. Paris symbolizes a community at peace, in contrast with the fragmented character of Vietnam. The goal of Paris is thus the pursuit of wholeness; it is a visionary dream not unlike Winthrop's vision of a "City upon a Hill." Paul Berlin, the lonely dreamer, recognizes himself as a creature of community, and the novel as a whole affirms the ideal of community.

Jeffords, Susan. *The Remasculinization of America: Gender and the Vietnam War*, pp. 170-179. Bloomington: Indiana University Press, 1989.
Jeffords in concerned with the transformation of Hasford's novel into Stanley Kubrick's film *Full Metal Jacket*. Focusing on three crucial scenes (involving snipers and prostitutes), she argues that "a shift has occurred between 1979 to 1987—from an ambivalent gender construction to a reaffirmed and confident masculinity that defines itself in opposition to an enemy feminine." Jeffords finds the novel "one in which the masculine struggles against itself and loses." The "undelineated boundaries between masculine and feminine" in Hasford are turned into firmly defined, opposed territories in Kubrick's film.

Melling, Philip H. *Vietnam in American Literature*, pp. 8-12. Boston: Twayne, 1990.
Melling argues that the novel "exposes our complacent affiliations with literary language in order that Joker, as narrator, might work undercover and promote himself to an eminent position in the text." We should be suspicious of the way that he uses his charisma and authority to exercise social control: "The pacification of others through violent action is affirmed as a social achievement in the concluding line of the book."

Myers, Thomas. *Walking Point: American Narratives of Vietnam*, pp. 112-124. New York: Oxford University Press, 1988.

"A first-person narrative told entirely in the present tense, the novel is a moment-to-moment study in cultural overload, a spare but minutely rendered poetics of evil." Myers stresses the black humor strategy, particularly the way in which Hasford's "violent caricature" remains connected to his "historical referent" while continually interpreting it. Hasford's handling of the grunts' relationship with the enemy underscores their true status: Gook and grunt are identified as bonded victims of the war.

Reaves, Gerri. "From Hasford's *The Short-Timers* to Kubrick's *Full Metal Jacket*: The Fracturing of Identification." *Literature/Film Quarterly* 16, no. 4 (1988): 232-237.

Hasford's novel provides a cohesive narrative and a "modern nihilistic hero" with whom the reader can easily identify. *Full Metal Jacket* offers "fractured, panoramic identification techniques" that alienate the viewer. Reaves explores other contrasts between the film and its source. Three other essays in this issue examine *Full Metal Jacket*, while David Everett Whillock offers "Defining the Fictive American Vietnam War Film: In Search of a Genre" (pp. 244-250).

Larry Heinemann

Bonetti, Kay. *Larry Heinemann: Interview with Kay Bonetti*. Sound recording. Columbia, Mo.: American Audio Prose Library, 1988.

The focus is on Heinemann's method of bringing the flavor of oral storytelling to readers, as in *Paco's Story*.

Close Quarters

Beidler, Philip D. *Re-writing America: Vietnam Authors in Their Generation*, pp. 90-97. Athens: University of Georgia Press, 1991.

The conventional narrative development is cast in a "larger poetic of design" through "essentially poetic formal divisions." The "dialectic of fact and imagination" gives the book resonance and links it with other central texts of the Vietnam War. Heinemann's genius, and the book's difficulty, lies in the way in which "one mode of consciousness slides into the other."

Cronin, Cornelius A. "Historical Background to Larry Heinemann's *Close Quarters*." *Critique* 24, no. 2 (Winter, 1983): 119-129.

Cronin sees Heinemann's novel as a representative literary reflection of "changes in training methods and tactical and strategic goals which occurred in

the United States Army between World War II and the Vietnam War." The
abundance of graphically violent scenes with their macabre sexual overtones
reflects the consciousness of one trained under methods first recommended by
Col. S. L. A. Marshall, who sought a means of making men aggressive fighters
under the conditions of modern infantry warfare. Marshall's attention to fire
ratio is a key element.

Jason, Philip K. "Sexism and Racism in Vietnam War Fiction." *Mosaic* 23, no. 3
(Summer, 1990): 129-133.
Heinemann's plot and imagery project a forceful connection between woman and
enemy, between sexual aggression and killing. Philip Dosier's relationships with
three women—Claymore Face (the Vietnamese battlefield whore), Susie (the
refined Japanese prostitute), and Jenny (the girl back home whom he mar-
ries)—echo one another in ways that collapse the social and psychological
distance between woman as loving partner and woman as enemy-victim.

Paco's Story

Anisfield, Nancy. "After the Apocalypse: Narrative Movement in Larry Heinemann's *Paco's Story*." In *America Rediscovered: Critical Essays on Literature
and Film of the Vietnam War*, edited by Owen W. Gilman, Jr., and Lorrie
Smith. New York: Garland, 1990.
The typical fictional narrative of the war reaches a late climax dependent upon
intensified violence. This feature is even carried over into fiction that deals with
the returned veteran. Heinemann avoids this convention, both in *Close Quarters*
and in *Paco's Story*. In the latter, "a passive, tightly focused internal event
draws the narrative to its close." The rejection of apocalyptic closure allows
thoughtful examination of the war and its consequences.

Beidler, Philip D. *Re-writing America: Vietnam Authors in Their Generation*, pp.
97-103. Athens: University of Georgia Press, 1991.
Beidler examines the "complex experimentalism" through which Heinemann
raises questions about the nature of storytelling. By puzzling us with a ghost
narrator and a named but still unspecified listener, Heinemann dares himself and
the reader to find the terms by which to value another Vietnam story. Each
chapter is a relatively self-contained story, having in common the narrator, the
listener, and Paco himself, in which the Vietnam War reaches into the unfolding
present, continuing to change the history and historical vision of Americans and
America.

Canfield-Reisman, Rosemary M. "*Paco's Story*." In *Magill's Literary Annual,
1988*. Pasadena, Calif.: Salem Press, 1988.

Heinemann's narration alternates through three worlds: the battlefield, the postcombat world of small-town America, and the supernatural world inhabited by the spirits of the dead men in Paco's company. The narration is notable for skillful and purposeful shifts in tone, sometimes quiet and objective, sometimes strident and mocking. Paco's failed search for relationship is an effective dramatization of the post-Vietnam agony of many veterans.

Jeffords, Susan. "Tattoos, Scars, Diaries, and Writing Masculinity." In *The Vietnam War and American Culture*, edited by John Carlos Rowe and Rick Berg. New York: Columbia University Press, 1991.
Jeffords finds in this novel a sinister pattern in which masculine suffering seeks retribution and relief in the raping of women. Heinemann, she feels, has discovered a strategy for displacing the violence of rape by "desexualizing" and "metaphorizing" it. The polarization of women and victims turns women into oppressors. In this latest stage in the gender wars, men, especially Vietnam veterans, have usurped the power of victimhood. Jeffords makes fascinating connections among the various images of scars, tattoos, and other inscriptions. Instructive contrasts with Maxine Hong Kingston's *The Woman Warrior*.

Michael Herr

Beidler, Philip D. *Re-writing America: Vietnam Authors in Their Generation*, pp. 264-287. Athens: University of Georgia Press, 1991.
Dispatches is "still in many ways the ultimate Vietnam experience and myth-text" and thus a point of reference for all Vietnam-related art. Beidler examines the classic status of this book as both a work of witness and interpretation and also as the central text about writing (or rewriting) the war. He shows how it seems to absorb even those texts written after it. Beidler then discusses Herr's contributions to the scripts of *Apocalypse Now* and *Full Metal Jacket*. Herr's "intertextual" career continues in his collaboration with painter Guy Peellaert on *The Big Room*, a study of Las Vegas.

Schroeder, Eric James. "Interview with Michael Herr: 'We've All Been There.'" *Writing on the Edge* 1, no. 1 (Fall, 1989): 39-54.
Discusses Herr's background and purposes as well as the process by which *Dispatches* came into being. Herr reveals that "when the book was finished there was some question as to whether it should be published as journalism or as a novel." Herr privately thinks of it as a novel. Much material on Herr's personal experience, his view of Vietnam as "a writer's war" rather than television's war, and his views on other journalists and Vietnam writers, including Stone, O'Brien, and Mailer.

Dispatches

Beidler, Philip D. *American Literature and the Experience of Vietnam*, pp. 141-
148. Athens: University of Georgia Press, 1982.
   Beidler credits Herr with writing one of the first books about the Vietnam War
   to gain authority by finding its own method of literary representation. The truth
   revealed by *Dispatches* "is allowed to seek its own context, create or invent its
   own matrix of signification." The book's structure and style enact an exploration
   of consciousness, mixing memory, imaginative reconstruction, and the dispersion
   and manipulation of fact. Herr succeeds at establishing a literary coherence that
   is appropriate to the fractured coherence of the war and to the range of polemics
   surrounding it.

Cobley, Evelyn. "Narrating the Facts of War: New Journalism in Herr's
   Dispatches and Documentary Realism in First World War Novels." *Journal of
   Narrative Technique* 16, no. 2 (Spring, 1986): 97-116.
   In *Dispatches*, fact and fantasy intermix so that even the narrator cannot always
   tell which is which. Moreover, "factual assertions lose their reputation for
   innocent objectivity." In World War I novels, facts are presented as reliable—"the stable ground on which the verisimilitude of fictional elements
   depends." For Herr, facts no longer have an "authorizing function." Cobley
   stresses the importance of the narrator's voice on the impact and meaning of this
   work.

Hellmann, John. *American Myth and the Legacy of Vietnam*, pp. 150-160. New
   York: Columbia University Press, 1986.
   Hellmann reviews the acclaim accorded Herr's book, the style and structure of
   the book, and Herr's journey in memory in which "he risks confrontation with
   the most dangerous truths of his psyche, American truths of an American
   psyche, to bring back to the culture needed information for its survival of the
   Vietnam experience." Kennedy's "counterinsurgency experts" were "carriers of
   American mythic expectations who were unable to force Vietnam into the
   configuration of the inner romance they projected upon it."

_____. "The New Journalism and Vietnam: Memory as Structure in
   Michael Herr's *Dispatches*." *South Atlantic Quarterly* 79, no. 2 (Spring, 1980):
   141-151.
   Dispatches is a blend of previously published articles and unpublished materials
   worked over laboriously. It takes full advantage of the new journalism as a
   literary strategy for dealing with this war. The book is partly about what we
   mean by information and partly "about its own language and form." Herr finds
   vividness in "an intensely felt act of shaping memory" rather than in presenting
   immediate experience. He tells us that without a new structure of consciousness

no array of facts can bring essential truths. This essay is transformed into "Memory, Fragments and 'Clean Information': Michael Herr's *Dispatches*" in Hellmann's *Fables of Fact: The New Journalism as the New Fiction* (Urbana: University of Illinois Press, 1981).

Jakaitis, John M. "Two Versions of an Unfinished War: *Dispatches* and *Going After Cacciato.*" *Cultural Critique* no. 3 (Spring, 1986): 191-210.
Jakaitis examines these principal Vietnam War texts to "illuminate the more deeply embedded causes of delayed stress syndrome and reveal the deep structures which inform everyday life in our culture." *Cacciato* "depicts a young soldier's efforts to reshape his Vietnam experience into a more digestible form." *Dispatches* is an attempt "to dispatch [eliminate] the horror of Vietnam, or to demonstrate that such a process is impossible." Jakaitis stresses the philosophical dimensions of both works.

James, David E. "Rock and Roll in Representations of the Invasion of Vietnam." *Representations* 29 (Winter, 1990): 78-98.
"The invasion and rock and roll are intertwined so thoroughly that their interdependence is an exemplary instance of the operationality of modern culture." James refers briefly to Terry's *Viet Rock* and Mailer's *Why Are We in Vietnam?* before giving a comprehensive discussion of how rock and roll is "a ubiquitous tapestry" in Herr's book (pp. 83-86). Most of the essay deals with cinematic representation.

Jeffords, Susan. *The Remasculinization of America: Gender and the Vietnam War*, pp. 22-35. Bloomington: Indiana University Press, 1989.
Comparing Herr's work to Norman Mailer's *The Armies of the Night* and Richard Nixon's *No More Vietnams*, Jeffords argues that "these texts share a strategy of representation that becomes a spectacle itself, one that paralyzes rather than enables effective political action." Beginning as an outsider, Herr becomes part of the war's reality "by accepting its consensus, assuming its voices." Moreover, by assuming "the position of both actor and audience," Herr and the other authors blur the lines between fact and fiction and usurp the reader's position.

Jones, Dale W. "The Vietnams of Michael Herr and Tim O'Brien: Tales of Disintegration and Integration." *Canadian Review of American Studies* 13, no. 3 (Winter, 1982): 309-320.
See annotation under Tim O'Brien, *Going After Cacciato*, below.

Kazin, Alfred. "Vietnam: It Was Us vs. Us: Michael Herr's *Dispatches*: More Than Just the Best Vietnam Book." *Esquire*, March, 1978, 120-123.
In this significant review, Kazin praises Herr's ability to evoke "the specific

environment that sooner or later hallucinated Americans at war." He applauds Herr's sad humor, his "ear for bitter soldier talk," and his inventive style.

Kuberski, Philip Francis. "Genres of Vietnam." *Cultural Critique*, no. 3 (Spring, 1986): 168-188.
Herr's book is the key text in this careful examination of the ways in which various representations of the war conceal "their own mediation of the truths offered as unconcealment." Herr, it would seem, shows the most heightened awareness of the traps inherent in genre and in the act of representation. This essay is a fine mix of theory and application.

Melling, Philip H. *Vietnam in American Literature*, pp. 67-84. Boston: Twayne, 1990.
Herr's "cameo revelations" are part of "an act of frenetic salesmanship" in which the author borrows the authority of both fact and fiction to convey his version of modernist experience. The work is less difficult than Herr's strategies make it seem; "the narrator creates a strict allegorical framework" in which "easy, reductive equations" make idiot-villains of the powerful and heroes of "those who suffer the abuses of power." For Melling, "*Dispatches* is a concoction that has little to do with Vietnam," but much to do with Herr, America, "and the expectations of its reading public."

Myers, Thomas. *Walking Point: American Narratives of Vietnam*, pp. 146-171. New York: Oxford University Press, 1988.
"Herr's Vietnam . . . seems the product of the combined imaginative resources of Lewis Carroll, Samuel Coleridge, and the most fearsome, uncontrolled acid dream." His prose style resembles "a manic teletype . . . always in danger of being short-circuited by the plenitude of words and images being fed through it." Myers explores the structure of *Dispatches* as well as Herr's orchestration of symbolic details. Herr's romantic sensibility remakes the journalistic-historical enterprise; he recognizes "that Vietnam is not an American historical aberration."

Ringnalda, Donald. "Unlearning to Remember Vietnam." In *America Rediscovered: Critical Essays on Literature and Film of the Vietnam War*, edited by Owen W. Gilman, Jr., and Lorrie Smith. New York: Garland, 1990.
Sharable truths about the war do not reside in fact-oriented appeals to authenticity. Herr's "genius lies in the way he prevents us from remembering them [facts] simplistically." Herr worked to unlearn the cultural myths and literary paradigms embedded in American culture in order to perceive and transmit the realities of the war freshly. He succeeded as well as anyone is likely to succeed.

Stewart, Matthew C. "Style in *Dispatches*: Heteroglossia and Michael Herr's Break with Conventional Journalism." In *America Rediscovered: Critical Essays on Literature and Film of the Vietnam War*, edited by Owen W. Gilman, Jr., and Lorrie Smith. New York: Garland, 1990.
The novelistic techniques in *Dispatches* include "elaborating and typifying even minor characters through their dialogue." Sometimes the narrative voice mixes with that of the GIs or leaders, often through unmarked dialogue that has "its most provocative presence . . . within the parenthetical remarks with which Herr's narrative is replete." Other stylistic features include key word repetition that explores various shades of meaning and contexts.

Taylor, Gordon O. "American Personal Narrative of the War in Vietnam." *American Literature* 52 (May, 1980): 294-308.
After giving an overview of the collective enterprises of both novels and personal narratives of the war, Taylor develops an extended treatment of *Dispatches* in which he explores the relationship between Herr's work and Greene's *The Quiet American*. Herr's book represents others that "consist of an inward questing for personal clarification of all that is confusing and chaotic in their subject." Herr uses Greene as a moral reference point, but finally Herr (and others) distance themselves from Greene in order to go beyond him. Reprinted as "Debriefed by Dreams: Michael Herr," in Taylor's *Chapters of Experience: Studies in Twentieth Century American Autobiography* (New York: St. Martin's Press, 1983).

Van Deusen, Marshall. "The Unspeakable Language of Life and Death in Michael Herr's *Dispatches*." *Critique* 24, no. 2 (Winter, 1983): 82-87.
In his drive to find "a language beyond the language of factual reporting" to reveal his experience, Herr has developed a style that is filled with literary echoes and allusions on the one hand and the "latrine language" of war stories on the other. The former include references to *Huckleberry Finn*, *The Red Badge of Courage*, *The Sun Also Rises*, and a poem by Thomas Hardy. The cross-referential ties made by the allusions connect the Vietnam war to the larger sweep of history.

Wilson, James C. *Vietnam in Prose and Film*, pp. 45-47. Jefferson, N.C.: McFarland, 1982.
Wilson considers *Dispatches* an "evasion," placing it in his chapter on "The Dope and Dementia Theory." The discontinuous nature of Herr's book blocks any "discovery of meaning," and his representation of the war's surrealistic quality captures only the surface. Furthermore, "Herr betrays a fascination with the glamour of war" and does not present "a consistent moral stance." Finally, "the book fails to transcend the limits of its self-reflexive stance."

David Huddle

Beidler, Philip D. *Re-writing America: Vietnam Authors in Their Generation*, pp.
162-171. Athens: University of Georgia Press, 1991.
Though best known as a short-story writer, Huddle has emerged as a significant
poet of the Vietnam War. In Huddle's poems one finds the story of an American
family etched against visions of the war by which a son was changed; thus,
"amidst all the old contextualizations, Vietnam remains the secret crux. It is the
long foregrounding of a departure. It is the latest ritual of return."

William Turner Huggett

Body Count

Jeffords, Susan. *The Remasculinization of America: Gender and the Vietnam War*,
pp. 65-67. Bloomington: Indiana University Press, 1989.
The war environment enhances tendencies to overcome differences between men
(through the masculine bond) and to accentuate differences between men and
women. Scenes with prostitutes underscore the way in which men's racial and
class differences, for example, are subsumed into their bonding masculinity:
"While the American soldier can cross racial barriers to share the bond of war
with his enemy, he is still alienated from women, who also share cross-racial
bonds, but only with other women, not with men." *Body Count* seems to
demonstrate the need to affirm "that the structure of gender difference is
'universal'" rather than merely national or cultural.

Ward Just

Gilman, Owen W., Jr. "Ward Just's Vietnam: Where Word and Deed Did Not
Meet." *South Atlantic Quarterly* 84, no. 4 (Autumn, 1985): 356-367.
After discussing the lure of war to writers, Gilman introduces Just's credentials
as a Vietnam War correspondent for *The Washington Post*. He then summarizes
the plots and themes of *Stringer* and *In the City of Fear*. Stringer, whose name
is symbolic, seems to suffer from an "existential malaise" reflecting the
country's uncertainty about Vietnam. *In the City of Fear* examines the centrality
of language to power (and mismatches of fact and rhetoric) in its exploration of
political life and responsibility in Washington, D.C.

Just, Ward. "Vietnam—Fiction and Fact." *TriQuarterly* 65 (Winter, 1986): 215-
220.
Just describes his experiences as a journalist and how they impelled him to write

about the war in various genres. He lists five realities related to writing about the war: the personal reality of participant or observer; the reality of visual records and the effect of the camera on the action; the reality of the reporter; poetic reality; and the reality of the novel and imagination. His comments are part of a symposium in this special issue of *TriQuarterly* that also includes statements by Robert Stone and Gloria Emerson. All three respond to questions.

The American Blues

Beidler, Philip D. *Re-writing America: Vietnam Authors in Their Generation*, pp. 289-296. Athens: University of Georgia Press, 1991.
Just's novel "announces from the outset its primary purpose as ongoing response to the experience of Vietnam: the depiction of the continuing immense purchase of the war upon the American soul." Meditations on language and media interrupt and comment on the protagonist's attempt to write about the peace that followed the war. It is a work dedicated to stripping away pretense, about seeing and abandoning "his own very Americanness . . . before the deepest American secrets of writing about Vietnam may be unlocked."

Myers, Thomas. *Walking Point: American Narratives of Vietnam*, pp. 213-221. New York: Oxford University Press, 1988.
By struggling in peacetime with his unfinished six-hundred-page history of the war, Just's unnamed journalist lives a marginal life haunted by the past. His obsession isolates him and makes the war and people's relationship to it the touchstone for his relationships to them. Myers reveals how skillfully Just exposes his narrator's memory: "an intricate mixture of structure and improvisation, sadness, and fatalism." The narrator's inability to forget or to finish reflects the continuing impact of the Vietnam War on the American psyche.

Takeshi Kaiko

Heberle, Mark A. "Darkness in the East: The Vietnam Novels of Takeshi Kaiko." In *Fourteen Landing Zones: Approaches to Vietnam War Literature*, edited by Philip K. Jason. Iowa City: University of Iowa Press, 1991.
Heberle examines the themes and techniques of Kaiko's related novels, *Into a Black Sun* and *Darkness in Summer*. Both works appear to be autobiographical novels in which the detached Japanese correspondent-narrator explores "the self by means of the war and the war by means of the self." The narrator's experiences, however, do not lead to enlightenment; "experiential, cognitive, and moral darkness" prevails. Ideologues who think they can see through the darkness, it is implied, are among those responsible for the catastrophe.

Yoshida, Sanroku. "Takeshi Kaiko's Paradox of Light and Darkness." *World Literature Today* 62, no. 3 (Summer, 1988): 391-396.
After providing biographical information leading up to Kaiko's assignment as a journalist in Vietnam, Yoshida examines "the dehumanized world of the Vietnam War" found in *Into a Black Sun* and then "Kaiko's exploration of human darkness" based on his own experiences as transmitted through *Darkness in Summer*. Kaiko's work exhibits an existential, Sartrean view of fundamental human tendencies.

Adrienne Kennedy

Blau, Herbert. "The American Dream in American Gothic: The Plays of Sam Shepard and Adrienne Kennedy." *Modern Drama* 27, no. 4 (December, 1984): 520-539.
Blau discusses the centrality of the "confusion of gender" in Kennedy's plays as well as her "obsession with powerlessness" and her ambivalent relationship to Black Power. Audiences may "admire the passion and imagination of the plays but reject them for [their] apolitical naivete." No comments on *An Evening with Dead Essex*, but useful general observations.

Diamond, Elin. "An Interview with Adrienne Kennedy." *Studies in American Drama, 1945-Present* 4 (1989): 143-158.
Diamond provides detailed biographical and career information. Much of the interview concerns Kennedy's *People Who Led to My Plays* (1987), a book designed to answer the questions most frequently asked about the sources of her work. She discusses her secure identity as a black, Off-Broadway playwright. Some sense of Kennedy's play-crafting process comes through in the interview.

Sollors, Werner. "Owls and Rats in the American Funnyhouse: Adrienne Kennedy's Drama." *American Literature* 63, no. 3 (September, 1991): 507-532.
Though he provides the most comprehensive examination of Kennedy's plays to date, Sollors fails to treat *An Evening with Dead Essex* and seems unaware that the play has been published. After examining seven of her plays, he judges them to be "the condensed expression of a theatrical mind that has integrated the diverse autobiographical elements of family history, the tragic paradox of American race relations in the twentieth century, and the impulses of popular culture as well as of high modernism, of European as well as African art, into an effective aesthetic form." Despite its glaring omission, an important article.

An Evening with Dead Essex

Murray, Timothy. "Screening the Camera's Eye: Black and White Confrontations of Technological Representation." *Modern Drama* 28, no. 1 (March, 1985): 119-120.
Murray explores how Black American dramatists have employed and addressed technological innovation. He discusses how *An Evening with Dead Essex* works through a collage of artifacts, employing and exposing film and documentary techniques.

Zinman, Toby Silverman. "'In the presence of mine enemies': Adrienne Kennedy's *An Evening with Dead Essex.*" *Studies in American Drama, 1945-Present* 6, no. 1 (Spring, 1991): 3-13.
This detailed examination of the thematic concerns and theatrical devices of Kennedy's play questions its status in the Kennedy canon by pointing to how it contrasts with her other plays. Zinman provides background on the play and explores its various polarities including the racial and the presentational. She also discusses Kennedy's directions for acting style, the play's confrontational nature, and its unresolved dramaturgical problems.

Maxine Hong Kingston

Aubrey, James R. "'Going Toward War' in the Writings of Maxine Hong Kingston." *Vietnam Generation* 1, no. 3/4 (Summer/Fall, 1989): 90-101.
Aubrey finds Kingston's *Tripmaster Monkey* to be, though in an oblique way, about the impending war in Vietnam. Kingston's tendency to write about war is also evident in her three earlier books: *The Woman Warrior*, *China Men*, and *Hawai'i One Summer*. Aubrey discusses these works is the context of Kingston's participation in the antiwar movement. Her writings "teach how to change war into peace, how to transcend conflict through narratives about conflict."

Victor Kolpacoff

The Prisoners of Quai Dong

Wilson, James C. *Vietnam in Prose and Film*, pp. 63-65. Jefferson, N.C.: McFarland, 1982.
Kolpacoff's novel faces the "question of moral responsibility." His dark prison room is a "transparent metaphor for Vietnam" in which captors and captive are alike entrapped. The novel exposes the hollow argument that shared responsibility lessens individual accountability. "Whoever enters the dark room, whoever

enters Vietnam, sinks into the quagmire of guilt." Not only participants, but also observers, share in the guilt. Wilson contrasts Kolpacoff's vision with that of Caputo in *A Rumor of War*.

Wolfe, Geoffrey A. "Vietnam Allegory." *New Leader*, November 6, 1967, 22-23. The novel "turns Vietnam into a metaphor for our own unrestrained willfulness and luxurious cruelty." Wolfe likens the book to a classical drama and stresses its allegorical nature, asserting that "it is about the crime of letting compassion be trapped by external systems of logic and illogic that feed upon themselves and generate their own insane energies."

Yusef Komunyakaa

Beidler, Philip D. *Re-writing America: Vietnam Authors in Their Generation*, pp. 171-182. Athens: University of Georgia Press, 1991.
Komunyakaa's early collections tell about Vietnam "mainly by telling about America, and particularly about black America." They form the context for the Vietnam-centered collection *Dien Cai Dau*, which speaks to us "of the black American in the Vietnam era and its aftermath." The Vietnam poems are less musical than Komunyakaa's other work, more consciously flat, but some find the essential "moments of reflexive epiphany" that suggest a "redemptory vision."

Gotera, Vicente F. "'Lines of Tempered Steel': An Interview with Yusef Komunyakaa." *Callaloo* 13, no. 2 (Spring, 1990): 215-229.
The interview explores Komunyakaa's apprenticeship as a poet, early influences on his work, his New Orleans background, and his habits of composition. Gotera raises questions about jazz and blues music; line break, and Komunyakaa's place in the community of poets. In readings, we learn, Komunyakaa often defies or counterpoints the printed version of the poem. Improvisation plays a part in performance.

Dien Cai Dau

Gotera, Vicente F. "'Depending on the Light': Yusef Komunyakaa's *Dien Cai Dau*." In *America Rediscovered: Critical Essays on Literature and Film of the Vietnam War*, edited by Owen W. Gilman, Jr., and Lorrie Smith. New York: Garland, 1990.
By waiting almost two decades to publish poems on Vietnam, Komunyakaa has polished his craft and "achieved a distance on his Vietnam experience." His "academic grounding in modernist and contemporary poetics as well as classic

surrealism" marks his work as "an aesthetic advance not only of poetry about the Vietnam War but also of war literature in general." Komunyakaa's poetry is unusual among the work of Vietnam veterans in offering "self-renewal and solace."

_____. "Killer Imagination." *Callaloo* 13, no. 2 (Spring, 1990): 364-371.
Though essentially a review of Komunyakaa's collection of Vietnam War poetry, this article reaches back to trace the poet's development. Gotera discusses Komunyakaa's technique of yoking opposites, of "crunching together the dissimilar . . . at several levels." After introducing the poet's "montage approach to lyricism," Gotera examines the fruits of this approach in *Dien Cai Dau*, a retrospective "odyssey through the Vietnam of memory." Several poems are examined in detail.

Arthur Kopit

Dasgupta, Gautam. "Arthur Kopit." In *American Playwrights: A Critical Survey*, by Bonnie Marranca and Gautam Dasgupta. New York: Drama Book Specialists, 1981.
This overview of Kopit's career describes his connection with absurdist theater, his depiction of "a horrific world where logic holds no sway." Dasgupta's brief comments on *Indians* (pp. 22-23) place that work in the context of Kopit's other major plays: "Without being dogmatic or overly pedantic he devised provocative theatrical forms to argue his perceptive social vision." The vision and the forms are elucidated here.

Hennessy, Brendan. "Arthur Kopit." *Transatlantic Review* 30 (Autumn, 1968): 68-73.
Interviewed soon after the world premier of *Indians* at the Aldwych Theatre in London, Kopit discusses why a New York production was then impossible. The interchange includes remarks on the parallels between the destruction of the Indians and present-day U.S. problems stemming from an "inheritance of violence." There are remarks on other Kopit plays as well.

King, Kimball. "Arthur Kopit." In his *Ten Modern American Playwrights: An Annotated Bibliography*. New York: Garland, 1982.
King provides, under primary sources, editions of plays, films, translations, and interviews. His annotations of secondary materials—critical essays and production reviews—are helpful and concise.

Weaver, Laura H. "Arthur Kopit." In *American Playwrights Since 1945: A Guide to Scholarship, Criticism, and Performance*, edited by Philip C. Kolin. New York: Greenwood Press, 1989.
A brief assessment of Kopit's reputation is followed by a primary bibliography of plays, essays, and interviews. Weaver provides the production history for *Indians* and Kopit's other plays as well as a survey of secondary sources, analyses of individual plays, and an extensive bibliography of secondary sources, including reviews.

Indians

Auerbach, Doris. "A Myth Reconsidered: *Indians*." In her *Sam Shepard, Arthur Kopit, and the Off Broadway Theater*. Boston: Twayne, 1982.
This detailed and cogent analysis describes the genesis of the play (a comment by Gen. Westmoreland) and then develops the parallels between Kopit's interpretation of a cavalry charge on an American Indian village and his vision of American involvement in Vietnam. Kopit places the war "in the larger context of American history and American mythology." William Cody's attempt to turn the American heritage into show business parallels the television coverage of the Vietnam War.

Beidler, Philip D. *American Literature and the Experience of Vietnam*, pp. 65-69. Athens: University of Georgia Press, 1982.
Most viewers did not catch the indirect, "symbolic exploration of the war's relationship with a larger body of collective mythic assumption." Kopit develops Cody as "a violent, bullheaded, self-torturing do-gooder who actually seems to believe . . . that one can destroy things in order to 'save' them." *Indians* examines not only the way in which the Vietnam War was fought but also the way in which policymakers conceived it. Kopit parallels one "grand tragedy of mass cultural misperception" to another.

Grant, Thomas M. "American History in Drama: The Commemorative Tradition and Some Recent Revisions." *Modern Drama* 19, no. 4 (December, 1976): 327-339.
After reminding readers that theater historically "has been a prime media for promoting glorified notions about the national past," Grant discusses a more recent tradition in which playwrights have sought to "demythify the past." Among the examples of this new impulse is Kopit's *Indians*, a discussion of which closes Grant's survey. Grant provides a useful context for examining Kopit's work.

Hughes, Catharine. *Plays, Politics, and Polemics*, pp. 61-66. New York: Drama Book Specialists, 1973.
Hughes contrasts the London and New York productions then gives a thematic overview: "Kopit is concerned with past and present, with the Indians and the blacks we destroyed, and with the Asians we are destroying." She finds that the diffuseness of the play keeps it from moving us as much as it should, that it does not quite fulfill its ambition.

Jones, John B. "Impersonation and Authenticity: The Theatre as Metaphor in Kopit's *Indians.*" *Quarterly Journal of Speech* 59, no. 4 (December, 1973): 443-451.
"The central argument of *Indians* is that the United States has always had to fabricate myths about her more unpleasant behavior in order to conceal or justify the actualities of bare historical facts." Impersonation, "a basic tool of myth-creation," is the raw material and method of Kopit's drama—especially self-impersonation in which historical figures play themselves. Detailed presentation of evidence.

Lahr, John. "Arthur Kopit's *Indians*: Dramatizing National Amnesia." In his *Up Against the Fourth Wall: Essays on Modern Theater*. New York: Grove Press, 1970.
Perhaps the shrewdest appreciation of Kopit's play and a work that avoids making the Vietnam connection disproportionately significant. Kopit's Buffalo Bill "must make the Indian an enemy in order to make himself just," and the process by which he does so "continues to mushroom into political suicide" while Cody "covers up his myopia with moral outrage." Lahr praises Kopit's technical skill and finds the play unique in the scope of its inquiry. Originally published in *Evergreen Review* 13 (October, 1969): 19-21, 63, 67. See also *Evergreen Review* 13 (January, 1969): 55-58, 84-87.

Lahr, John, and Arthur Kopit. "A Dialogue Between Arthur Kopit and John Lahr," edited by Anthea Lahr. Unpaginated insert. In *Indians,* by Arthur Kopit. New York: Bantam, 1971.
This extensive "dialogue" is probably the richest and most accessible discussion of Kopit's themes and techniques. The Vietnam experience is set into the context of Kopit's broader concerns about the American vision and its capacity for self-blinding: "this man [Buffalo Bill] who like the Indians inadvertently destroyed their food," says Kopit. Says Lahr, "The Indians were America's first Vietnam." Illustrated.

O'Neill, Michael C. "History as Dramatic Present: Arthur L. Kopit's *Indians.*" *Theater Journal* 34, no. 4 (December, 1982): 493-504.
Kopit achieved a new form that avoided avant-garde excess. His mosaic

structure has musical affinities, allowing him to use techniques that parallel counterpoint and recapitulation. Kopit takes license with historical fact to expand his play's meaning and build links between America's past and its Vietnam-focused present. A persuasive, thorough analysis of method and message.

Weiher, Carol. "American History on Stage in the 1960's: Something Old, Something New." *Quarterly Journal of Speech* 63, no. 4 (December, 1977): 405-412.
Many historically based plays of the 1960s "treat the American past with less reverence and thereby evoke from audiences new responses to their national legacy." Martin Duberman's *In White America* and Kopit's *Indians* are selected as representative and explored through comparisons and contrasts. Weiher shows no concern for the Vietnam connection, but she address how Kopit "reflects upon the process of history-making in America."

Westarp, Karl-Heinz. "Myth in Peter Shaffer's *The Royal Hunt of the Sun* and Arthur Kopit's *Indians*." *English Studies: A Journal of English Language and Literature* 65, no. 2 (April, 1984): 120-128.
Westarp examines how *Indians* embodies and undermines the "American hero-cult that grew up around the figure of 'Buffalo Bill.'" Kopit, he feels, exposes the emptiness and paradoxical nature of white American beliefs while granting Indian myths more positive power and validity. Both Shaffer and Kopit are demythologizers.

Wolter, Jurgen. "Arthur Kopit: Dreams and Nightmares." In *Essays on Contemporary American Drama*, edited by Hedwig Bock and Albert Wertheim. Munich: Max Hueber, 1981.
Within this comprehensive yet compact career study is a careful analysis of *Indians* (pp. 65-70), which Wolter calls "Kopit's most mature play to date." The play is viewed not only as a Vietnam War commentary but also as an investigation of "how a group with a false conception of its superiority will destroy its outsiders either by suppression or assimilation." Kopit's techniques are perfectly adapted to his themes.

Ron Kovic

Born on the Fourth of July

Beidler, Philip D. *American Literature and the Experience of Vietnam*, pp. 153-154, 158-161. Athens: University of Georgia Press, 1982.
More explicitly experimental than Caputo's *A Rumor of War*, Kovic's work is characterized by a "fractured chronology" that is "free, shifting, reflexive," and

thus evocative of "the motion of consciousness itself." Beginning with the wound that brings Kovic's combat experience to an end, the book interweaves Kovic's attempt to come to terms with his own pain and loss with his sense of the nation's parallel journey. Only in the final chapters does Kovic reveal the events leading up to his personal tragedy, a strategy that recontextualizes the rest of the narrative in significant ways.

Fleming, George J. *"Born on the Fourth of July."* In *Magill's Literary Annual, 1977.* Englewood Cliffs, N.J.: Salem Press, 1977.
Fleming summarizes the major events, describes Kovic's use of flashbacks as a major device, and underscores the employment of irony. He argues that Kovic's changes of attitude are not sufficiently explained. Also, the principles by which Kovic commits himself to various protest activities are not clearly stated. The emotional truths, however, hit home forcefully. Kovic's individuality, not the war or the issues surrounding it, is the book's center of interest.

Kunz, Don. "Oliver Stone's Film Adaptation of *Born on the Fourth of July*: Redefining Masculine Heroism." *War, Literature, and the Arts* 2, no. 2 (Fall, 1990): 1-26.
Kunz sheds light on the strategies and themes of Kovic's memoir while examining Stone's screen adaptation. He argues that the film is "more coherently focused and positively concluded." Stone straightens out Kovic's "bifurcated chronology," and he emphasizes Kovic's theme by employing "an extended sexual trope." Stone "partially fictionalizes Kovic's non-fiction narrative, taking license with some facts in the interest of articulating more significant and moving conceptual truths about America's Vietnam involvement."

Melling, Philip H. *Vietnam in American Literature*, pp. 56-58. Boston: Twayne, 1990.
Kovic's book exemplifies the fulfilled "quest for strength and authority" by which the veteran overcomes "the attempt to emasculate him in civilian and military life." Its title is an ironic echo of the process of rebirth for the betrayed superpatriot American born again as agitator. It works like a religious text to convert the unknowing through the power of its testimony.

William J. Lederer and Eugene Burdick

The Ugly American

Christie, Clive. "From *The Quiet American* to *The Ugly American*: American Literature on Indochina in the 1950s." In his *"The Quiet American" and "The Ugly American": Western Literary Perspectives on Indo-China in a Decade of*

120

Transition, 1950-1960. Occasional Paper 10. Canterbury, England: University
of Kent Centre of South-East Asian Studies, 1989.
Christie examines the ideological fixation of the "Cold War" as the general
backdrop and John F. Kennedy's "New Frontier" as the immediate context for
the novel. He establishes the origin of the novel as a nonfiction project that
turned into what is essentially a collection of "short stories, or parables,
illustrating 'how' and 'how not' to fight communism in South-East Asia."
Christie demonstrates how the book was pitched at Middle America.

Hellmann, John. *American Myth and the Legacy of Vietnam*, pp. 15-38. New York:
Columbia University Press, 1986.
Hellmann reviews the historical context in which the book appeared and the
controversy that it raised: "The impact of *The Ugly American* resulted from its
providing the American public with a purgative ritual of self-criticism and
warning." The true American is represented as incorporating those Puritan
virtues from which the "ugly" have fallen away. Much of the inner conflict is
dramatized by having Indochina function "as a symbolic landscape embodying
the opposed mythic values of city and country." In a return to the fundamental
values of nature, the American character could find redemption. An earlier
version of this material appears as "Vietnam as Symbolic Landscape: *The Ugly
American* and the New Frontier," in *Peace and Change* 9, no. 2/3 (Summer,
1983): 40-54.

Mary McCarthy

Goldman, Sherli Evens. *Mary McCarthy: A Bibliography*. New York: Harcourt,
Brace & World, 1968.
This analytic bibliography lists only primary sources, beginning with books
through *Vietnam*. Other sections list contributions to books, contributions to
periodicals, and translations of McCarthy's work into foreign languages.

Taylor, Gordon O. "Cast a Cold 'I': Mary McCarthy on Vietnam." *Journal of
American Studies* 9, no. 1 (April, 1975): 103-114.
Taylor explores "as a continuous sequence" McCarthy's three short books about
America in Vietnam: *Vietnam, Hanoi*, and *Medina*. He assesses McCarthy's
awareness and handling of "problems and possibilities involving self-representa-
tion." McCarthy's narratives fuse her roles of critic, polemicist, autobiographer,
and reporter. This material is absorbed in the chapter "The Word for Mirror:
Mary McCarthy," in Taylor's *Chapters of Experience: Studies in Twentieth
Century American Autobiography* (New York: St. Martin's Press, 1983).

Walter McDonald

Beidler, Philip D. *Re-writing America: Vietnam Authors in Their Generation*, pp. 182-191. Athens: University of Georgia Press, 1991.
McDonald's work evolves around the theme of living in America "After the Noise of Saigon" has shaped one's senses and sensibilities. Though pain and emptiness are often the rewards of attempted sense-making, still "such odysseys of consciousness toward experiential and imaginative reconstitution continue to get made." Beidler gives special attention to how in the recent collection, *Night Landings*, "the war fades eventually altogether from explicit reference, becoming an uninscribed presence."

Frank, Robert. "Walter McDonald: Poet of Sight and Insight." *Poet Lore* 80, no. 4 (Winter, 1986): 220-226.
This brief overview of McDonald's work remarks on "the movement from death to life" in his first book, *Caliban in Blue*, as well as in the next two: "Cruelty and death are met at every turn, not just on the battlefields of Vietnam." Frank also discusses broader concerns, such as self-affirmation, that include, but also go beyond, McDonald's Vietnam poems. The essay introduces a sampling of previously unpublished poems.

Phillip K. McMath

Native Ground

Calloway, Catherine. "'Quentin Broke His Watch': The Theme of Time in Phillip K. McMath's *Native Ground*." *Publications of the Arkansas Philological Association* 14, no. 2 (Fall, 1988): 11-19.
By alternating scenes in Vietnam with flashback scenes in the protagonist's "native ground" in southern Arkansas, McMath develops a complex representation of time. The pressure of time consciousness, the absence of sure demarcations in warfare situations, and the imagined time of memory all contribute to McMath's theme. References to Quentin Compson's breaking of his watch in Faulkner's *The Sound and the Fury* underscore McMath's concern with time's relationship to fate.

Norman Mailer

Adams, Laura. "Criticism of Norman Mailer: A Selected Checklist." *Modern Fiction Studies* 17, no. 3 (Autumn, 1971): 455-463. Special issue on Mailer.
Contains general essays on Mailer's work as well as investigations of individual

titles. Adams' checklist, like the issue of which it is part, includes a section on general studies and another in which essays on particular works are listed. A third section lists Mailer's books and uncollected essays chronologically.

_____. *Norman Mailer: A Comprehensive Bibliography*. Metuchen, N.J.: Scarecrow Press, 1974.
Updates and elaborates Adams' earlier "Checklist." Primary sources include books, periodical pieces and prefaces, selected excerpts and anthologizations, films, plays, and unpublished manuscripts. Secondary sources include reviews and critical articles, full-length studies and collections, theses and dissertations, interviews, nonprint media, and bibliographies. Thorough, but dated.

Anderson, Chris. "Norman Mailer: The Record of a War." In his *Style as Argument: Contemporary American Nonfiction*. Carbondale: Southern Illinois University Press, 1987.
Anderson considers *Of a Fire on the Moon* as the thematic and structural counterpart of *The Armies of the Night*. Both belong to an informal nonfiction trilogy completed by *The Executioner's Song*. Anderson makes useful comparisons of Mailer's work to that of Truman Capote and Tom Wolfe. Along with these authors, Mailer has "offered a high style as a war against the poverty of the American spirit." He battles the "antiverbal." Close attention paid to Mailer's rhetoric.

Hollowell, John. "Mailer's Vision: 'History as a Novel, the Novel as History.'" In his *Fact and Fiction: The New Journalism and the Nonfiction Novel*. Chapel Hill: University of North Carolina Press, 1977.
This detailed assessment of Mailer's nonfiction stresses *The Armies of the Night*, *Miami and the Siege of Chicago*, and *Of a Fire on the Moon*. Mailer's competitive spirit drives him beyond the arena of the conventional novel. These three works "comprise a kind of impressionistic history of the sixties as seen through the distorting lens of a participant-observer." Hollowell is attentive to the genre of the nonfiction novel and to Mailer's playfulness in *Armies*.

Ruas, Charles. "Norman Mailer." In his *Conversations with American Writers*. New York: Alfred A. Knopf, 1985.
This interview is interesting mainly for insights into Mailer's political views. The focus is on *The Executioner's Song* and *Ancient Evenings*.

The Armies of the Night

Adams, Laura. *Existential Battles: The Growth of Norman Mailer*, pp. 121-136. Athens: Ohio University Press, 1976.
Armies is the culmination of Mailer's "search for a hero and for an effective style for that hero." His own participation in the antiwar movement has been fashioned as the metaphorical heroic action. The mode of the book bridges the gap between heroic and mock-heroic while establishing itself as a foremost representative of the hybrid narrative enterprise that blends fiction and nonfiction. It can be argued that the book made and changed history.

Begiebing, Robert J. "*The Armies of the Night.*" In his *Acts of Regeneration: Allegory and Archetype in the Works of Norman Mailer*. Columbia: University of Missouri Press, 1980.
"Mailer's primary achievement in *Armies* is that he discovers and communicates large implications and hope for a human renaissance in an event of absurdity, compromise, human weakness, and mass movements." Begiebing's prose is not usually that bad as he discusses Mailer's persona of "Mailer-the-fool" and demonstrates how *Armies* continues Mailer's response to conventional journalism. Mailer's major theme has to do with turning losses into gain.

Benoit, Raymond. "Norman Mailer's *Moby-Dick*." *Notes on Modern American Literature* 1, no. 3 (Summer, 1977): 26-27.
The Armies of the Night is a contemporary parallel to Melville's epic. The Pentagon replaces the whale; the map echoes Ahab's charts. Benoit develops other ingenious yet not totally convincing parallels.

Breslin, James E. "Style in Norman Mailer's *The Armies of the Night*." *Yearbook of English Studies* 8 (1978): 157-170.
Armies, a National Book Award winner, "launched the restoration of Mailer's reputation." Breslin feels that Mailer's stance stresses his role as "Mailer the writer," a role that emphasizes "style as value." Style becomes not only a literary issue but also a "manner of being," and certainly a matter of political behavior. The kind of intimacy and immediacy that is Mailer's goal eludes him as the work becomes forcefully totalitarian in its own way.

Champoli, John D. "Norman Mailer and *The Armies of the Night*." *Massachusetts Studies in English* 3, no. 1 (Spring, 1971): 17-21.
Champoli praises and illustrates Mailer's brilliance of wit and intellect, finding his "verbal pyrotechnics not simply incestuous celebrations of style" but a means of coming to terms with reality. There is little here on the issues, more on Mailer's tone, his "self-conscious control over his artistic machinery," and his essential patriotism.

Gutman, Stanley T. "*The Armies of the Night*: Resolution in Mid-Career." In his *Mankind in Barbary: The Individual and Society in the Novels of Norman Mailer*. Hanover, N.H.: University Press of New England, 1975.
The book pivots on two conflicts: that between the young and the old, and that between the individual and the state. Mailer, projected as a representative figure, "refers to himself as schizophrenic, divided by antithetical urges and needs." The antithetical elements include humanity's civilized nature and its animality. The work is "existential in both purpose and form" in its "attempt to understand the modern world . . . by coming to grips with an existent situation."

Hellmann, John. "Journalism as Metafiction: Norman Mailer's Strategy for Mimesis and Interpretation in a Postmodern World." In his *Fables of Fact: The New Journalism as the New Fiction*. Urbana: University of Illinois Press, 1981.
Hellmann examines Mailer's experimental strategies in *Armies* as well as *Of a Fire on the Moon* and *The Executioner's Song*. Each work has a distinct version of a shared quality: "the focus on the consciousness of characters as they view facts, rather than on a direct, seemingly objective view of facts, and on the authorial consciousness shaping the overall text." Hellmann looks closely at Mailer's portrait of the U.S. Marshals.

Johnson, Michael L. "Journalist." In *Will the Real Norman Mailer Please Stand Up*, edited by Laura Adams. Port Washington, N.Y.: Kennikat Press, 1974.
Johnson describes how *Armies* grows out of and develops Mailer's earlier journalistic enterprises. The success of *Armies* as journalism is the result of "Mailer's remarkable ability to combine poetry and objectivity into a greater whole." The first part of the book lets us "know the character of the journalist-historian of the second." The technique and aesthetic realized here informs later works, in particular *Miami and the Siege of Chicago*. This material originally appeared in Johnson's *The New Journalism* (Lawrence: University of Kansas Press, 1971).

Louvre, Alf. "The Reluctant Historians: Mailer and Sontag as Culture Critics." In *Tell Me Lies About Vietnam: Cultural Battles for the Meaning of the War*, edited by Alf Louvre and Jeffrey Walsh. Philadelphia: Open University Press, 1988.
Mailer's book and Sontag's "Trip to Hanoi" (both published in 1968) share a confessional strategy as a means of balancing the authors' need to make fruitful connection to the antiwar movement with their antipathy toward the masses and their hostility toward many of their fellow intellectuals. These writers both "engage in self-examination and analysis, to offer their personality, their psyche, their instinctive reflexes as an index of the culture as a whole."

Merideth, Robert. "The 45-Second Piss: A Left Critique of Norman Mailer and *The Armies of the Night*." *Modern Fiction Studies* 17, no. 3 (Autumn, 1971): 433-449.

Merideth argues that Mailer's leftist vision, as expressed in *Armies*, has not caught up with the maturing of the new left that his earlier works helped to inspire and energize. In particular, the idea of self that dominates this work is one that "the left is now obliged to repudiate." Mailer's macho, egocentric model is stale in a new age of responsible and nonaggressive masculinity—of the new man.

Merrill, Robert. "*The Armies of the Night.*" In *Norman Mailer*, edited by Harold Bloom. New York: Chelsea House, 1986.
Merrill focuses on the book's unique structure, specifically how the account of personal actions that constitutes the first section "is an elaborate preparation" for the more general historical treatment of the second part. Mailer transforms himself "from comic hero to mildly exalted initiate" as a prototype for the mass of demonstrators. First published in *Illinois Quarterly* 37, no. 1 (September, 1974): 30-44. Also collected in *Norman Mailer* (Boston: Twayne, 1978), edited by Merrill.

Mierau, Maurice A. "Carnival and Jeremiad: Mailer's *The Armies of the Night.*" *Canadian Review of American Studies* 17, no. 3 (Fall, 1986): 317-326.
Mierau applies Sacvan Bercovitch's understanding of the "jeremiad," a fusion of sermon and political persuasion, to Mailer's effort. Its "carnivalesque" qualities have to do with breaking down the boundaries between art and life. By applying the conventions of jeremiad and carnival to Mailer's work, Mierau is able to underscore its fundamental American qualities.

Seib, Kenneth A. "Mailer's March: The Epic Structure of *The Armies of the Night.*" *Essays in Literature* 1, no. 1 (Spring, 1974): 89-95.
Most critics fail to realize that Mailer works in "traditional and clear-cut forms." The classical epic is the model for *Armies*. Mailer treats the march on the Pentagon "as an historical event of the first magnitude" with Mailer himself filling the role of epic hero by sharing traits of Achilles and Odysseus. Seib notes epic structural features and "epic similes of Homeric proportion."

Weber, Ronald. *The Literature of Fact: Literary Nonfiction in American Writing*, pp. 80-97. Athens: Ohio University Press, 1980.
Weber addresses the mix of narrative, speculative, and dialectic modes in Mailer's effort. He finds in the work's "strong inflations, an air of self-mockery." He argues also that "Mailer's personal journalism is not really very personal." It is more of a personality portrait: the creation of a Mailer who is a quasi-historical, quasi-fictional character. Weber praises Mailer's style, especially in his "flights of amateur philosophizing."

Why Are We in Vietnam?

Aldridge, John W. "From Vietnam to Obscenity." In *Norman Mailer: The Man and His Work*, edited by Robert F. Lucid. Boston: Little, Brown, 1971.
Mailer's novel seems to be "a modernized and even rather banal retelling of the classic American mythic tale of quest, initiation and ultimate absolution." Yet the obscenity is purgative, given the noble, saintly rhetoric with which our involvement in Vietnam was defended. Aldridge examines the types and functions of obscenity that Mailer employs. First published in *Harper's Magazine*, February, 1968, 91-97.

Begiebing, Robert J. "*Why Are We in Vietnam?*" In his *Acts of Regeneration: Allegory and Archetype in the Works of Norman Mailer*. Columbia: University of Missouri Press, 1980.
The novel employs "a narrative consciousness of complexity unparalleled in the previous fiction." Earlier critics have failed to understand the significance of the Alaskan setting as a "force field" that becomes "a heightened battleground for God and Devil." D. J.'s profanity "is a response to his own sense of guilt" and "is satirically directed against all that he hoped to surmount." Also published as "Norman Mailer's *Why Are We in Vietnam?*: The Ritual of Regeneration," in *American Imago* 37, no. 1 (Spring, 1980): 12-37.

Beidler, Philip D. *American Literature and the Experience of Vietnam*, pp. 34-36, 42-46. Athens: University of Georgia Press, 1982.
Mailer's "calculated literariness" in writing a book about the war without ever mentioning it after the title demonstrates that no understanding of the war is possible without an examination of American culture: "The book is media event, X-rated soap opera, adventure romance, epic quest, pastoral idyl, ultimate power and death trip . . . Vietnam, summoned up at its very springs in the American soul." The Harlem to Texas to Alaska locales are made into a symbolic landscape.

Bufithis, Philip H. "An Alaskan Odyssey: *Why Are We in Vietnam?*" In his *Norman Mailer*. New York: Frederick Ungar, 1978.
The hunting party represents the American military, while the animals subjected to aerial machines are the Vietnamese victims of napalm. This work of "anarchic but creative flux" defies categorization, suggesting in its gathering of "linguistic waves" that no one answer or method can explain the confused and contradictory elements in the American psyche that find their outlet in Vietnam. The common element in the voice and mind of the undetermined narrator is violence.

Cooperman, Stanley. "American War Novels: Yesterday, Today, and Tomorrow." *Yale Review* 61 (Summer, 1972): 517-529.

"War and violence, for American writers, has been a basic subject, almost a cultural inevitability," writes Cooperman as he begins his discussion of Mailer's novel. Mailer's vision is that war is part of the fabric of American life, that "the United States is not simply at war, it is in war, of war" — hence Mailer's title and approach. Cooperman pays some attention to Kolpakoff's *The Prisoners of Quai Dong*, but only to set off his comments on Mailer, who, along with Hemingway, presents "the phallic impact of war: the iron penis raping the world, yet impotent without violence."

Fair, Alan. "The Beast in the Jungle: Mailer, Eastlake, and the Narrating of Vietnam." In *Tell Me Lies About Vietnam: Cultural Battles for the Meaning of the War*, edited by Alf Louvre and Jeffrey Walsh. Philadelphia: Open University Press, 1988.
See annotation under William Eastlake, *The Bamboo Bed*, above.

Gordon, Andrew. "*Why Are We in Vietnam?*: Deep in the Bowels of Texas." *Literature and Psychology* 24, no. 2 (1974): 55-65.
Gordon points outs the images of disembowelment and links them as symbols of castration. He finds that "D. J. identifies himself so strongly with his mother" that his actions involve "both incest and a masochistic attempt to eviscerate the female part of himself." This work is "an excessively manic and . . . sadistic novel" whose aggression is directed at the reader and somewhat redeemed by humor.

Gutman, Stanley T. "*Why Are We in Vietnam?*: The Dialectic of Authentic and Inauthentic Existence." In his *Mankind in Barbary: The Individual and Society in the Novels of Norman Mailer*. Hanover, N.H.: University Press of New England, 1975.
D. J.'s compromised initiation demands that he cope with the violence of both the natural world and American civilization. Mailer considers natural violence to be authentic, even beneficial, while the violence connected with American corporate life is destructive and malicious. The hunt motif is one kind of institutional violence, making war is another, but the former—in certain circumstances—partakes of the natural.

Hassan, Ihab. "Focus on Norman Mailer's *Why Are We in Vietnam?*" In *American Dreams, American Nightmare*, edited by David Madden. Carbondale: Southern Illinois University Press, 1970.
Stresses the functional importance of obscenity, Mailer's love of America, images of power, narrative stance, and tone in an odd imitative meditation presented in outline form. Hassan claims to be searching for a critical voice or style responsive to Mailer's achievement.

Hellmann, John. *American Myth and the Legacy of Vietnam*, pp. 78-82. New York: Columbia University Press, 1986.
The title question is worked out by asking "what a contemporary frontier means for a society that has given itself over to corporation and machine." Mailer's strategy is to "link a clearly perverse activity to the . . . imagery of the American frontier myth and to the disturbing contemporary images of Vietnam." Lyndon Johnson's America is seen as having transformed the frontier myth into something revealing "the worst European rapacity."

Kaufman, Donald L. "Catch 23: The Mystery of Fact (Norman Mailer's Final Novel?)". *Twentieth Century Literature* 17, no. 4 (October, 1971): 247-256.
Kaufman views this novel as evidence that Mailer's well is running dry. Mailer's recycled ideas now play in the background of a work whose "culture shock runs on language." The novel is a cross between Heller's *Catch-22* and William Burroughs' *Naked Lunch*. Kaufman was quite wrong in guessing that this novel would be "Mailer's footnote to fiction," but his reasoning is intriguing.

Pearce, Richard. "Norman Mailer's *Why Are We in Vietnam?*: A Radical Critique of Frontier Values." *Modern Fiction Studies* 17, no. 3 (Autumn, 1971): 409-414.
"Escalation," argues Pearce, "may be the stylistic key—social and literary—to the tall tale, to Mailer's novel, and to our cultural history." Having run out of space (even given the space mission), the United States makes of Vietnam a fabricated frontier for maintaining and justifying the enormous psychic and material investments that have made American culture into a massive network of appetites and providers. Mailer's novel points to the destructive potential of forces hidden beneath the idyllic illusion of frontier values.

Poirier, Richard. *Norman Mailer*, pp. 119-155. New York: Viking, 1972.
Poirier makes this work the centerpiece of his chapter called "The Minority Within." He argues that "few are prepared for his unique mixtures of daily news, the world we take for granted, with the world of nightmare and psychotic imagining." Mailer is concerned with how the mind (and the collective psyche) turns its contents and itself into waste. An excellent discussion of style, with references also to *An American Dream* and *The Armies of the Night*. Included in *Norman Mailer* (New York: Chelsea House, 1986), edited by Harold Bloom.

Rabinovitz, Rubin. "Myth and Animism in *Why Are We in Vietnam?*" *Twentieth Century Literature* 20, no. 4 (October, 1974): 298-305.
Here, as elsewhere, Mailer's thoughtfulness is masked by "a brash facade." While his novel interweaves derivative mythic themes, his handling of them shows his originality. Mailer describes "animistic phenomena in scientific language" to diminish the distance between primitive humankind and contempo-

rary technological humankind. Mailer's obscenity hides "the deeper level of his story in an effort to duplicate the subtlety of psychological forces at play in daily life."

Ramsey, Roger. "Current and Recurrent: The Vietnam Novel." *Modern Fiction Studies* 17, no. 3 (Autumn, 1971): 415-431.
Ramsey insists that this novel is primarily "about" its protagonist, D. J., and that Mailer's achievement is primarily an achievement in form. The novel is a dazzling rehearsal of Mailer's previously fashioned concerns with American culture, his main lines of criticism appearing over and over again outside of, and within, this novel. By once more formulating his vision of America, Mailer supplies the answer(s) to his title question.

Emily Mann

Kolin, Philip C., and Lanelle Daniel. "Emily Mann: A Classified Bibliography." *Studies in American Drama, 1945-Present* 4 (1989): 223-266.
Here is an excellent overview of Mann's career prefacing an exhaustive bibliography that lists Mann's plays, translations and adaptations, screenplays, interviews, criticism, reviews (including five pages on *Still Life*), Mann's work as a director, and biographical and information sources.

Savran, David. "Emily Mann." In his *In Their Own Words: Contemporary American Playwrights*. New York: Theatre Communications Group, 1988.
Mann answers questions about her career in general and her Vietnam play, *Still Life*, in particular. The interview provides background material on Mann's early theater experience, the genesis of *Still Life*, and its connection to her earlier documentary drama *Annulla*. We find out about the influence of Brecht on her work, the interaction of her writing and directing roles, and her reactions to foreign productions of *Still Life*.

Shteir, Rachel. "'I Became an Optimist': An Interview with Emily Mann." *Theater* 22, no. 1 (Fall/Winter, 1990/1991): 20-26.
Mann speaks on "the brutality of the human condition" as it is reflected in her work as well as on her movement toward healing and affirmation. The focus is on *Betsey Brown*, but other works are addressed, including *Still Life*. Mann comments on David Rabe's success, theater economics, and the place of women in the theater power structure.

Still Life

Kolin, Philip C. "Mann's *Still Life*." *The Explicator* 48 (Fall, 1989): 61-63.
Kolin examines the suggestiveness of Mann's title by pointing to Mark's photographs "that concretize violence" and the slides that frame isolated body parts. Stillness communicates death within life. The characters "live a still life on stage" by almost never communicating with, or acknowledging, one another. Life processes are stilled by sexual attitudes that ignore the procreative urge. Kolin calls this work "one of the best plays yet written about the Vietnam War."

Meyers, Kate Beaird. "Bottles of Violence: Fragments of Vietnam in Emily Mann's *Still Life*." In *America Rediscovered: Critical Essays on Literature and Film of the Vietnam War*, edited by Owen W. Gilman, Jr., and Lorrie Smith. New York: Garland, 1990.
Still Life suggests that American involvement in Vietnam may result from "a dichotomy . . . in the American psyche between two epistemologies" that Richard Slotkin associates with the hunter-warrior and the shaman. Each of the play's three characters represents some aspect of these roles. Mann's dramatic dialogue echoes "the chaotic pattern of the veteran's experience during and after the war." Mark's slide show imposes "a second narrative layer on top of the drama itself."

Bobbie Ann Mason

Bonetti, Kay. *Bobbie Ann Mason: Interview with Kay Bonetti*. Sound recording. Columbia, Mo.: American Audio Prose Library, 1985.
Mason discusses her concerns of craft and her interest in writing about the impact of popular culture on her characters' lives. This interview sheds light on her use of rock and roll, brand names, shopping habits, television, and other textural aspects of *In Country*.

Kling, Vincent. "A Conversation with Bobbie Ann Mason." *Four Quarters*, 2d ser. 4, no. 1 (Spring, 1990): 17-22.
Interviewed in October, 1988, Mason discusses her methods of composition, her concern for surface details, and the absence of critical theory in her day-to-day attention to craft. She considers *In Country* her favorite work, and she gives interesting comments about Emmett's skirt-wearing. Also covered are Mason's reading habits and her attitude toward being labeled as a Southern writer.

Lyons, Bonnie, and Bill Oliver. "An Interview with Bobbie Ann Mason." *Contemporary Literature* 32, no. 4 (Winter, 1991): 449-470.
The interviewers extract useful information on the backgrounds of Mason's

stories and novels as well as her interest in Nabokov. Mason discusses the evolution of *In Country*, which did not originate with a strong Vietnam theme. Lyons and Oliver elicit comments on the importance of place and on the celebratory moods that conclude some of Mason's works.

Wilhelm, Albert E. "An Interview with Bobbie Ann Mason." *Southern Quarterly* 26, no. 2 (Winter, 1988): 27-38.
In this November, 1986, interview, Mason talks of her rural upbringing, of her early writing, and of the background for *In Country*. She addresses in particular the *M*A*S*H* references and the quest motif and structure. There are comments on various short stories as well.

In Country

Booth, David. "Sam's Quest, Emmett's Wound: Grail Motifs in Bobbie Ann Mason's Portrait of America After Vietnam." *Southern Literary Journal* 23, no. 2 (Spring, 1991): 98-109.
Booth draws upon Jessie Weston's classic *From Ritual to Romance* (1920) to explore the grail legend in Mason's novel, finding that "every element of the legend remains recognizably present though transfigured." Images of blight and impotence, fecundity and vitality reflect the patterns of the legend. Emmett figures as the wounded king. Our involvement in Vietnam is our moral wasteland.

Brinkmeyer, Robert H., Jr. "Finding One's History: Bobbie Ann Mason and Contemporary Southern Literature." *Southern Literary Journal* 19, no. 2 (Spring, 1987): 22-33.
After first surveying Mason's short fiction, Brinkmeyer turns to *In Country* as "Mason's most significant and forceful statement of personal growth through the challenge of history." He traces the sporadic and partial nature of Sam's development that leads her to "a deeper knowledge of the dark complexities that shadow all human experience." The novel has a "distinctly Southern insistence on keeping hold of history, on probing rather than forgetting, on immersing oneself in the experience of defeat so as to rise transfigured above it."

_____. "Never Stop Rocking: Bobbie Ann Mason and Rock-and-Roll." *Mississippi Quarterly* 42, no. 1 (Winter, 1988/1989): 5-18.
Rock and roll music permeates the texture of Mason's settings and touches the lives of her characters. The influence of Bruce Springsteen is particularly notable, especially as it affects Samantha in *In Country*. So is a previously unreleased Beatles record. Rock music can have "transforming power" for Mason and for some of her characters.

Carton, Evan. "Vietnam and the Limits of Masculinity." *American Literary History*
3, no. 2 (Summer, 1991): 308-318.
In a powerful and persuasive reading of Mason's novel, Carton shows how it
"subverts the ideological function" of the analogy between war and childbirth
as essential and exclusive destinies for men and women "by insisting upon the
analogy itself and making Sam's female sexuality—a putative disqualification for
understanding 'the Vietnam experience'—the means by which she enters into that
experience." Generally useful in exploring how Mason demystifies a range of
cultural codes through Sam's quest.

Durham, Sandra Bonilla. "Women and War: Bobbie Ann Mason's *In Country*."
Southern Literary Journal 22, no. 2 (Spring, 1990): 45-52.
Durham stresses Mason's use of popular culture images and identifies Psyche's
search as the archetype of Sam's journey. As a concretization of the feminine
principle, Sam must contend with the insistent nonfeminine in her quest for
understanding. Her visit to Cawood's Pond is motivated, in part, by her need to
experience corruptness. Intriguing threads are never quite woven together in this
article.

Ehrhart, W. D. "Who's Responsible. *Vietnam Generation* 4, no. 1-2 (Spring,
1992): 95-100.
Ehrhart explains the special thanks accorded him on the novel's copyright page
by recalling his exchanges with Mason regarding the authenticity of her
presentation of Vietnam veterans, jargon, technical accuracy, and other matters.
Ehrhart praises many features of the book, including Mason's way of showing
how Americans, through the media and popular culture, obtain marginal
understandings of important historical events.

Jeffords, Susan. *The Remasculinization of America: Gender and the Vietnam War*,
pp. 62-65. Bloomington: Indiana University Press, 1989.
This novel, though "written by a woman and told from a woman's point of
view, confirms collectivity as a function of the masculine bond." In her quest
for information about the war and particularly about her father's death,
Samantha Hughes is constantly rebuffed. The war is felt by the other characters
to be privileged male terrain. Women are exclude not only from participation but
also from understanding. By finding a name similar to her own on the Vietnam
Memorial, Sam is symbolically reborn as a man and thus finally included in the
Vietnam experience.

Kinney, Katherine. "'Humping the Boonies':·Sex, Combat, and the Female in
Bobbie Ann Mason's *In Country*." In *Fourteen Landing Zones: Approaches to
Vietnam War Literature*, edited by Philip K. Jason. Iowa City: University of
Iowa Press, 1991.

Samantha Hughes's attempt to understand what happened in Vietnam is undermined not only by men asserting that, by definition of her gender, she cannot understand, but also by the fact that her investigation is conducted largely through language. Because the sexual metaphors and similes with which she contends are not universal but rooted in male experience, Samantha's opportunities are circumscribed. Mason's plot and uses of language explore difference and sameness in gender constructions.

McCabe, Stephen. "The Literature Born of Vietnam." *Humanist* 46, no. 2 (March/April, 1986): 30-31.
McCabe reviews what he considers to be the best of Vietnam War writing as a preamble to honoring *In Country* as "the most ambitious assimilation of the Vietnam War experience into the realm of fiction to be published to date." He raises important questions about the contrasts between works that focus on the actual conflict and those that search its meaning and effects without actually taking us there.

Melling, Philip H. *Vietnam in American Literature*, pp. 150-157. Boston: Twayne, 1990.
In Mason's work as well as in Wright's *Meditations in Green*, there remains the belief that nature teaches significant lessons. Emmett can get outside of himself by thinking about birds. Cawood's Pond offers Sam at least an approximation of the wisdom that she seeks. *In Country* also concerns itself with the surrogate histories offered by movies and television and the personalization of the myths and icons of popular culture. Melling explores the way in which Sam's imagination deals with Agent Orange as "a science fiction disease."

Ryan, Barbara T. "Decentered Authority in Bobbie Ann Mason's *In Country*." *Critique* 31, no. 3 (Spring, 1990): 199-212.
Ryan points out Mason's use of postmodernist *Bildungsroman* conventions, underscoring "the heroine's changing conception of the authority she seeks." Though the jargon is a bit thick, Ryan's insights into the nature and context of Sam's search are provocative, particularly her analysis of Sam's responses to "texts": *M*A*S*H* reruns, movies, her father's letters and diaries, and the names of veterans at the memorial.

Stewart, Matthew C. "Realism, Verisimilitude, and the Depiction of Vietnam Veterans in *In Country*." In *Fourteen Landing Zones: Approaches to Vietnam War Literature*, edited by Philip K. Jason. Iowa City: University of Iowa Press, 1991.
The story of Emmett Smith, Samantha Hughes's uncle, is co-equal in importance with Sam's own. In her portrait of Emmett and his circle of friends, Mason has created "a microcosm of Vietnam veterans' feelings, complaints and problems

regarding reintegration into civilian society." Mason's description of their
symptoms in complete and trustworthy. Only at the end of the novel does Mason
abandon a "scrupulous verisimilitude" for a fanciful happy ending.

White, Leslie. "The Function of Popular Culture in Bobbie Ann Mason's *Shiloh
    and Other Stories* and *In Country*." *Southern Quarterly* 26, no. 4 (Summer,
    1988): 69-79.
    Mason risks destruction by parody. She allows "the fictional context to generate
    every cliché possible, and parody is neutralized by the sheer accumulation of
    cliché." Mason's characters, much like her readers, receive their understandings
    secondhand through the dynamics of popular culture, which can "tighten the
    breach between cultural images and individual perceptions."

Robin Moore

The Green Berets

Hellmann, John. *American Myth and the Legacy of Vietnam*, pp. 53-66. New York:
    Columbia University Press, 1986.
    Moore's portrayal of the Special Forces is a "transmutation of an 'official'
    myth." The legend of the Green Berets echoes the long tradition of Western
    myth, especially the frontier hero represented by Daniel Boone. The myth
    sanctions "a lawless ruthlessness in pursuit of a morality superior to institutional
    and social restraint." Hellmann argues that *The Green Berets* "spoke to a part
    of the American mind only weakly repressed by its conscious ideals and
    purposes."

Spark, Alasdair. "The Soldier at the Heart of the War: The Myth of the Green
    Beret in the Popular Culture of the Vietnam Era." *Journal of American Studies*
    18, no. 1 (April, 1984): 29-48.
    Spark traces the growing popularity of the Green Berets during the 1960s
    culminating in Moore's novel and its film version. The popular image was based
    on a threefold appeal: It was an elite body, its members had highly specialized
    knowledge, and it realized itself in action. Spark examines the Defense
    Department's reaction to Moore's treatment and then assesses later treatments
    of special forces in *The Deerhunter* and *Apocalypse Now*.

Wilson, James C. *Vietnam in Prose and Film*, pp. 36-39. Jefferson, N.C.:
    McFarland, 1982.
    The best example of a novel that repeats the official distortions of the govern-
    ment regarding the purposes and conduct of the war. "Rather than illuminating
    his subject, Moore obscures it in clichés." Moore's characters are stereotypes

rather than individuals, and his version of history not only is irresponsibly shortsighted but also denies humanity to the Vietnamese, thus robbing the novel of any semblance of moral vision. Wilson is appalled at the popular success of the novel and its movie version.

David Morrell

Polak, Maralyn Lois. "David Morrell: Father of Rambo." *Philadelphia Inquirer Magazine*, August 19, 1990, 9-10.
This interview provides biographical information about the Canadian-born novelist's career as a literature professor. Morrell feels that his distance on the subject of the war enabled him to write a successful antiwar novel, one that also dealt with veterans' problems of adjustment. He speaks of the relationship between the novels and the subsequent movies and also of his other successful work, such as *The Brotherhood of the Rose*.

First Blood

Kunz, Don. "*First Blood* Redrawn." *Vietnam Generation* 1, no. 1 (Winter, 1989): 94-112.
Kunz provides a careful summary of the plot, tone, and vision of the novel in order to point out how the sequence of "Rambo" movies based on it sanitize Morrell's rendering of American's involvement. "David Morrell's complex and disturbing protagonist is simplified and softened in order to transform the public's concept of America's Vietnam veteran from psychotic loser to incorruptible and invincible superpatriot."

Walsh, Jeffrey. "*First Blood* to *Rambo*: A Textual Analysis." In *Tell Me Lies About Vietnam: Cultural Battles for the Meaning of the War*, edited by Alf Louvre and Jeffrey Walsh. Philadelphia: Open University Press, 1988.
Four works—Morrell's original novel, the movie based on it, the sequence to that movie, and Morrell's novelistic expansion of the movie—"have clear individual identities relating to and constituted by different phases of post-Vietnam American culture." The novel *First Blood* "concentrates less upon traditional formulations of heroism than upon Oedipal collisions." Morrell's second Rambo novel has as subtext "conservative assumptions and myths about personal conduct in society."

Tim O'Brien

Bates, Milton J. "Tim O'Brien's Myth of Courage." *Modern Fiction Studies* 33, no. 2 (Summer, 1987): 263-279.

O'Brien's approach to the issue of courage is more philosophical, more domestic, and more civilized than that of America's earlier war novelists. *Northern Lights* makes explicit the myth of courage that is implicit in *If I Die in a Combat Zone* and *Going After Cacciato*. This myth involves the synthesis of masculine and feminine modes of courage, each inadequate by itself. Courage is an "androgynous virtue" growing out of "a happy coincidence of character and event." Bates follows his detailed analysis of *Northern Lights* with shorter discussions of the Vietnam narratives.

Beidler, Philip D. *Re-writing America: Vietnam Authors in Their Generation*, pp. 11-37. Athens: University of Georgia Press, 1991.

Beidler traces O'Brien's developing craft and vision across five books, noting the sweep of genre and formal experiment. He observes that O'Brien's themes have been "the great ones: discipline, honesty, integrity, understanding, acceptance, endurance." Beidler makes connections between O'Brien's Vietnam texts and the books that less obviously reflect his Vietnam-influenced outlook.

Calloway, Catherine. "Tim O'Brien: A Checklist." *Bulletin of Bibliography* 48, no. 1 (March, 1991): 6-11.

Primary source subdivisions are books, short fiction and published excerpts, essays and nonfiction, and audiovisual materials. Secondary sources are grouped as biography, interviews, book reviews, criticism, and general articles and books. Clearly the place to begin for materials published through 1988.

Lyons, Gene. "No More Bugles, No More Drums." *Entertainment Weekly*, February 23, 1990, 50-52.

This celebrity portrait of O'Brien draws connections between his three major Vietnam titles: *If I Die in a Combat Zone*, *Going After Cacciato*, and *The Things They Carried*, with the emphasis on the latter. Based on interview questions and public statements, the portrait includes O'Brien's comments on the nature of truth in fiction. O'Brien insists that he is not a war writer and that his book "is really about peace."

McCaffery, Larry. "Tim O'Brien." In *Anything Can Happen: Interviews with Contemporary American Novelists*, conducted and edited by Tom LeClair and Larry McCaffery. Urbana: University of Illinois Press, 1983.

In this interview conducted in April, 1979, O'Brien asserts that though his war experience impelled him to write he does not consider himself a war writer. He provides biographical information, comments on the relationship between *If I Die in a Combat Zone* and *Going After Cacciato*, and discusses the then-in-progress *The Nuclear Age*. We learn that O'Brien designs the chapters of his novels to have an independent wholeness, and we hear his views on the relationship between teaching and storytelling. First appeared in *Chicago Review* 33, no. 2 (1982): 129-149.

Naparsteck, Martin J. "An Interview with Tim O'Brien." *Contemporary Literature* 32, no. 1 (Spring, 1991): 1-11.
Conducted in April, 1989, during the final revisions of *The Things They Carried*. O'Brien is embarrassed by *Northern Lights*, which he finds overwritten and overly influenced by Hemingway and Faulkner. He may go back and rewrite this first novel, as he rewrote passages of *Going After Cacciato* for its latest edition. O'Brien is fond of *Cacciato*'s scrambled chronology. The issues of courage and obligation found there run throughout his Vietnam and non-Vietnam writings. O'Brien comments on the composition and manner of *The Things They Carried*, which he believes may introduce a new genre.

Nelson, Marie. "Two Consciences: A Reading of Tim O'Brien's Vietnam Trilogy." In *Third Force Psychology and the Study of Literature*, edited by Bernard J. Paris. Rutherford, N.J.: Fairleigh Dickinson University Press, 1986.
O'Brien's first three books (*If I Die in a Combat Zone, Northern Lights*, and *Going After Cacciato*) may be seen as a trilogy confronting a single question: "What law must a man who wants to be good obey?" In each work, O'Brien presents "responses to the demands of authoritarian and humanistic consciences." His early reading in Erich Fromm probably influenced O'Brien's personal credo. Fromm's ideas inform Nelson's analysis, which reveals a pattern of growth and commitment to life in O'Brien's writings.

Schroeder, Eric James. "Two Interviews: Talks with Tim O'Brien and Robert Stone." *Modern Fiction Studies* 30, no. 1 (Spring, 1984): 135-164.
The O'Brien interview focuses on the background and intentions of *If I Die in a Combat Zone* and *Going After Cacciato*. Schroeder probes O'Brien's thinking on the distinction between fiction and nonfiction and on Vietnam narratives by other authors. Stone answers questions about the personal experiences behind the writing of *Dog Soldiers*, the characters Converse and Hicks, and the distinction between the truth telling of fiction and journalism. Rich material for studies of either author.

Schumacher, Michael. "Writing Stories from Life." *Writer's Digest*, April, 1991, 34-37.
Essentially an interview with O'Brien on his version of the writing process. O'Brien attempts (once again) to distance himself from the Vietnam-writer label while acknowledging that he will continue to use Vietnam as a setting or

backdrop—a vehicle to engage readers in broad, universal concerns. O'Brien comments on the writer's relationship to facts and truth, and he offers contrasts among his three Vietnam books: *If I Die in a Combat Zone, Going After Cacciato,* and *The Things They Carried.*

Zins, Daniel L. "Imagining the Real: The Fiction of Tim O'Brien." *Hollins Critic* 23, no. 3 (June, 1986): 1-12.
This biographical and critical essay covers O'Brien's first four books, though *Going After Cacciato* and *Northern Lights* get the most attention. The treatments are essentially detailed plot summaries with some interpretive comment.

Going After Cacciato

Beidler, Philip D. *American Literature and the Experience of Vietnam,* pp. 172-179. Athens: University of Georgia Press, 1982.
O'Brien recognizes the disparity between facts and interpretation yet strives for a synthesis in which the disparity is somehow resolved. He recognizes also the interplay between memory and imagination: Each depends on, and colors, the other. What "happened" to Paul Berlin (or any other veteran) is just as much what his imagination experienced as what he recalls, and the latter is as true or truer than any rehearsal of facts. O'Brien presents a sophisticated and self-conscious exploration of the nature of truth in storytelling. O'Brien "brings the truth of what was and the truth of what might have been into strange illuminating congruency."

Busby, Mark. "Tim O'Brien's *Going After Cacciato*: Finding the End of the Vision." *CCTE Proceedings* 47 (September, 1982): 63-69.
Although O'Brien draws upon other American literature, his allusions do not make the book derivative but rather enrich it and underscore its themes. Busby explores connections to Hemingway's *A Farewell to Arms,* Twain's *The Adventures of Huckleberry Finn,* Heller's *Catch-22,* and Vonnegut's *Slaughterhouse-Five.* In not allowing Paul Berlin to become the redemptive Adam- or Christ-figure, O'Brien separates him from the American mythic traditions with which he is structurally and situationally identified.

Calloway, Catherine. "Pluralities of Vision: *Going After Cacciato* and Tim O'Brien's Short Fiction." In *America Rediscovered: Critical Essays on Literature and Film of the Vietnam War,* edited by Owen W. Gilman, Jr., and Lorrie Smith. New York: Garland, 1990.
O'Brien's concern with the impossibility "of knowing the reality of the war in absolute terms" is manifest in *Cacciato* as well as in several short stories later modified and integrated into the novel. By examining these different versions of

O'Brien's text, one can observe the pursuit of a multidimensional vision in his fiction. The stories are "The Fisherman," "Going After Cacciato," "The Way It Mostly Was," "Keeping Watch by Night," "Speaking of Courage," and "Where Have You Gone, Charming Billy?"

Couser, G. Thomas. "*Going After Cacciato*: The Romance and the Real War." *Journal of Narrative Technique* 13, no. 1 (Winter, 1983): 1-10.
While expressing "radical skepticism about both the nature and the narratability of war," the novel manages to shape a narrative that expresses a participant's experience. It conveys both "the disruption of a coherent sense of time and the erosion of the distinction between reality and dream." These two effects on Berlin's consciousness are "grounded in the essence of war and conditioned by the circumstances of this one."

Gilman, Owen W., Jr. "Vietnam and John Winthrop's Vision of Community." In *Fourteen Landing Zones: Approaches to Vietnam War Literature*, edited by Philip K. Jason. Iowa City: University of Iowa Press, 1991.
See annotation under Gustav Hasford, *The Short-Timers*, above.

Griffith, James. "A Walk Through History: Tim O'Brien's *Going After Cacciato*." *War, Literature, and the Arts* 3, no. 1 (Spring, 1991): 1-34.
The particular terms of Paul Berlin's escape to Paris show that "the implied author directs his route through history, a six-hour fantasy that blends six months of Paul's history with the country's." Griffith points out the parallels between the incidents and characters in Berlin's imaginary journey, his earlier experiences of the war, and recent historical events of which he has little knowledge. He pays attention to, and builds upon, earlier critical discussions.

Hellmann, John. *American Myth and the Legacy of Vietnam*, pp. 160-167. New York: Columbia University Press, 1986.
"The protagonist . . . begins in this anti-frontier utterly separated from his proper mythic role, and imagines himself into a frontier stretching west from Vietnam all the way back to the Europe where the American errand commenced." Paul Berlin "locates the important moments he has shared with his father in symbolic frontier settings of a preserved wilderness." In Vietnam, the land is the enemy, and Cacciato himself is a reduced, regressive version of the American hero. The frontier spirit of boundless optimism is thwarted by the need to accept limits.

Herzog, Tobey C. "*Going After Cacciato*: The Soldier-Author-Character Seeking Control." *Critique* 24, no. 2 (Winter, 1983): 89-95.
The Vietnam veteran "author's difficulty in gaining control of literary materials mirrors the American soldier's problem of handling his Vietnam experiences by

establishing meaning, order, and control in his life." O'Brien's novel "explores the formal and thematic implications of this struggle" and involves the reader in the "pursuit of control." O'Brien's method involves the juxtapositioning of "three narrative strands . . . roughly equal to past, present, and future."

Jakaitis, John M. "Two Versions of an Unfinished War: *Dispatches* and *Going After Cacciato.*" *Cultural Critique* no. 3 (Spring, 1986): 191-210.
See annotation under Michael Herr, *Dispatches*, above.

Jones, Dale W. "The Vietnams of Michael Herr and Tim O'Brien: Tales of Disintegration and Integration." *Canadian Review of American Studies* 13, no. 3 (Winter, 1982): 309-320.
Jones distinguishes the formal differences in the uses of fact and imagination in these two works. He also notes how "their depictions of the war's daily realities more often than not coincide," pointing out a number of parallel passages. O'Brien's limitation of scope makes his novel "a more sensitive portrayal of what the average soldier experienced" than Herr's insistence on portraying almost everything and involving the reader in sensory overload. The two works are most divergent in their treatments of courage.

Lyons, Gene. "Pieces of a Vietnam War Story." *The Nation*, January 29, 1977, 120-122.
Before *Cacciato* was published, Lyons assessed several of the sections that were published as self-contained stories in various literary magazines. He praises the lyrical qualities of O'Brien's prose, its special kind of lyricism, and its discipline. Some brief comments also on *Northern Lights* and *If I Die in a Combat Zone*.

McWilliams, Dean. "Time in O'Brien's *Going After Cacciato.*" *Critique* 29, no. 4 (Summer, 1988): 245-255.
After describing the three narrative lines, McWilliams examines how they intersect and interact in order to answer a series of questions including why Berlin's imagination is overwhelmed by memory. Berlin's "repressed memories haunt the fantasy and finally cause it to collapse" because they are charged with guilt. They emerge "unbidden and out of sequence" for this reason. Berlin's dialogue with Sarkin Aung Wan "ironically undercuts Berlin's rhetoric of commitment."

Myers, Thomas. *Walking Point: American Narratives of Vietnam*, pp. 171-185. New York: Oxford University Press, 1988.
Cacciato is the most experimental of the Vietnam War fictions. The protagonist, Paul Berlin, "attempts to meld the data of memory and imagination into an interpretive strategy that is both a departure and a pursuit." Myers examines

both the "intricate weave of fact and fantasy" and the moral core of the novel, showing how technique and vision interact. He argues that "*Cacciato* seems an intensely classical work, a feeling instilled by O'Brien's placing the problematic history of the war in an expansive moral and philosophical context."

Palm, Edward F. "The Search for a Usable Past: Vietnam Literature and the Separate Peace Syndrome." *South Atlantic Quarterly* 82 (Spring, 1983): 115-128.
The title character represents the "separate peace" option that has its forebears in Hemingway's *A Farewell to Arms* and Heller's *Catch-22*, yet O'Brien seems to reject that option. Cacciato illustrates "the absurdity of withdrawal." Paul Berlin, the true central character, articulates "the consequences of leaving that Hemingway and Heller do not really address." His loyalty is not to abstract principles, but to people. O'Brien "has presented the first serious challenge to Heller's particular form of tyranny over the literature of war."

Raymond, Michael W. "Imagined Responses to Vietnam: Tim O'Brien's *Going After Cacciato*." *Critique* 24, no. 2 (Winter, 1983): 97-104.
Cacciato contains a mimetic narrative of Berlin's experience that is not chronological and only vaguely distinguished by markers of time and place. Its second narrative, a sequence of chapters each called "The Observation Post," forms "a series of indirect interior monologues or meditations." The third narrative is the "fantastic picaresque fiction" of Cacciato's flight and the squad's pursuit of him. Each narrative holds distinct and sometimes conflicting truths.

Saltzman, Arthur M. "The Betrayal of the Imagination: Paul Brodeur's *The Stunt Man* and Tim O'Brien's *Going After Cacciato*." *Critique* 22, no. 1 (1980): 32-38.
For the protagonists of both novels, "the war presents itself as a series of challenges designed for them alone, and the only meaningful commitment for either one is to his own protection." Berlin disqualifies imagination as a way of overcoming reality. Cacciato's alternative to submission is not refusal or imaginative flight "but an inability to participate." In both novels, "dreams die from their own irrelevance."

Schroeder, Eric James. "The Past and the Possible: Tim O'Brien's Dialectic of Memory and Imagination." In *Search and Clear: Critical Responses to Selected Literature and Films of the Vietnam War*, edited by William J. Searle. Bowling Green, Ohio: Bowling Green State University Popular Press, 1988.
After exploring the structural and stylistic resemblance to fiction of O'Brien's memoir (*If I Die in a Combat Zone*), Schroeder examines the way *Cacciato* places its focus upon the process by which Paul Berlin attempts to resolve his moral ambivalences. The novel tests the nature of reality and the reliability of

perception. The search for Cacciato "really becomes a search for Paul Berlin's own self" in which Berlin has it both ways: "He runs away and he doesn't run away." A first-rate study.

Slabey, Robert M. "*Going After Cacciato*: Tim O'Brien's 'Separate Piece.'" In *America Rediscovered: Critical Essays on Literature and Film of the Vietnam War*, edited by Owen W. Gilman, Jr., and Lorrie Smith. New York: Garland, 1990.
O'Brien gives a special twist to the "separate piece" tradition of Hemingway and Heller by having Paul Berlin go AWOL (absent without leave) only in his mind. The novel combines three styles: realism for combat scenes, black humor to underscore the absurd, and lyricism for the fantasy of the journey. It "celebrates the imagination's way of resisting the destructive powers of immediate experience, but it also questions the imagination."

Stephenson, Gregory. "Struggle and Flight: Tim O'Brien's *Going After Cacciato*." *Notes on Contemporary Literature* 14, no. 4 (September, 1984): 5-6.
Like Melville's *Billy Budd*, O'Brien's tale asks "how to reconcile or choose between the reality principle and the pleasure principle . . . the world as it is and the world as we would wish it to be." Lt. Corson is likened to Melville's Captain Vere. Melville aside, this piece is a brief book report.

Vannatta, Dennis. "Theme and Structure in Tim O'Brien's *Going After Cacciato*." *Modern Fiction Studies* 28, no. 2 (Summer, 1982): 242-246.
This concise analysis outlines the three-part structure of the novel: chapters of recollected war experiences, observation post chapters, and fantasy-pursuit chapters. These various narrative lines intersect to enact O'Brien's theme concerning "the struggle and eventual failure to impose order on the flux of experience." Vannatta considers O'Brien "a throwback to the great modernists." Probably the best brief discussion of how the novel works.

West, Richard. "Vietnam and the Imagination." *Books and Bookmen* 24, no. 5 (February, 1979): 57-58.
A brief summary of earlier Vietnam War literature introduces this odd review in which *Going After Cacciato* is praised as a fine war novel but not as essentially a novel about the Vietnam War. West addresses the various levels at which the novel operates. An interesting British perspective.

Wilhelm, Albert E. "Ballad Allusions in Tim O'Brien's `Where Have You Gone, Charming Billy?'" *Studies in Short Fiction 28*, no. 2 (Spring, 1991): 218-222.
Before it was rewritten as the "Night March" chapter in *Going After Cacciato*, this short story (which appeared in *Redbook*) contained many more allusions to folk ballads. These references provide "ironic resonance" and help amplify the

themes of initiation and imaginative transformation. According to Wilhelm, even as Berlin's imagined telegram to Billy Boy Watkins' parents comically masks his real terror.

Wilson, James C. *Vietnam in Prose and Film*, pp. 56-60. Jefferson, N.C.: McFarland, 1982.
O'Brien "portrays the confusion of his young American soldiers sent to Vietnam with no social or historical understanding of the Vietnamese people." Because their own government has made it impossible for them to understand why they are there, men such as the fictional Paul Berlin are forced into a kind of insanity. In his fantasy of flight from the war, Berlin "keeps brushing up against reality, just as the imaginary [government] progress reports . . . kept smashing against the reality of Vietnam." The novel shows how "official distortions of the war proved self-defeating for the United States."

If I Die in a Combat Zone

Beidler, Philip D. *American Literature and the Experience of Vietnam*, pp. 99-105. Athens: University of Georgia Press, 1982.
Commends O'Brien's attempt "to locate the truth of experience within some more or less traditional sense of achieved context, to use the literary process as a way of investigating individual conduct and belief with what may still remain of older ideas of human representativeness and centrality." Rather than depending on traditional plot or growth of character, O'Brien presents a series of "linked epiphanies" in the manner of a lyric poet. O'Brien's allusive manner evokes versions of heroism that are measured against the narrator's "heroism of consciousness." O'Brien projects meaning as process rather than conclusion.

Myers, Thomas. *Walking Point: American Narratives of Vietnam*, pp. 77-89. New York: Oxford University Press, 1988.
O'Brien frequently mixes classical and Christian allusions, creating an "inverted parable, brief illustrations of the effects of American practice and attitude in Vietnam." His "deductive project" marks "a new direction in American war memoir" in which inherited myths are undermined as the personal meditation becomes a cultural indictment. O'Brien discovers that for which he is not searching: "a capacity for malice, indifference, and revenge" that Western and American storytelling had kept largely hidden.

The Things They Carried

Beidler, Philip D. *Re-writing America: Vietnam Authors in Their Generation*, pp. 28-37. Athens: University of Georgia Press, 1991.
At the latest stage of his career, O'Brien creates a "literature of personal sense making and cultural revision." The work is at once a novel, a private confessional, "an ancient romance of consciousness and a postmodern epic of something that looks like . . . heroism." It is also a "treatise on the possibilities of language and representation" that makes us reconsider our "categories of factual and fictive structure."

Morace, Robert A. "*The Things They Carried.*" In *Magill's Literary Annual, 1991*. Pasadena, Calif.: Salem Press, 1991.
Though certain devices of this complex work may seem self-serving to the cynical reader, they are actually "self-examining in ways and to the extent that no work on the same subject has been." Morace reviews the interactions of genre and the relationships among the several parts that make this book both strange and familiar, forthright and evasive. He considers it "the most thorough examination yet to appear of the failure not simply to understand but even to find an appropriate means for depicting what has been insufficiently described as the American experience in Vietnam."

Jayne Anne Phillips

Bonetti, Kay. *Jayne Anne Phillips: Interview with Kay Bonetti*. Sound recording. Columbia, Mo.: American Audio Prose Library, 1991.
Phillips discusses her interest in voice and her curiosity about nontraditional families. She also expresses her concern with capturing the way that the mind works.

Nichols, Capper. "Jayne Anne Phillips: An Annotated, Primary, and Secondary Bibliography." *Bulletin of Bibliography* 47, no. 3 (September, 1990): 177-185.
Under primary works Nichols first groups books, then uncollected items in periodicals, and finally anthology appearances. Secondary works are classified as biographical sources, interviews, articles, and reviews (including many on *Machine Dreams*). Brief, well-focused annotations.

Machine Dreams

Driskell, Leon V. "*Machine Dreams.*" In *Magill's Literary Annual, 1985*. Englewood Cliffs, N.J.: Salem Press, 1985.

Though "neither remarkable for its story nor memorable for its characters," *Machine Dreams* "suggests that each generation somehow perpetuates the legacy which it receives from the previous generation." Driskell shows how the structure, imagery, and other techniques reveal the generational relationships, including the ways in which the family dynamics of the World War II era are echoed by those of the Vietnam War.

Gainey, Karen Wilkes. "Jayne Anne Phillips's *Machine Dreams*: Leo Marx, Technology, and Landscape." *Journal of the American Studies Association of Texas* 21 (October, 1990): 75-84.
Exploring the implicit metaphor in Phillips' title, Gainey points out the ways in which machines figure in the novel's action and setting. Billy's prophetic dream of being shot down from his helicopter in Vietnam is the most directly accessible machine dream in the novel. According to Gainey, Phillips sees contemporary American society as one in which the border between the human and the machine has become blurred. The machine dimension of our lives is limiting rather than liberating.

Lassner, Phyllis. "Jayne Anne Phillips: Women's Narrative and the Recreation of History." In *American Women Writing Fiction: Memory, Identity, Family, Space*, edited by Mickey Pearlman. Lexington: University of Kentucky Press, 1989.
Lassner explores how the dreams and memories that constitute *Machine Dreams* create connections among otherwise isolated individuals. Mitch's inability to make sense of his memories creates a pattern of loss that reaches its nadir when his son, Billy, bails out of a helicopter in Vietnam "and is missing in action forever." Feminine connectedness is set in contrast to masculine building of boundaries. Essay followed by primary and secondary bibliography.

John Clark Pratt

The Laotian Fragments

Aubrey, James R. "Conradian 'Darkness' in John Clark Pratt's *The Laotian Fragments*." In *Fourteen Landing Zones: Approaches to Vietnam War Literature*, edited by Philip K. Jason. Iowa City: University of Iowa Press, 1991.
Aubrey meticulously reveals how "Pratt uses Conrad's *Heart of Darkness* as a pattern for his narrative about the war in Southeast Asia." He examines the parallel between the psychological journey of Conrad's Marlow and Pratt's Blake while elucidating other literary allusions in Pratt's novel. Pratt's use is not systematic, and Aubrey offers a number of candidates for the Kurtz figure. Biographical material on Pratt is included.

Nicholas Proffitt

Gardens of Stone

Jeffords, Susan. *The Remasculinization of America: Gender and the Vietnam War*,
pp. 140-143. Bloomington: Indiana University Press, 1989.
This discussion is about Francis Ford Coppola's film rather than Proffitt's novel;
still, it is instructive in pointing out the ways in which antiwar constructs tend
to demand a version of the "new man"—a character who incorporates the
feminine—while still "establishing the masculine point of view as a position from
which to teach meaning to society as a whole." Clel Hazard is seen in this
complex dynamic. His fathering role is examined in detail, with Jeffords
asserting that the "affirmation of masculine . . . parenting" compromises the
film's antiwar impulses. Includes comparisons to *Platoon*.

David Rabe

Beidler, Philip D. "American Dramatist: David Rabe." In his *Re-writing America:
Vietnam Authors in Their Generation*. Athens: University of Georgia Press,
1991.
Beidler traces the Vietnam connection (in vision, in rereading American culture),
in those four major plays by Rabe that are not generally assigned as Vietnam
artworks: *The Orphan*, *In the Boom Boom Room*, *Goose and Tomtom*, and
Hurlyburly. The works conveniently labeled the "Vietnam Trilogy" are
intelligently probed. Beidler notes that in all Rabe's plays "the dramatic site
remains at once itself and a field of overarching mythic possibility as
well—myths of genealogy, authority, cultural origin, and their vindications of
institutional violence."

Bigsby, C. W. E. "The Theater of Commitment." In *Beyond Broadway*. Vol. 3
in his *A Critical Introduction to Twentieth-Century American Drama*. Cambridge, England: Cambridge University Press, 1985.
Bigsby briefly discusses *The Basic Training of Pavlo Hummel*, *Sticks and Bones*,
and *The Orphan* (pp. 324-331) as part of a larger section on the drama of the
Vietnam War. Of the Vietnam playwrights, only Rabe has gone beyond the
isolated, topical treatment of the war to create a significant body of work.

Christie, N. Bradley. "Still a Vietnam Playwright After All These Years." In *David
Rabe: A Casebook*, edited by Toby Silverman Zinman. New York: Garland,
1991.
Christie examines the causes of Rabe's identification as a Vietnam playwright
and the unease with which the label is applied and qualified. He suggests that

because Rabe must always write from "that insistent, destabilizing experience" of the Vietnam War, the war will in some way always remain his inevitable subject. Christie reviews some of the critical commentary on Rabe in order to demonstrate the problems of Vietnam writers and contemporary canon formation. He also comments on the "trilogy" of Vietnam dramas, pointing out the power of Vietnam as a metaphor for American society. The issues that Christie raises have broad application for the study of Vietnam War representation.

Cohn, Ruby. *New American Dramatists: 1960-1980*, pp. 31-36. New York: Grove Press, 1982.
In a five-page, relatively superficial summary of Rabe's career, Cohn links him with Ronald Ribman, John Guare, and David Mamet as an Off-Broadway sensibility who managed to reach Broadway. There are also fleeting comments on Kopit, Terry, Kennedy, and Valdez.

DeMastes, William W. "David Rabe's Assault on Rationalism and Naturalism." In his *Beyond Naturalism: A New Realism in American Theatre*. New York: Greenwood Press, 1988.
Rabe's plays assert "that the irrational violence he witnessed throughout his experiences during the Vietnam conflict . . . is not some localized anomaly but a fundamental fact of life that permeates all current American experience." DeMastes shows the thematic and stylistic links between Rabe's Vietnam plays and his other theater pieces. They all attach the rationalism and logic that is expressed in naturalism.

Herman, William. "When the Battle's Lost and Won: David Rabe." In his *Understanding Contemporary American Drama*. Columbia: University of South Carolina Press, 1987.
Herman provides a brief biography and a survey of approaches to Rabe's work. Then each of the major plays is discussed thematically and structurally. Some stage history is given. "Rabe has searched for the right forms of ritual theater to embody his high sense of overriding purpose." Herman makes some instructive comparisons between Rabe's plays and those of other playwrights.

Homan, Richard L. "American Playwrights in the 1970s: Rabe and Shepard." *Critical Quarterly* 24, no. 1 (Spring, 1982): 73-82.
These men are the two new playwrights who produced a substantial amount of significant work in the 1970s. Rabe's Vietnam plays exhibit "a progression from an experimental style to realism" and an "extraordinary use of language." Rabe's theme is "our struggle to comprehend violence and death." In each play, "Rabe chooses a situation in which the horror of violence can be juxtaposed with

the assumptions of everyday life." Brief comments on *Pavlo Hummel, Sticks and Bones*, and *Streamers*.

King, Kimball. "David Rabe." In his *Ten Modern American Playwrights: An Annotated Bibliography*. New York: Garland, 1982.
Under primary sources, King provides editions of plays, film scripts, translations, and interviews. Secondary sources include astutely annotated critical essays and reviews of productions.

Kolin, Philip C. *David Rabe: A Stage History and a Primary and Secondary Bibliography*. New York: Garland, 1988.
This first full-length work on Rabe has three parts. First comes a biographical essay that stresses his early years, his work as a reporter, and the stage history of his plays. Next comes the authoritative primary bibliography of Rabe's writings. The third part is a secondary bibliography that includes an annotated list of critical studies. All Rabe research should begin with this book.

_____. "David Rabe." In *American Playwrights Since 1945: A Guide to Scholarship, Criticism, and Performance*, edited by Philip C. Kolin. New York: Greenwood Press, 1989.
Kolin provides an overview of Rabe's reputation; a primary bibliography of plays, screenplays, articles and letters, and interviews; a production history for each of Rabe's plays; brief analyses of individual plays; and a detailed overview of secondary sources. This work is an abbreviated version of Kolin's book-length study listed above.

_____. "An Interview with David Rabe." *Journal of Dramatic Theory and Criticism* 3, no. 2 (Spring, 1989): 135-156.
Rabe addresses his habits of composition and revision, his thoughts on ritual in life and in drama, the ways in which the central symbols of his various plays emerged, and a wide range of thematic and theatrical concerns. Kolin elicits a number of useful remarks on Rabe's intentions regarding the Vietnam plays. Asked about his overall goal, Rabe says, "I feel like exploding things. I always feel like I'm trying to break something open." A concise career overview precedes the interview.

Phillips, Jerrold A. "Descent into the Abyss: The Plays of David Rabe." *West Virginia University Philological Papers* 24 (February, 1979): 108-117.
Rabe's plays are only superficially problem plays. At the core of each work is "a character who is led slowly, inexorably, and against his will to a recognition of . . . nothingness." Phillips examines Rabe's existentialist vision in *Pavlo Hummel, Sticks and Bones, In the Boom Boom Room*, and *Streamers*. He focuses, in turn, on Pavlo, Ozzie, Chrissy, and Richie.

Simard, Rodney. "David Rabe: Subjective Realism." In his *Postmodern Drama: Contemporary Playwrights in America and Britain*. Lanham, Md.: University Press of America, 1984.
Simard connects Rabe to "the school of anger which dominated the 1950s" while observing how he draws upon "absurdist and epic techniques." Rabe's vision is essentially existentialist. Each of Rabe's plays "suggests a framework of objective reality but dramatizes the individual perception of the characters on a subjective level." Simard applies this insight to the Vietnam plays and others. He finds Rabe to be essentially a social critic who uses the army as a metaphor for a dehumanized social system.

Zinman, Toby Silverman, ed. *David Rabe: A Casebook*. New York: Garland, 1991.
Twelve essays plus Zinman's interview with Rabe provide a rounded picture of the dramatist's achievement. Subjects treated include Rabe's theatrical techniques, his use of mass culture images, the cult of male identity, and his work on screenplays (especially *Casualties of War*). There are several essays on individual plays. Zinman juxtaposes portions of her interview with the critical material so that we can find Rabe's comments on issues being addressed by the critics. Her own "What's Wrong with This Picture? David Rabe's Comic Strip Plays" explores how Rabe's techniques force the theatrical experience into "the disturbing illusion of two-dimensionality" as a means of cultural critique. Zinman attends to *Pavlo*, *Streamers*, and other Rabe plays, making comparisons to Roy Lichtenstein's comic-strip paintings.

"Vietnam Trilogy"

Beidler, Philip D. *American Literature and the Experience of Vietnam*, pp. 112-118, 179-182. Athens: University of Georgia Press, 1982.
The Basic Training of Pavlo Hummel, *Sticks and Bones*, and *Streamers* constitute a major trilogy whose major theme involves "bringing the war home." *Pavlo Hummel* is a "pastiche of the American experience" that commingles "banality and terrifying waste." *Sticks and Bones* parodies the myth of happy American family life, a myth that the blocks the truth and pain of Vietnamese suffering and that of the Americans who fought there. *Streamers* deals with the shadow of Vietnam "upon a group of soldiers . . . who have to conceive of its threat as almost pure imaginative projection."

Hertzbach, Janet S. "The Plays of David Rabe: A World of Streamers." In *Essays on Contemporary American Drama*, edited by Hedwig Bock and Albert Wertheim. Munich: Max Hueber, 1981.
The dramas of the Vietnam trilogy "are not doctrinaire antiwar plays." The

Vietnam War is Rabe's vehicle for an exploration of "the inevitable, natural violence of American life." *Streamers*, *Sticks and Bones*, and *The Basic Training of Pavlo Hummel* receive brief analyses, as do other of Rabe's plays. *Streamers* is considered the most persuasive because it is the most dramatically straightforward. The others lack "texture and amplitude."

Hurrell, Barbara. "American Self-Image in David Rabe's Vietnam Trilogy." *Journal of American Culture* 4, no. 2 (Summer, 1981): 95-107.
Biography and production history preface Hurrell's discussion of how Rabe's plays deal with "the extent to which individuals (and, by extension, whole countries) will go to preserve a self-image, no matter how distorted." Rabe sees an America essentially racist, homophobic, materialistic, and militaristic, still trying to maintain its deluded self-image of virtuous and generous might.

Marranca, Bonnie. "David Rabe's Viet Nam Trilogy." *Canadian Theatre Review* 14 (1977): 86-92.
Marranca emphasizes that these are less antiwar plays than plays about the effects of war on individuals and the society. Taken together, the plays form a cycle that covers basic training, war, and returning home. Through the Vietnam focus, Rabe is able to reveal "attitudes towards heroism, maleness, alienation, violence, racism and interpersonal communication." Marranca reviews the themes and techniques of each play, stressing the range of theatrical conventions and devices that Rabe employs.

Werner, Craig. "Primal Screams and Nonsense Rhymes: David Rabe's Revolt." *Educational Theatre Journal* 30, no. 4 (December, 1978): 517-529.
The problem of language dominates the plays in Rabe's Vietnam plays: *Pavlo Hummel* shows "the alienating effect of the debased American language"; *Sticks and Bones* "links this debased language to a characteristic American refusal to accept reality"; *Streamers* presents "insurmountable barriers to human communication." A precise, forceful examination.

The Basic Training of Pavlo Hummel

Geis, Deborah. "'Fighting to Get Down Thinking It Was Up': A Narratological Reading of *The Basic Training of Pavlo Hummel*." In *David Rabe: A Casebook*, edited by Toby Silverman Zinman. New York: Garland, 1991.
The structure and patterns of repetition in *Pavlo* undermine narrative progression and instead emphasize "the inability of the characters to avoid the actions they are condemned to repeat." Geis's argument is attractive and compelling, though jargon almost gets the upper hand in her frequent references to theories of postmodern narrative.

Hughes, Catharine. *Plays, Politics, and Polemics*, pp. 77-82. New York: Drama
Book Specialists, 1973.
Hughes summarizes the sequence of events while pointing out the play's
unpredictability and Rabe's originality. She finds that Rabe's ambiguities raise
the play above other Vietnam War dramas. He does not fall into sentimentality
or "facile point-scoring." Pavlo is a willing participant in his own destruction.

Sticks and Bones

Adler, Thomas P. "Blind Leading the Blind: Rabe's *Sticks and Bones* and
Shakespeare's *King Lear*." *Papers on Language and Literature* 15, no. 2
(Spring, 1979): 203-206.
Rabe is indebted to *King Lear* "for certain symbols, character configurations,
and thematic motifs." Ozzie parallels Lear in his role as ineffective father;
David combines elements of the blind Gloucester as well as Edgar and
Cordelia's moral authority as misperceived children. Rabe echoes the mock trial
scene and other aspects of Shakespeare's drama.
Bernstein, Samuel. "*Sticks and Bones* by David Rabe." In his *The Strands
Entwined: A New Direction in American Drama*. Boston: Northeastern
University Press, 1980.
After a brief review of the commentary on this play, Bernstein presents an
examination of its social criticism, its theatricality, and its mixture of comic and
tragic elements. One hallmark of Rabe and other contemporary dramatists is the
entwining of realistic and surrealistic strands. *Sticks and Bones* is compared to
American Hurrah by Jean-Claude van Itallie.

Christy, James J. "Remembering Bones." In *David Rabe: A Casebook*, edited by
Toby Silverman Zinman. New York: Garland, 1991.
Christy directed the original production of *Sticks and Bones* at Villanova
University. He reviews the history of bringing the play to the stage, including
changes in the script as it further evolved for the New York production.

Cooper, Pamela. "David Rabe's *Sticks and Bones*: The Adventures of Ozzie and
Harriet." *Modern Drama* 29, no. 4 (December, 1986): 613-625.
After tracing the history of Rabe's Vietnam Trilogy, Cooper examines the ways
in which *Sticks and Bones* comments on the inability of media to present the
truth. By staging some of the futile action in the TV room and by presenting
David as a blind filmmaker, Rabe underscores his attack on media and popular
culture. The play presents the clash of a facile consumerism drugged by pleasing
appearances and the unacceptable reality of its mindless sanctioning of the
Vietnam adventure.

Davies, Lindsay. "Watching the Box: TV on Stage in *Sticks and Bones*." In *David Rabe: A Casebook*, edited by Toby Silverman Zinman. New York: Garland, 1991.

By borrowing television characters of the late 1950s and early 1960s and putting them on the stage, Rabe is able to project the American middle class as it prefers to see itself and then attacks that image. When the returned veteran, David, enters the set of the staged sitcom, the tensions of the incompatible worlds are released. Davies explores the variety of ways in which Rabe's play exploits television culture.

McDonald, David. "The Mystification of Vietnam: David Rabe's *Sticks and Bones*." *Cultural Critique*, no. 3 (Spring, 1986): 211-234.

The play's effects are built around significant absences: "It attempts to represent the American viewer's perspective as a text, which in its marginal relation to the actual war represents the displacement of the war and of Vietnamese culture as its subject and theme." McDonald stresses Rabe's deployment of parody as a way of underscoring the absence of meaning and, therefore, responsibility. A detailed, brilliant analysis of what he accomplishes and what he fails to address.

Robinson, James A. "Soldier's Home: Images of Alienation in *Sticks and Bones*." In *Search and Clear: Critical Responses to Selected Literature and Films of the Vietnam War*, edited by William J. Searle. Bowling Green, Ohio: Bowling Green State University Popular Press, 1988.

While images of disease probe "a national sickness which predates our involvement in Vietnam," the speechless character of Zung, the broken television, the silent film, and the soundless slide projections underscore the absence of communication on issues vital to the American family and the American nation. Rabe parodies and undermines "the idealized self-image of the bourgeois family" with his dysfunctional version of television's Nelson family, revealing a poisonous bigotry as a partial explanation for our involvement in Vietnam.

Streamers

Christie, N. Bradley. "David Rabe's Theater of War and Remembering." In *Search and Clear: Critical Responses to Selected Literature and Films of the Vietnam War*, edited by William J. Searle. Bowling Green, Ohio: Bowling Green State University Popular Press, 1988.

Bradley reviews, and tries to account for, Rabe's early critical and popular success with Vietnam War materials before treating the last part of Rabe's informal trilogy. "More singularly than either of the earlier plays, *Streamers* derives its power from the sharp delineation of figures forced to interact . . . in a consistent, contained, and rigidly regulated setting" as it "portrays the volatile situation of pent-up energies finally unleashed, this time upon ourselves."

Kolin, Philip C. "David Rabe's *Streamers.*" *The Explicator* 45 (Fall, 1986): 63-64.
Rabe's play examines "the rite of passage into manhood" of four soldiers. The father figures in the play "underscore Rabe's message about the failure of fatherhood for a Viet Nam generation." Cokes and Rooney represent "irresponsible Army fathers who are degenerate and degenerating."

Robert Roth

Sand in the Wind

Hellmann, John. *American Myth and the Legacy of Vietnam*, pp. 119-128. New York: Columbia University Press, 1986.
"Roth's technique, not always fully controlled or realized but never less than provocative, is to develop the fragmentation, tension, and circularity of the Vietnam experience toward episodes evoking the nightmares of the classic American romances." Hellmann compares this novel stylistically to those by Huggett and Webb, thematically to the memoirs of Caputo, Kovic, and O'Brien. The hero is traumatized by "his loss of belief in a unique American relation to nature as the sign of unique mission in the world."

James Park Sloan

War Games

Beidler, Philip D. *American Literature and the Experience of Vietnam*, pp. 89-92. Athens: University of Georgia Press, 1982.
Because Sloan is aware of the complex nature of fiction and of the sense-making task with regard to the war, his novel is a major achievement in spite of its "more than occasional arty oppressiveness." His is a "Vietnam as literary conceit . . . envisioned by someone well trained in philosophy who seems to have found Kafka and Borges at a particularly impressionable stage in his evolution." Sloan struggle productively with the task of achieving a balance between intellectualization and the rendering of experience. The ultimate content of this novel is its "intense self-consciousness."

Klinkowitz, Jerome. *Literary Disruptions: The Making of Post-Contemporary American Fiction*, pp. 112-118. Urbana: University of Illinois Press, 1975.
In a chapter in which Klinkowitz makes a risky paring of Sloan and Imamu

Amiri Baraka, he examines the techniques of both *War Games* and Sloan's second novel, *The Case History of Comrad V.* Klinkowitz discusses the organizational device of the protagonist's dental records, their very linearity underscoring the nonlinear, absurdist nature of the war. The war is so unreal that Sloan's protagonist will have to make one up (write one down) in order to have a real war.

Slabey, Robert M. "Fact, Fiction, and Metafiction in James Park Sloan's *War Games.*" In *Search and Clear: Critical Responses to Selected Literature and Films of the Vietnam War*, edited by William J. Searle. Bowling Green, Ohio: Bowling Green State University Popular Press, 1988.
Sloan explores the problems of writing the Vietnam War novel by having his nameless protagonist set about to write one. To prepare, he reads the classic literature of war, confronting the war through these and more contemporary, popular renderings. Finding that the models will not fit, Sloan and his protagonist explore the limits of various conventions while having the book "comment on its own fictionality."

Robert Stone

Beidler, Philip D. *Re-writing America: Vietnam Authors in Their Generation*, pp. 237-264. Athens: University of Georgia Press, 1991.
Beidler sees Stone as the "novelistic laureate of the post-Vietnam American soul." *A Hall of Mirrors* is already an exploration of "the intersection of contemporary history and myth in postmodern crisis." *Dog Soldiers* is the key text of "American virtue in flight" both in and after Vietnam; it is among the dominant portraits of a lost America. *A Flag for Sunrise* carries the paralyzing psychic strains of Vietnam to another venture and venue (Central America), while *Children of Light* uses the newest center of America's image-making enterprise, Hollywood, as the setting for postmodern (and post-Vietnam) American dread. This discussion is one of the best analyses of Stone's career.

Bonetti, Kay. *Robert Stone: Interview with Kay Bonetti.* Sound recording. Columbia, Mo.: American Audio Prose Library, 1982.
Stone discusses his thematic concerns, his attitude toward his craft, his religious and political views, and his ideas about the place of craft, vision, and plot in fiction. Comments on specific novels are weighted more toward *A Flag for Sunrise* than *Dog Soldiers*. An edited version of this interview (recorded in April, 1982) appears as "An Interview with Robert Stone," in *Missouri Review* 6, no. 1 (Fall, 1982): 91-115. Stone considers this recording to be his definitive interview.

Colonnese, Tom. "Robert Stone: A Working Checklist." *Bulletin of Bibliography* 39, no. 3 (September, 1982): 136-138.
Includes both primary and secondary sources. Useful for locating biographical material and especially for reviews of *Dog Soldiers* and *A Flag for Sunrise*.

Karagueuzian, Maureen. "Interview with Robert Stone." *TriQuarterly* 53 (Winter, 1982): 248-258.
Interviewed in the summer of 1980, Stone discusses his method of composition in which events proceed from character. He also comments on his habits of revision, his views on the transformation of his novels into films, and his relationship to the academic world. He notes similarities in plot between *Hall of Mirrors* and *Dog Soldiers*, and he speaks to the moral dilemmas of his main characters.

Melling, Philip H. *Vietnam in American Literature*, pp. 169-193. Boston: Twayne, 1990.
Melling treats *Dog Soldiers* and *A Flag for Sunrise* together in a lengthy discussion that explores Stone's fables of "the messianic fervor" of U.S. involvement in Indochina and Central America. America's imperial mission seems intact in spite of Stone's exposure of its diseased zealousness. In Stone's novels of U.S. ventures abroad, Melling sees (as he always does) American behavior cast as Puritan obsession with conquering the Antichrist. References to other contemporary works (fiction and film) as well as to Puritan texts help Melling elaborate this rather narrow and tedious thesis. He also pays attention to economic self-interest, the religion of capitalism.

Parks, John G. "Unfit Survivors: The Failed and Lost Pilgrims in the Fiction of Robert Stone." *CEA Critic* 53, no. 1 (Fall, 1990): 52-57.
This brief discussion of Stone's first four novels emphasizes the author's moral vision, a "vision of brokenness in our collective and personal lives." Comments on *Dog Soldiers* and on the Vietnam memory that "haunts the characters of *A Flag for Sunrise*" anchor Parks's overview of a body of works that see "American society as fractured and its people lacking a moral center." Cursory, but clear.

Ruas, Charles. "Robert Stone." In his *Conversations with American Writers*. New York: Alfred A. Knopf, 1985.
In this interview, conducted soon after the publication of *A Flag for Sunrise*, Stone discusses his New York Catholic upbringing, his navy and merchant marine experience, drugs and alcohol, and his work as a Vietnam War correspondent. He comments also on the moral issues in *Dog Soldiers* and the creation of setting in *A Flag for Sunrise*.

Schroeder, Eric James. "Two Interviews: Talks with Tim O'Brien and Robert
Stone." *Modern Fiction Studies* 30, no. 1 (Spring, 1984): 135-164.
See annotation under Tim O'Brien, above.

Dog Soldiers

Beidler, Philip D. *American Literature and the Experience of Vietnam*, pp. 108-
113. Athens: University of Georgia Press, 1982.
Portrays "how that war-anger and murderous confusion" of Vietnam spreads
"across the American landscape as well." The characters seem driven by "some
strange debased sense . . . of Nietzschean existential will." In the concluding
patterns of the novel, hunter and hunted, dog soldier and guerrilla, seem to
change places. The novel discovers that the horror of the war has always been
lodged back home, not in Vietnam. The final principle that they have defended
"is that nobody ever knows why they do what they do."

Elliot, Emory. "History and Will in *Dog Soldiers*, *Sabbatical*, and *The Color
Purple*." *Arizona Quarterly* 43, no. 3 (Autumn, 1987): 197-216.
Each work is examined as an instance of contemporary naturalism, with *Dog
Soldiers* assessed as the most traditional in method. Stone's novel evokes the
historical context of the Vietnam War era "as a force that determines the fate of
the characters." Although Stone challenges his readers morally and intellectually,
the novel's determinism seems to cancel the possibilities for free will or reform.

Hellmann, John. *American Myth and the Legacy of Vietnam*, pp. 139-150. New
York: Columbia University Press, 1986.
Stone presents Vietnam as "the murderous field that has finally forced frontier-
marching America to gaze upon its self-projected image, stripped of its dreams
and myths, and find nothing but brute behavior." Stone's vehicle exploits and
yet undermines the conventions of the thriller genre. In Converse, Stone presents
"a bitter parody of the American liberal" whose mission goes sour in Vietnam
and whose heroin smuggling reflects his disillusionment and his perception that
the idealized "American mythic landscape . . . overlays a moral desert."

Jordan, Clive. "The Viet Nam Connection: New Novels." *Encounter* 45, no. 3
(September, 1975): 71-76.
Despite the title, only three of the novels have anything to do with Vietnam and
only one—Stone's *Dog Soldiers*—is examined in detail. Jordan praises Stone's
"grasp of a particular kind of everyday American speech—vivid, vulgar, and
direct." Jordan admires Stone's ability to mix various fictional modes and yet
contain them within the conventions of realism. Reviewed also are the
marginally relevant *The Virtues of Hell* by Pierre Boulle and the barely relevant
The Shadow Knows by Diane Johnson.

Karagueuzian, Maureen. "Irony in Robert Stone's *Dog Soldiers*." *Critique* 24, no. 2 (Winter, 1983): 65-73.
Dog Soldiers, though little of it is set in Southeast Asia, provides a direct parallel to American's involvement in Vietnam and describes the effects of the war on the American sensibility. Allusions to works by Hemingway, especially to *The Sun Also Rises*, provide an ironic commentary on the limitations of the Hemingway ethic that affected a generation of Americans. The ironic, nonjudgmental acceptance of a Jake Barnes is inherited by Frank Converse and found wanting in its unwillingness to recognize evil and to make moral choices.

Klein, Jeffrey. "The Vietnam Connection." *American Scholar* 44 (Autumn, 1975): 686-688.
Dog Soldiers is "a cultural thriller" whose very plot brings the war home—and "leaves it there." In this appreciative review, Klein observes the sting of Stone's understated irony, the "anti-intellectual twists," and the creation of "an orphan's world where the worst can arrive at any time." Klein's assessment is as penetrating as much of the later academic criticism.

Knox, Stephen H. "A Cup of Salt for an O.D.: *Dog Soldiers* as Anti-Apocalypse." *JGE: The Journal of General Education* 34, no. 1 (Spring, 1982): 60-68.
One must catch the satiric edge to Stone's episodes of visionary intensity in order to understand how *Dog Soldiers* "nullifies the apocalyptic interpretation of the Vietnam War." Knox explores Stone's central metaphor that equates violence with narcotics as well as Stone's concern with how dangerous "long view" perspectives can be when they ignore "immediate reality as a ground for making choices."

Sale, Roger. "Robert Stone." In his *On Not Being Good Enough*. New York: Oxford University Press, 1979.
Sale stresses the grim vision of *Dog Soldiers* and Stone's commitment to straightforward, realistic storytelling. He praises Stone's craft, especially his art of characterization and scene making. Sale, however, feels that Stone finally betrays his characters by forcing their natures to conform to the demands of the plot. Originally appeared in *The New York Review of Books*, April 3, 1975.

Shelton, Frank W. "Robert Stone's *Dog Soldiers*: Vietnam Comes Home to America." *Critique* 24, no. 2 (Winter, 1983): 74-81.
In this interpretive summary, Shelton points out how "brutality and illegality are the norm and not the exception" in Stone's world, and how the novelist "has implicitly linked that condition to the Vietnam War." The war is not the cause of the situation. Rather, it is a consequence of the same moral disease. Shelton's analysis tends to focus more on Hicks than on Converse.

Wilson, James C. *Vietnam in Prose and Film*, pp. 65-69. Jefferson, N.C.:
McFarland, 1982.
Stone presents the war as both a consequence and a cause of "disintegrating
American culture." Vietnam serves as a metaphor for a world in which death
and violence have permeated human experience so as to become a norm. Though
the novel quickly leaves the battlefields of Vietnam behind, the later events are
a continuation and mirror of the war's violence. Stone shows us how moral
laxity snowballs until people readily descend into bestiality: "In the allegory of
Dog Soldiers, the war was fought and all the lives were lost for an illegal stash
of narcotics."

Megan Terry

Hart, Lynda. "Megan Terry." In *American Playwrights Since 1945: A Guide to
Scholarship, Criticism, and Performance*, edited by Philip C. Kolin. New York:
Greenwood Press, 1989.
Viet Rock is treated along with other plays by Terry in this article that includes
discussion of Terry's reputation, the stage history of her plays, and the plays
themselves. Hart provides a primary bibliography, an assessment of scholarship
on Terry, and a secondary bibliography that includes reviews.

Klein, Kathleen Gregory. "Language and Meaning in Megan Terry's 1970's
'Musicals.'" *Modern Drama* 27, no. 4 (December, 1984): 574-583.
Although this article treats four plays written and produced after *Viet Rock*,
Klein's analysis of Terry's techniques and themes can be effectively applied to
the earlier play. Terry's passionate demonstration of the power and abuses of
language and her ongoing parodies of popular media inform *Viet Rock* as well
as the plays discussed by Klein.

Leavitt, Dinah L. "Interview with Megan Terry." In *Women in American Theatre*,
edited by Helen Krich Chinoy and Linda Walsh Jenkins. New York: Crown,
1981.
This 1977 interview records Terry's thoughts on the function of theater and the
purposes and possibilities of feminist drama. Of all her plays, only *Viet Rock*
developed from structured improvisation. Terry finds the play tame at the
distance of a decade, though it was shocking in its moment. She finds it
important to identify with audiences. See also David Savran's *In Their Own
Words* (New York: Theatre Communications Group, 1988.)

Londre, Felicia Hardison. "An Interview with Megan Terry." *Studies in American
Drama, 1945-Present* 4 (1989): 177-186.
This interview provides biographical material and Terry's comments on the

importance of community concerns in her writing and theater managing. She also remarks on the importance of music in her plays.

Schlueter, June. "*Keeping Tightly Closed in a Cool Dry Place*: Megan Terry's Transformational Drama and the Possibilities of Self." *Studies in American Drama, 1945-Present* 2 (1987): 59-69.
Schlueter sets Terry's early transformational plays, including *Viet Rock*, in the context of Off-Broadway concepts of character during the 1950s and 1960s. The focus here is on the play named in the title. Schlueter writes, "Transformational drama acknowledges the extent to which the modern self is shaped by popular culture."

Weales, Gerald. *The Jumping-Off Place: American Drama in the 1960's*, pp. 238-241. New York: Macmillan, 1969.
Weales' comments on Terry's early work, including *Viet Rock*, are not very flattering. He compares her method unfavorably to that of Jean-Claude van Itallie, noting two basic types of plays: "those . . . in which the performers assume ever-changing roles, and those in which the transformations work out of a dramatic context rather than a playing situation."

Viet Rock

Hughes, Catharine. "The Theatre Goes to War." *America*, May 20, 1967, 759-761.
Hughes compares and contrasts *Viet Rock* with the improvisational *US* directed by Peter Brooks. She sees both plays as too polemical and too filled with cliches. Mere sensationalism will have to give way to more serious probing before a significant drama of the war can emerge.

Marranca, Bonnie. "Megan Terry." In *American Playwrights: A Critical Survey*, by Bonnie Marranca and Gautam Dasgupta. New York: Drama Book Specialists, 1981.
This discussion describes Terry's use of "transformations" defined as "a nonpsychological, action and image-oriented conception of character which negates the notion of a fixed reality of situation in favor of the continuous displacement of one reality with another." Marranca traces the employment of this concept in various plays of Terry including *Viet Rock* (pp. 187-189), which she considers Terry's most accomplished play in this style. In *Viet Rock*, Terry's vision of America "evolves from advertising slogans, antiwar chants, rock and roll dances, and movie-style gestures, all of them set in relief against the militaristic, sexist, racist machine that grinds out soldiers for a war in Southeast Asia." The play's impact depends on audience contact, a sense of improvisation and open shape. It was one of the first rock musicals.

Tran Van Dinh

Blue Dragon, White Tiger: A Tet Story

Christopher, Renny. "*Blue Dragon, White Tiger*: The Bicultural Stance of
Vietnamese-American Literature." In *Reading the Literatures of Asian America*,
edited by Shirley Lim and Amy Ling. Philadelphia: Temple University Press,
1992.
Not only is the theme of this autobiographical novel the attempt to negotiate
American and Vietnamese cultures, the author's attitude (reflected in his
protagonist's actions) is also that such a bridging can be successfully accomplished. Moreover, "the novel itself attempts to be bicultural in structure."
Christopher explores the various devices through which a bicultural experience
is projected.

Luis Valdez

Brown, Edward G. "The Teatro Campesino's Vietnam Trilogy." *Minority Voices*
4, no. 1 (Spring, 1980): 29-38.
For this theater group, the emergence of the Vietnam theme accompanies a shift
in philosophy from improvisational collaborations to play scripts. Luis Valdez,
the group's "principal creative force," is credited with bringing each play to its
final form. Each represents a different perspective on the "Chicano Vietnam
experience": *Vietnam Campesino* shows the connection between wartime
profiteering and a discriminatory selective service system; *Soldado Razo* presents
a barrio family's upheaval as a son prepares for Vietnam; *Dark Root of a
Scream* stages the wake held for a Chicano Medal of Honor winner. Brown
provides details on each play and discusses their interrelationships.

Herms, Deiter. "Luis Valdez, Chicano Dramatist: An Introduction and Interview."
In *Essays on Contemporary American Drama*, edited by Hedwig Bock and
Albert Wertheim. Munich: Max Hueber, 1981.
Although neither the introduction nor the interview makes mention of Valdez's
Vietnam-related plays (see David J. DeRose's "Soldados Razos," published in
Vietnam Generation 1, no. 2. [Spring, 1989]: 38-55), insights into the
playwright's other works and his relationship with the acclaimed theater
company, El Teatro Campesino, make this work a useful reference. These works
receive fleeting mention in John W. Brokaw's "Mexican-American Drama"
found in the same volume.

James Webb

Beidler, Philip D. *Re-writing America: Vietnam Authors in Their Generation*, pp. 63-79. Athens: University of Georgia Press, 1991.
Alone among the significant Vietnam novelists, Webb presents a revisionist career. *Fields of Fire, A Sense of Honor,* and *A Country Such as This* affirm "the old soldierly values of dignity, honesty, and integrity." *Fields of Fire* captures the "ecstasy of horror" in its revisionary mythmaking while *A Sense of Honor* pursues the theme "of a military-political tradition at war with itself." The third novel "becomes a [neoconservative] museum of major fifties, sixties, and seventies issues."

Fields of Fire

Beidler, Philip D. *Re-writing America: Vietnam Authors in Their Generation*, pp. 64-69. Athens: University of Georgia Press, 1991.
Webb assembles a traditional cast of characters (mainly young, undereducated, and socially marginal) and moves them through a series of traditional actions to the "primal scene of Vietnam narrative, some ultimate confrontation with atrocity." The pain and suffering is not redeemed by the confused political or military agendas but by personal honor and group loyalty. Goodrich's "repentant liberalism" is not enough to heal "the deep anguish of our own larger spirit of national irresolution."

Palm, Edward F. "James Webb's *Fields of Fire*: The Melting-Pot Platoon Revisited." *Critique* 24, no. 2 (Winter, 1983): 105-118.
Views Webb's novel as "a technically flawed but moderately successful attempt to adapt the realistic pattern established by Mailer, and Dos Passos before him, to the demands of Vietnam fiction." The third-person point of view shifts among three major characters and a series of lesser ones. The novel's theme "of selfless, mutual concern" at the small-unit level is carefully managed through the manipulation of point of view and through its three-part structure. Palm considers the handling of the major character, Lt. Hodges, "an embarrassment."

Puhr, Kathleen M. "Four Fictional Faces of the Vietnam War." *Modern Fiction Studies* 30, no. 1 (Spring, 1984): 103-108.
Webb's message is that only those who have been there have a right to criticize the war and that the Vietnam veteran deserves compassion. He stresses the camaraderie of men in combat. Puhr takes the unusual stance that, in terms of plot, Goodrich is the most important character. She praises Webb's successful handling of realistic action and character, his treatment of draft evasion, and the inclusion of a parable: "the parable of the ice."

Bruce Weigl

Beidler, Philip D. *American Literature and the Experience of Vietnam*, pp. 182-191. Athens: University of Georgia Press, 1982.
Weigl establishes a context of romance conventions against which to play both the expectations of an American youth and the grim realities of his experience soldiering in Vietnam. By interspersing poems that treat the war and poems that treat stateside experiences, Weigl suggests the private and collective wars, the ways in which the war exists in the individual psyche and in American culture as well as in the landscape of Vietnam. Weigl conjures "the imagination of romance in a world of remembered madness" as a means to illumination.

_____. *Re-writing America: Vietnam Authors in Their Generation*, pp. 191-205. Athens: University of Georgia Press, 1991.
Perhaps more than the work of any other poet of his generation, Weigl's work (as marked by his series of book titles) "may be said to chart the enactment of a poetic career as an evolution of mythic consciousness distinctly tied to the American experience of Vietnam." Beidler traces this evolution through examining key poems and groupings in *A Romance*, *The Monkey Wars*, and *Song of Napalm*. The latter has some resemblances to the shape of Vietnam novels and to the pattern of Herr's *Dispatches*.

The Monkey Wars

Gotera, Vicente F. "Bringing Vietnam Home: Bruce Weigl's *The Monkey Wars*." In *Search and Clear: Critical Responses to Selected Literature and Films of the Vietnam War*, edited by William J. Searle. Bowling Green, Ohio: Bowling Green State University Popular Press, 1988.
Weigl avoids the self-consciously avant-garde in his use of the short lyric. His vision of the war is unusual among veteran writers in that, rather than seeing the American soldier as victim, Weigl recognizes, if only with hindsight, his culpability. His poems enact "the penance of memory." The juxtapositioning of poems suggests that Weigl sees "no separation between the [moral] landscape of Vietnam and that of America." Gotera examines key poems in some detail.

Stephens, Michael G. *The Dramaturgy of Style: Voice in Short Fiction*, pp. 148-154. Carbondale: Southern Illinois University Press, 1986.
Stephens admires the epiphanic nature of many of Weigl's poems: "By a kind of purposeful utterance grown into a dramatic complication, his narratives lead to recognition."

Song of Napalm

Jason, Philip K. *"Song of Napalm."* In *Magill's Literary Annual, 1989.* Pasadena, Calif.: Salem Press, 1989.
By collecting all of his Vietnam poems in one volume, Weigl has stripped them of the charged interaction with domestic poems that they had in earlier collections. Still, there are gains in the cumulative impact of the narrator's Vietnam story. Weigl's poems insist that violence and rage exist first in the warrior, then in the war itself. By extension, then, we are all capable of the cruelty that war demands. A number of the poems are briefly examined.

Peter Weiss

Viet Nam Discourse

Hughes, Catharine. *Plays, Politics, and Polemics*, pp. 91-97. New York: Drama Book Specialists, 1973.
Technically and stylistically Weiss's most complex play to date, a blend of "highly stylized writing and agitprop rhetoric which employs chorus and choreography, an elaborate structure with characters who are at one moment anonymous representations of their epoch, at another specific figures in history." Hughes explores the structure and themes to argue for a failed link between the two. The play also fails because the spectators are never allowed to decide anything for themselves.

Kalma, Thomas A. "A Remobilization from the Left: Peter Weiss's *Viet Nam Discourse.*" *Modern Drama* 18, no. 4 (December, 1975): 337-348.
Kalma examines the origins of Weiss's brand of documentary drama as well as the technical means by which Weiss represents twenty-five hundred years of Vietnamese history. The playwright's critique of colonialism and capitalism develops "from the standpoint of a dialectic process predicated on Marxist revolutionary theory." The play, written during 1966 through 1968, seems directed at inspiring "criticism of the U.S. war effort in Viet Nam."

John A. Williams

Bonetti, Kay. *John A. Williams: Interview with Kay Bonetti.* Sound recording. Columbia, Mo.: American Audio Prose Library, 1989.
Williams gives the background behind many of his eleven novels, comments on the craft of fiction, and discusses the degree of compulsion in his career.

Nadel, Alan. "My Country Too: Time, Place, and Afro-American Identity in the Work of John Williams." *Obsidian II* 2, no. 3 (Winter, 1987): 25-41.
Williams uses "modernist narrative conventions to reflect a sense of displacement . . . endemic to Afro-American experience." *Captain Blackman* is one of those works that illustrates Williams' characteristic blend of autobiography, history, and fantasy. Its structure "is more cumulative than linear, one that moves forward by accumulating the past."

Captain Blackman

Harris, Norman. "*Captain Blackman* and Cultural Literacy." In his *Connecting Times: The Sixties in Afro-American Fiction*. Jackson: University Press of Mississippi, 1988.
The novel reveals why black youths joined the military and how they viewed the role of the black soldier in Vietnam. Many black soldiers felt that their service might "connect the American and African halves of themselves and assure acceptance by white America." Captain Blackman, seeing himself and other blacks "repeatedly duped into service" and learning the lessons of black military history, becomes a revolutionary who destroys America's defense systems.

Muller, Gilbert H. "Dark and Bloody Ground: *Captain Blackman*." In his *John A. Williams*. Boston: Twayne, 1984.
Muller examines Williams' use of the Vietnam War as a "springboard" for a panoramic treatment of all America's major wars. He places the work in the context of American war literature and also that of the Brechtian epic concept. Williams' mountain of research connects *Captain Blackman* to the nonfiction novel. Muller's discussion of the themes and various formal devices is concise and persuasive. He sees Blackman's journey as "an unsentimental education" in militarism and the black experience. This chapter forms a part of a comprehensive study of Williams' career. Bibliography.

Tobias Wolff

Bonetti, Kay. *Tobias Wolff: Interview with Kay Bonetti*. Sound recording. Columbia, Mo.: American Audio Prose Library, 1985.
Vietnam is directly or obliquely conjured up in a number of Wolff's stories (collected in *The Garden of North American Martyrs* and *Back in the World*) and in his novel *The Barracks Thief*. Wolff addresses matters of craft in this wide-ranging interview. Working with other writers at Stanford was helpful to him. All of his writing is autobiographical in some way (though not necessarily in a literal way); thus, he finds some sympathy for all of his characters. He would

not write of people about whom he only feels negatively. Endings are most difficult.

Lyons, Bonnie, and Bill Oliver. "An Interview with Tobias Wolff." *Contemporary Literature* 31, no. 1 (Spring, 1990): 1-16.
The focus is on Wolff's memoir *This Boy's Life*, but the interview ranges over Wolff's entire career with some attention to how his experience in Vietnam hangs in the background of all of his work. Useful comments on *Back in the World*, *The Barracks Thief*, and on other contemporary writers—including those who have dealt with the Vietnam War.

The Barracks Thief

Glatzer, Richard. "*The Barracks Thief.*" In *Magill's Literary Annual, 1986*. Englewood Cliffs, N.J.: Salem Press, 1986.
This novella has a multipart structure clearly defined by shifts in point of view. It develops themes of "male honor and male bonding" and handles the details of army protocol especially well. Though not completely successful, the work is "beautifully written and evocative." Glatzer pays little attention to the Vietnam connections.

Stephen Wright

Meditations in Green

Beidler, Philip D. "Re-writing America: Literature as Cultural Revision in the New Vietnam Fiction." In *America Rediscovered: Critical Essays on Literature and Film of the Vietnam War*, edited by Owen W. Gilman, Jr., and Lorrie Smith. New York: Garland, 1990.
Beidler applauds the generative, or regenerative, vision in O'Brien's *Going After Cacciato* and Wright's *Meditations in Green*. Both novels point in the direction of the artwork as "redemptory cultural fact." Both share intricate narrative structures that make each three books at once. *Cacciato* has a narrative of "Observation Post" interchapters, a "fact-book," and a "fantasy-book," while *Meditations* has the "Meditations" interchapters, a first-person narration, and a third-person narration. Some of this argument is refashioned in the final pages of Beidler's book, *Re-writing America: Vietnam Authors in Their Generation*.

Brink, Jeanie R. "*Meditations in Green.*" In *Magill's Literary Annual, 1984*. Englewood Cliffs, N.J.: Salem Press, 1984.
A dependable summary of plot, characterization, and theme, this essay considers

the use of cinematic and photographic references, especially the "symbolic reveries which link the war to films about war." The protagonist's stateside experience parallels those that he had during the war. Wright's vision is one of "unrelenting cynicism and nihilism." Sometimes Wright loses control over his structural design.

Melling, Philip H. *Vietnam in American Literature*, pp. 121-124, 163-168. Boston: Twayne, 1990.
Despite disturbances in Griffin's personality and in the text's structure, this novel's "vision of history is coherently expressed through reference to Puritan design and vision." Griffin's Puritanism undergoes a change: "In Vietnam he is instrumental in rooting out the signs and providences of God's mission in the wilderness." In the United States he is "more preoccupied with the cultivation of a garden."

Metress, Christopher. "'Hopeless Tatters': The American Movie Tradition and Vietnam in Stephen Wright's *Meditations in Green*." *Studies in the Humanities* 16, no. 2 (December, 1989): 111-120.
Though examples of "cinematic sensibility" influencing soldiers' attitudes are plentiful in Vietnam War fiction, Wright's novel explores "most fully the dimensions of American movie mythology" and its connection to the experience of this war. Metress examines Wright's cinematic metaphors and the direct use of film viewing and filmmaking in the plot. Horror film iconography is more relevant to Vietnam than is the iconography of the Western.

Myers, Thomas. *Walking Point: American Narratives of Vietnam*, pp. 197-210. New York: Oxford University Press, 1988.
Like Stone's *Dog Soldiers*, Wright's novel assumes "cultural continuity between war and postwar sensibility" by tracing Griffins' attempt to achieve a balanced, productive life within a debilitating American city: "For Wright's veteran, postwar America is not fertile ground for personal retrieval but the likelihood that the cultural possibilities that the war illustrated and energized will achieve increasingly virulent permutations." Myers elucidates style and the functions of secondary characters.

Ringnalda, Donald. "Chlorophyll Overdose: Stephen Wright's *Meditations in Green*." *Western Humanities Review* 40, no. 2 (Summer, 1986): 125-140.
Wright's novel orchestrates the multilevel symbology of the color green, "the color of the cosmic Southeast Asian jungle." The main character, Griffin, "overdoses on the rioting vegetation of Vietnam," and his meditative therapy involves identification with "a humble plant." Ringnalda also examines Wright's manipulations of point of view and his experimental structure of "overlapping, spiraling circles" and "texts within texts."

THE VIETNAM WAR
IN
LITERATURE

INDEX

Note: Entries appearing in boldface direct the reader to authors of Vietnam War literature.

Adair, Gilbert 75
Adams, Laura 121-123
Adler, Thomas P. 151
Agent Orange 27
Aichinger, Peter 52
Aldridge, John W. 126
Alexander, David 35
Allen, Douglas, and Ngo Vinh Long, eds. 8
Allott, Miriam 96
Alvarez, Everett, Jr., and Anthony S. Pitch 8
Anderegg, Michael, ed. 75
Anderson, Chris 122
Anglade, Jean 67
Anisfield, Nancy 52, 104
Antiwar movement, the 11, 14, 16, 28, 66
Anzenberger, Joseph F., Jr., ed. 8
Asahina, Robert 72
Aubrey, James R. 113, 145
Auerbach, Doris 116
Aulich, James, and Jeffrey Walsh, eds. 48
Auster, Albert, and Leonard Quart 76
Australians and Vietnam 11, 35, 42, 43

Baber, Asa 39, 78
Bagguley, John, and Cecil Woolf, eds. 28
Bailey/Howe Library 5
Baker, Mark 32, 44, 50, 51
Balaban, John 38, 39, 46, 48, 68-72, **78-79**
Baldwin, Neil 53
Balk, H. Wesley 75
Baritz, Loren 8
Barry, Jan 45, 49, 69, 70
Bates, Milton J. 30, 136
Baughman, Ronald, ed. 30
Bausch, Robert 66, **79-80**
Begiebing, Robert J. 123, 126
Behr, Edward, and Mark Steyn 80
Beidler, Philip D. 30, 41, 53, 54, 78, 80-84, 86, 92-95, 100, 103-106, 110, 111, 114, 116, 118, 121, 126, 136, 138, 143, 144, 146, 149, 153, 154, 156, 161, 162, 165
Bell, Pearl K. 31
Bellamy, Michael 31
Bellhouse, Mary L., and Lawrence Litchfield 31
Benoit, Raymond 123
Berg, Rick, and John Carlos Rowe, eds. 44
Bergonzi, Robert 54
Berkley, Gerald W. 54

Bernstein, Samuel 151
Berry, D. C. 69, 80
Bigsby, C. W. E. 146
Blacks and Vietnam 25, 40, 57, 58, 100, 112-114, 164
Blau, Herbert 112
Bly, Robert 69-72
Bonetti, Kay 83, 87, 103, 130, 144, 154, 163, 164
Bonn, Maria S. 84
Books on Southeast Asia and the Indochina Wars 29
Booth, David 131
Boublil, Alain, Richard Maltby, Jr., and Claude-Michel Schonberg 80
Boulle, Pierre 67, 156
Bowman, John S., ed. 8
Braestrup, Peter 9
Breslin, James E. 123
Briley, John 64, 66
Brink, Jeanie R. 165
Brinkmeyer, Robert H., Jr. 131
Brossard, Chandler 81
Brown, Constance A. 31
Brown, Corinne 55
Brown, D. F. 69-71, **81**
Brown, Dale E., and Lloyd J. Matthews, eds. 19
Brown, Edward G. 160
Brown, F. C. 50
Brown, F. C., and B. Laurie 54
Brown, Wesley 58
Broyles, William 32
Bryan, C. D. B. 31, 35, 36, **81-82**
Budge, Alice, and Pam Didur 9
Bufithis, Philip H. 126
Bunting, Josiah 53-55, 61
Burdick, Eugene, and William J. Lederer 17, 56, 119
Burns, Richard Dean, and Milton Leitenberg 9, 17
Busby, Mark 138
Butler, Deborah A. 32
Butler, Robert Olen 29, 46, 47, 53, **82-83**
Butterfield, Fox, Neil Sheehan, Hedrick Smith, and E. W. Kenworthy 23

Cable, Larry E. 9
Calloway, Catherine 32, 79, 121, 136, 138

INDEX

INDEX

ACS-0679   1/16/95

PS
228
V5
Z995
1992